Student Resistance

Student Resistance

A History of
the Unruly Subject

MARK EDELMAN BOREN

Routledge
New York   London

For Kate

Published in 2001 by
Routledge
29 West 35th Street
New York, NY 10001

Published in Great Britain by
Routledge
11 New Fetter Lane
London EC4P 4EE

Routledge is an imprint of the Taylor & Francis Group.
Copyright © 2001 by Routledge

Printed in the United States of America on acid-free paper.

10 9 8 7 6 5 4 3 2 1

Library of Congress Cataloging-in-Publication Data

Boren, Mark Edelman.
    Student resistance : a history of the unruly subject / Mark Edelman Boren
        p.   cm.
    Includes bibliographical references and index.
    ISBN 0-415-92623-8 (hbk.) — ISBN 0-415-92624-6 (pbk.)
        1. College students—Political activity—History.   2. Student
    movements—History.   I. Title.
LB3610.B665 2001
378.1'981—dc21

00-056139

The age of complacency is ending . . .
　　　　　　　　—*C. Wright Mills*

Contents

Acknowledgments   ix

Introduction   Student Resistance: The Fourth "R"   1

1 | Riotus Interruptus?: Early Defiance and Medieval Violence   8

2 | The Student Body Inflamed   22

3 | The Modernization of Student Power and Rise of the Student Leader   38

4 | Success, Sabers, and Sacrifice, 1900–1919   57

5 | Reform and Terrorism in the 1920s and 1930s   75

6 | Student Militancy and Warfare, 1940–1959   98

7 | Student Resistance in the 1960s   122

8 | 1968 and 1969: Student Power, Part I   149

9 | 1968 and 1969: Student Power, Part II   166

10 | The 1970s: Campus Killings and Student Fury   184

11 | Revolution in a Postmodern World, 1980–1989   201

12 | Student Unrest on the Eve of a New Millennium   221

Epilogue   Whither Student Resistance?   248

Notes   251

Bibliography   285

Index   299

Acknowledgments

Several generations of American activists—both past and present—inspired my interest in student resistance. During the writing of this book, my own students taught me much on the subject, and I owe a great deal of my understanding of modern student concerns to them. My professional colleagues at the University of Georgia and at the University of North Carolina at Wilmington have shared their own insights and stories, for which I am deeply grateful. Librarians and staff at numerous institutions helped me locate materials, and particularly helpful were those at the University of Georgia, Harvard, the Huntington, and the University of North Carolina at Wilmington. During 1998 and 1999, the University of Georgia contributed to research trips to Paris, London, Washington, and Mexico City; in 1999 the same university also made possible an extensive trip traveling and researching in California. In all my travels, I met people with stories, artifacts, and opinions that helped me deepen my understanding of specific conflicts and their outcomes; the enthusiasm I encountered for the subject confirmed that the effects of acts of student resistance not only are important to the participants but are socially profound and globally felt. I was particularly lucky to be able to visit Mexico City during the recent UNAM strikes and witness, as well, the massive student demonstration commemorating the 1968 Mexico City student massacre; students, riot police, professors, government officials, Mexico City residents—all willingly shared their views on present and past student actions, giving me a unique opportunity to see Mexico's student conflicts from different vantage points.

My greatest thanks go to individuals, however, who gave me their time, thoughts, and friendship. I am grateful to Tricia Lootens, Miranda Pollard, and Uri Vaknin, who confirmed for me that certain battles were worth fighting; they've given much of their lives to making the world a better place in which to live, and my respect for them is great. Frances

Teague is an inspiration. John Boyd, Tim Engels, Michael Hendrick, Elizabeth Kraft, Hubert McAlexander, Patrick McCord, Governor Raymond P. Shafer, Joe Sigalas, and Anne Williams have all contributed historical perspectives on student actions that expanded my understanding of student resistance in significant and very different ways. Bill Germano at Routledge offered advice on the manuscript and support. Special thanks to Debra Williams, Stewart Cauley, Enicia Fisher, and Ted Blake, all of whom provided me with knowledge, sanity, support, friendship, and lots of caffeine.

Doyle Boren can never know the gratitude I feel for his being my father. I owe much of who I am to his guidance. Jan Boren has taught me much about thoughtfulness and compassion. Bill and Nancy Montwieler have been tremendously supportive; Bill's knowledge of political history and Nancy's understanding of and involvement in the struggles of American labor have been invaluable, and their suggestions greatly improved the final book. My brother, Curt, has always been an inspiration and an example for me, and my sisters- and brother-in-law—Alice, Thea, and Jacob—have enthusiastically encouraged me on this project and have also had the good graces to at least feign interest when I rambled on too long about it. David's and Alicia's arrival in the world have made me understand what is at stake in making the world a more humane, thoughtful, and peaceful place.

My greatest debt I owe to two women who have had the most influence on my life. My mother, Nelda Edelman Boren, gave me love and taught me the meaning of personal strength. Her final battle, with cancer, was fought with the same ardor with which she lived her life. Katherine Montwieler's support and love are beyond measure. To my delight, my debt to her grows daily. As with all my endeavors, Kate had faith in this project from the start, and she also read, discussed, and corrected each draft of the manuscript. Thanks to her, the struggle of life is a joyous one.

Introduction

Student Resistance: The Fourth "R"

Like many people interested in student activism and resistance, I was first fascinated by the subject when I was a student; the idealism of youthful twenty-somethings who wanted to make the world a better place in some way, the war stories of older friends who had taken part—or wished that they had—in demonstrations in the 1960s, and the cultural myths surrounding student actions: all intrigued me. Student resistance was exotic in an era when political activism on U.S. campuses had become, well, quixotic. In discussions with current student activists, I noticed that many could refer to student heroes, movements, and organizations (recalling that the Student Nonviolent Coordinating Committee [SNCC], for instance, worked for civil rights or that the Weathermen were terrorists), but such cultural knowledge tended to be vague, and often limited to 1960s efforts in the United States and France. And once I began exploring the subject in libraries, I discovered that I had to immerse myself, become a student activist scholar of sorts, before I could even begin to piece together a general history of student activism. Many books studied specific student movements, mostly those occurring in 1968 and 1969, in depth, but to learn about the subject generally, one had to work through numerous books, memoirs, analyses, and articles. It took me a long time to build a lexicon of student resistance; no current text offered a general global history.

Numerous studies, however, pointed out that student activism and student movements were so diverse and ubiquitous that one could only study them individually. Granted, the premise is sound—if one is embarking on a scholarly career in academia; and yet the field itself is so vast, specialized, and separatist, and so rife with acronyms and jargon, that there is a real need for a general, comprehensive introduction to the subject. I thus present *Student Resistance* in the hope of making an extremely exciting field more accessible to the general reader: this study is an up-to-date chronological introduction, a concise history of student resistance. (For further and in-depth discussions of specific student movements, organizations, and actions, please refer to the notes included with individual chapters and the bibliography.)

This book simply would not have been possible had hundreds of journalists and scholars not paved the way, but *Student Resistance* does offer a unique perspective: it is a chronological global history of student actions, written for both the student of resistance and the layperson. It thus seeks to connect academic history with the public in a useful manner. A few foundational scholarly works gird this book. Lewis Feuer's *Conflict of Generations* (1969) amassed a tremendous history of student movements and organizations; it is a remarkable psychosocial analysis that seeks to understand student rebellion in terms of generational oedipal drives. Written in the immediate aftermath of the 1968 student riots, *Conflict of Generations* offers an explanation of why students rebel. Following those student uprisings, and the tremendous angst and excitement they caused, the public interest in student activism soared, igniting an explosion in activist scholarship. During the late 1960s and the 1970s, Seymour Martin Lipset produced a number of important studies on activism in the United States, while Philip G. Altbach wrote books and edited collections of essays devoted to understanding student movements in other nations. During these decades the field continued to gain depth and breadth. In 1989 Altbach edited *Student Political Activism: An International Handbook*, an essential resource that again defined and extended the still growing field. In 1998 Gerard J. DeGroot brought out a cultural study of student activism, *Student Protest: The Sixties and After*, and David F. Burg published *The Encyclopedia of Student and Youth Movements*, a much-needed reference text indispensable to both the student and the scholar. These studies not only offer detailed analyses of student activism but also serve as sterling examples of the theories, methodologies, and needs driving historical research.

The field continues to grow today. But even as it does so, the cultural parlance of student activism recedes. Che Guevara posters, Stokely

Carmichael, the peace sign, Aung San, "Red Rudi" Dutschke, the Baader-Meinhof Gang, SNCC, the Port Huron Statement, Tlatelolco, Daniel Cohn-Bendit—they've all become cultural icons . . . and distant memories. Thus when actions such as the 1989 Tiananmen Square uprising or the 1999 UNAM strike occur, they seem to lack historical context in the popular realm, when in fact they are heirs to a centuries-old global movement. This study attempts to uncover those connections and that legacy.

By chronologically describing a global history of student resistance, rather than isolating and describing movements nationally or the evolution of a given organization across many years, I would like to suggest that student resistance is a continually occurring, vital, and global social phenomenon. The student unionization efforts at New York University in 2000 can be related to the rise of the nineteenth-century German *Burschenschaften* and to the first medieval student collectives; the ways in which police troops carefully arrested striking UNAM students in 2000 had much to do with the massacre of hundreds of UNAM activists by military troops with machine guns in 1968; but both acts of suppression have parallels in other nations at other times. The connections are not forced; I believe they are specific to the nature and institution of the university itself.

Since the birth of the university, acts of student resistance and rebellion have had profound impacts on the political structures and the histories of many countries; today, student actions continue to have direct effects on educational institutions and on national and international politics. Throughout history, students have catalyzed local educational reform, transformed national political structures, and in more than a few instances spurred coups d'état. In the 1960s, university protests became major media events as students all over the world revolted against societal conventions, educational systems, and governments (and television beamed images of those events across oceans and mountains); although of relatively short duration, those acts of student resistance had tremendous cultural impact, significantly influencing government and institutional policies around the world and spawning popular mythologies that are still evident today—many of which involve somewhat exaggerated notions regarding the uniqueness, or uncommon militancy, of student resistance actions during that decade. The 1960s were watershed years for student activism around the world, but student resistance antedated and outlasted the decade.

Indeed, student resistance even predated the modern university (which had its roots in the early thirteenth century, when European students began forming collectives). And it has continued to thrive in the recent student-led political riots in Indonesia, the UNAM battles in Mexico City, and the anti-sweatshop-labor student boycotts in the United States. Although I highlight the student actions of the 1960s and the major incidents that have occurred since then (including the Chinese student demonstrations at Tiananmen Square), these events are only part of a rich and complicated history of student rebellion. This book places these well-known acts in an historical context that includes medieval student riots, student participation in the 1848 German revolutions, and the early-twentieth-century student uprisings that reformed education in many Latin American nations.

My approach to acts of student resistance—the flash points of rebellion—is based on the belief that once students cause a crisis significant enough to provoke a major response from opposing powers, then those actions in some ways move beyond a developmental context of student activist efforts, for in terms of power the contexts leading up to student actions often differ widely from those in which students find themselves after governments or institutions begin to respond. I suggest that at crisis moments, students are at the center of extremely powerful sociological, political, and physical forces for which they are generally unprepared. I sketch out the immediate contexts of given incidents of student resistance—the parties and the issues involved—but I focus on how the various forms of power play out at the sites of resistance.

The book is thus entitled *Student Resistance* for very specific reasons. A concept of "resistance" is historically primary to student actions; aggressors or not, students have necessarily taken the position that they are actively oppressed by the powers that be, whatever those powers are, and that in combating those forces (sometimes even violently), they are in actuality resisting aggression and suppression. Central to all the student actions in the following chapters is a resistance to oppression; student actions arise from conflicts between competing forces in complex systems of power, whether those forces are explicitly political or whether they are ideological, physical, economic, sexual, or generational.[1]

One of the legitimate generalizations we can make about student resistance actions is that much of their success lies in their ability to manipulate or provoke large-scale social or economic forces. From the beginning of the modern university, student power has been tied to the collective; when students band together, they can generate and wield significant economic or political power. But even large student collectives rarely constitute a great enough threat to a government (or an administration) to force change; thus the effectiveness of student actions often depends on their ability or potential to organize a larger uprising to bring greater public pressure to bear on their opponents. For example, when over 100,000 students calling for democracy gathered on Tiananmen Square in 1989, China's government was not particularly threatened and ignored them. When close to one million residents and workers joined those students, however, thus raising the specter of a large-scale worker uprising, the government acted, and with tremendous force. On a different scale, when a very small group of San Francisco State University students organized and threatened a hunger strike in 1999 to force the hiring of a number of "ethnic" professors, they did so with the knowledge that bad publicity and subsequent loss in revenues would encourage the university's administration to negotiate. Historically, powerful institutions—governmental or educational—generally do not notice if a student's stomach growls or if a student claims unfair treatment. And in direct physical confrontations with authority, students tend to lose, and lose big. However, images of students being outrageously treated, beaten, or killed by brutal forces of oppression can spark a massive popular response—even a revolution. Under the right conditions, a radical student with an issue can almost instantaneously become a public martyr for a righteous cause. While some students used nonviolent tactics to bring moral pressure to bear on their opposition in the late twentieth century, other activists purposely employed confrontational strategies of resistance aimed precisely at provoking police violence, preferably in the presence of media. Thus, even a few individuals can wield a tremendous amount of power, again, if the historical, social, and political conditions are right.

More than anything, the history of student resistance is a history of power relations. Students band together to try to generate enough force to overcome the forces of their oppression. Dramatic student actions and those in which governments respond with force are particularly informative because they sharply delineate power relations at work; those overt displays shed light on student actions occurring in more subtle forms, for even when institutions negotiate, they do so because they are forced to, not because they want to. After all, institutions are naturally conservative by nature. Some of the more evident fruits of negotiation are the appearance of women's studies, African-American studies, and Native American studies programs on U.S. campuses. Although their existence benefits both students and universities in measurable ways, they came about only after students exerted tremendous pressure on universities to begin negotiating reforms.

This text introduces a popular history of student resistance—what happened, where, when, and how—and it describes the various strategies employed by the rebellious and the gains they made or the losses they incurred. From Carl Follen's covert organization of conspiracy groups and Carl Sand's assassination of Auguste Kotzebue to Sammy Younge's SNCC efforts at Tuskegee and Tom Hayden's actions at Columbia, different situations demanded different methods of resistance and netted a wide variety of results, ranging from expulsion and sometimes brutal physical suppression to wars and peaceful large-scale social reforms. But those achievements reported in the media are only the obvious and immediate effects of student resistance. In the deployment and use of power, the forces of individuals, institutions, societies, and governments are reconfigured, reenergized, or used up.

Student Resistance outlines a concise history of student actions, of student-generated forces vying for validity, control, and survival in a sea of powerful, often violent, political and social forces. More often than not, student resistance withers and dies; but sometimes, often unpredictably, it thrives, and the effects on societies can be profound. Modern students live paradoxical existences; they face institutional restrictions, societal limitations, and political realities at the same time that they are intellectually empowered within universities, taught to challenge themselves, their beliefs, and the limits of what is known. Ironically, while students are meant to be learning the rules and regulations of a discipline, being prepared for a productive life in their society, resistance is what many students in the modern university end up learning on campus—it is the fourth "R," so to speak, the one that universities don't like to address; and it makes an unruly subject.

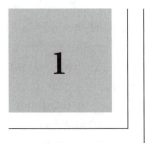

Riotus Interruptus?
Early Defiance and Medieval Violence

The Rise of the University and the Formation of Student Resistance

Although ancient complex educational systems existed in a number of countries—China, India, and Greece among them—universities as they exist today across the globe arguably descend from two specific mother institutions in Bologna and Paris.[1] Inspired by Arab scholars working in Spain, motivated youths and scholars banded together into academic guilds to share ideas, to study, and to discuss new trends in mathematics, astronomy, and literature in twelfth-century Europe.[2] Over the next two centuries these professional academic guilds appeared throughout Europe, and soon European imperialism ensured their establishment around the world as well.

Charters indicate that although numerous European schools existed prior to the twelfth century, these institutions catered only to very young boys training to be priests, monks, clerics, or literate laymen, focusing on fundamental skills of literacy and theological training.[3] Thus not until this early renaissance did Europe see the first phase of the evolution of "higher education," when an explosion of new knowledge allowed for—indeed demanded—a secular education in medicine and the law as well as in liberal arts and theology. Education soon became a fashionable way to rid wealthy homes of boisterous young men, while their less fortunate sisters generally remained "home-schooled," if they were educated at all.[4]

Universities originally referred simply to informal and rather loose guilds of scholars and students; the word *universitas* signaled only a collection of students, similar to the guilds formed of weavers or of carpenters. As students united, they realized they could affect their living conditions, and through collective action they lowered the costs of room and board, and in Bologna demanded reduced prices of books and supplies. Prior to the formation of such unions, townspeople, capitalizing on high rent and food costs, often victimized individual students, but with the recognition of their collective power, students began demanding their own terms with towns. As student collectives expanded in numbers, cities grew increasingly dependent on the revenues of universities, and students, realizing their greater bargaining power, found that they could threaten en masse to abandon a town if they did not receive fair economic treatment. Not infrequently students would simply pick up and move to other towns more willing to offer them better terms.

Universities were originally not founded as safe havens for the pursuit of knowledge but begun by the sons of the well-to-do and rising middle class for the express purpose of wielding economic power and for generating financial leverage against host towns and cities. Thus the powers of and behind modern universities have deep roots.[5] As a collective of students, the University of Paris, for instance, threatened to withdraw from the city in 1200 and successfully extorted significant legal and economic concessions from it; the events leading up to the threat centered around an already classic type of "town-and-gown" altercation: shortly after the cathedral school became a university, a student's servant was apparently thrown out of a Paris tavern after insulting the innkeeper and the innkeeper's wine.[6] In protest, the servant's master and a contingent of other students rushed into the establishment and attacked the innkeeper and a few inebriated locals; responding to the innkeeper's call for aid, town officials and a number of enraged townies retaliated by hunting down and viciously attacking the students, beating a number of them to death. Outraged, the university collective demanded justice from the sovereign and threatened to relocate, charging that the city was unfairly persecuting the students. The king sided with the collective, imprisoned the city provost, and granted a charter that exempted the students and the masters of the university from lay jurisdiction, giving them the privileges of clergy and freeing them from local taxes and prosecution. Thus the town's violent attack on the students resulted in a tremendous increase in the rights and privileges of the university; the power struggle resulted in a radical realignment of local power.[7] Such events became a classic formula for "gainful" medieval student actions, and similar actions would occur in other European cities and in Paris many times over. Of course tensions did not ease between universities and their host cities, and repeatedly, citizens would bear student unruliness only so far, retaliate, and face further sanctions for their actions.[8]

Students in Bologna founded the university as a guild, which Emperor Frederick Barbarossa officially acknowledged in 1158 by granting protection to those doing scholarship there. The university's power over Bologna was at first primarily economic. In 1217, for example, the students removed the university from Bologna to a nearby city to protest against the former's unfair economic practices and did not return until 1220, when city officials agreed to tax reform and to enforce decreases in local costs of room and board.[9] During this same strike, students complained that their masters treated them unethically and agreed to return only if the university's masters would abide by rules demanding that, among other things, masters would no longer be tardy to or skip lectures. The teachers complied with the demands; thus in 1220 in Bologna students learned the extent of their power. Not only could they demand fair economic treatment, but they could also as a collective institute their own educational reforms. Such straightforward student power may be hard to imagine in the modern developed world, but that is in large part due to the carefully orchestrated reorganization of power relations within universities by administrators and professors. In 1562, for example, Pope Pius IV generously donated a building to the University of Bologna, and while the gift was generous and sizable, it also effectively neutralized the threat of students moving the university from the city in the future.

Of course the students of the early universities hailed from different social classes and regions than the residents of the towns housing the collectives, and these differences, combined with the increasing privileges granted European universities by state and church, ensured further conflict. Not invested economically or socially in the towns in which they studied, students of medieval Europe, much like university students today, felt neither personal nor social pressures to conform to their foster towns' notions of proper behavior or proper respect for person or property. When a university was founded in Vienna in 1365, Duke Rudolf IV instituted severe punishments to dissuade town-and-gown wars, predicting that violent conflicts would ensue. He proclaimed, for example, that if a nonstudent attacked a student, and the student lost a body part in the assault, then the nonuniversity assailant was to suffer the loss of a similar member as punishment.[10] Regardless of initial causes, in scraps between students and townies, European university students generally received preferential treatment by the state. And so, as disturbances between universities and their host towns continued, universities inevitably gained more and more power, and towns continued to lose power to the student collectives.

A series of violent town-and-gown clashes rocked Cambridge and Oxford in the mid-fourteenth century, resulting in both the deaths of a number of students and the universities' subsequent economic control over both towns. The first two decades of the century witnessed a series of bloody but relatively minor clashes between students and townspeople in Cambridge, but in 1322 bailiffs and many citizens of Cambridge, fed up with the havoc privileged students were wreaking on the town, commenced a large-scale assault on the university. Armed with clubs and swords, they attacked the university and the student dormitories, severely injuring many students and destroying much of their personal property. The university immediately took steps to withdraw from Cambridge, and the sympathetic king had the principals and several hundred townspeople tried for the attack. For a few decades afterward, calm generally prevailed, though a few small riots, some started by students and others by townspeople, disturbed the relative peace and kept the relations between the university and the city strained. The Peasants' Revolt of 1381 was a more violent encounter. The mayor of Cambridge and a contingent of townspeople banded together with peasants to attack university students with swords, axes, pitchforks, and scythes. The bloody onslaught ended only when a neighboring aristocrat's army engaged the mob, definitively quelling the uprising. The king responded to the Cambridge battle by giving the university complete authority over the city's market economy.[11] Similar to the events and outcome of local violence against the University of Paris over a hundred years earlier, the conflict at Cambridge resulted in a substantial increase in the university's power over the town.

At the turn of the thirteenth century, the strained relationship between the town of Oxford and the university residing there erupted in a series of deadly exchanges. Thousands of students roamed the streets, randomly attacking the hapless citizens and sheriffs who could not touch the marauding students out of fear of state retaliation. For years the city had complained of the university's autocratic rule, and of the violent altercations and riots that occurred annually; the citizens charged that the students consistently flouted city laws, repeatedly destroyed property, and harmed them physically. In the face of complaints, the university threatened to leave the town, but King Edward, demanded that the university stay, reaffirming its rights and privileges over the town. By the end of the thirteenth century, it was clear that against the university the town of Oxford could not win.

A notorious town-and-gown mêlée, the St. Scholastica's Day Riot (February 10, 1354), took place at Oxford. The riot began in an inn where a group of students disparaged the quality of the wine they'd been drinking and insulted the innkeeper; as Oxford historian Antony Wood recounts, "The vintner giving them stubborn and saucy language, they threw the wine and vessel at his head."[12] Following the students' assault, the merchant's alarmist friends rang a nearby church bell to muster a group of townspeople who, armed with bows, ruthlessly fell upon a completely different group of students loitering in the neighborhood. Hearing of the townspeople's ambushing of students, the university chancellor rushed to the scene to stop the violence, and was himself greeted with a flurry of arrows. Indignant at the assault on his person, the chancellor responded by raising a group of students, and they attacked the bellicose townsfolk in a pitched battle that lasted the remainder of the day and into the night. The next day a mob of townsmen with bows and arrows, axes, and swords gathered at another church, ambushing some students who were unfortunate enough to pass them. They killed one student outright and injured several others.

Sensing serious trouble brewing and wanting to get ahead of it, the mayor quickly rode to Woodstock to see the king, to explain the town's position on the violence to him, and to voice chronic grievances with the students. While the mayor was gone, however, the angry townspeople went into the neighboring countryside to enlist more muscle (those living in the country had no great fondness for students either), and the combined forces attacked the students and scholars in Beaumont fields. Recording the event, Wood writes,

> [Students were] wounded mortally, others grievously and the rest used basely. All of which being done without any mercy, caused an horrible outcry in the town and ... divers Scholars issued out armed with bows and arrows in their own defense.... Then entered the town by the west gate about two thousand countrymen ... of which the Scholars having notice, and being unable to resist so great a force and fierce a company, they withdrew themselves to their lodgings. The countrymen advanced crying, "Slea, Slea.... Havock, Havock.... Smyt fast, give gode knocks!" ... They broke open five Inns, or Hostles of Scholars with fire and sword ... and such Scholars as they found in said Halls or Inns they killed or maimed. Their books and all their goods they spoiled, plundered and carried away. All their victuals, wine and other drink they poured out; their bread, fish etc. they trod under foot.[13]

The mob attacking the students and scholars ceased their rampage as night fell, but the next day the violence grew even worse, "with hideous noises and clamours they came and invaded the scholars' houses ... and those that resisted them and stood upon their defense (particularly some chaplains) they killed or else in a grievous sort wounded."[14] Many students and scholars were killed; some carried "their entrails in their hands in a most lamentable manner," while others were scalped: "The crowns of some chaplains, that is, all the skin so far as the tonsure went, these diabolical imps flayed off in scorn of their clergy."[15] What began with an insult given by a drunken student to an innkeeper, or by an innkeeper to a student, in serving the wine he did, turned into the worst riot the city had ever seen. For a while, enrollment at Oxford University was dramatically diminished. But the town too was to suffer greatly for the attacks, as the king awarded economic power to the university in retribution.

As a result of the violence, Edward III imprisoned in the Tower of London a number of the townsmen who led the attacks, and significantly increased the power of the university, granting Oxford University sovereignty over the town and, most importantly, its market. Additionally, the mayor and bailiffs of Oxford were forced to swear an annual oath observing the supremacy of the university over the town. The church was not to stand idly by, either, with such an opportunity to display power: the bishop of Lincoln quickly placed the town under interdiction, and in addition to the ecclesiastical censure denying the town sacraments, he further commanded the mayor and city officials to attend an annual mass at St. Mary's Church every St. Scholastica's Day to commemorate the slain students, a practice that continued well into the nineteenth century.

Thus although the cost in human life and property was high, the massacre was enormously beneficial for the university in the long run. Such struggles, though on a lesser scale, between universities and hosting towns occurred all over Europe throughout the Middle Ages, generally with similar results; local riots erupted from insignificant altercations and escalated in size and violence until the state was forced to intercede, which in most cases meant punishment for the towns and new privileges for the students, as well as increased economic and political power for the universities.

Medieval conflicts between universities and towns, regardless of initial causes, were primarily and explicitly struggles for physical and political power. Often sons of privilege, students had recourse to different political channels than mayors and bailiffs, but it was their numbers and group cohesion that allowed them to succeed where individuals alone could do little. In the modern world, the power that universities hold does not appear to rest primarily with the student body; but this myopia might indicate a lack of historical perspective and the sophistication of institutional strategies of student control and domination. Generally, university students (or a significant portion of them) are still directly connected to avenues of power, material wealth, and the classes of citizens who can effect institutional, political, or social change. This trend is especially true in developing nations in which upper-class youth make up the majority of university students, but it is also true of developed nations in which the offspring of the middle and upper classes form a substantial part of the university and in which the entire student body can represent a powerful block of consumers. Resources of power—economic, political, legal, and social—exist for university students today, as they did for Oxford students during the reign of Edward III, even if they are more sophisticated and varied than they were in England in the Middle Ages.

Medieval universities, of course, had internal struggles as well, although masters and students would momentarily suspend their differences to repel an attacking mob of townies when needed. Strict guidelines concerning student behavior and discipline within universities developed almost upon their inception, for students were immediately infamous for causing trouble within as well as without the confines of the colleges. When students were not studying or warring against local residents, they were often warring against rival student groups or competing "nations" within the universities, which were organized around students' geographical origins. Students, of course, also struggled against their masters and college authorities, and transgressed university codes of behavior and regulations. At Oxford University in 1432, the "unrestrained continuance of execrable [student] dissentions almost blackened [the university's] charming manners, its famous learning and its sweet reputation," and university authorities retaliated by fining students for inappropriate conduct, which included carrying weapons (swords or axes) on campus, attacking other students, speaking English rather than Latin within the halls, speaking during lectures, or simply being late to these (in the fifteenth century, tardiness would cost you quite a few shillings).[16] In time, stipulated offenses grew to include staying out past curfew, keeping the wrong kind of animals (e.g., ferrets) as pets, disturbing other students in their studies, and smuggling women from the town into university hostels. When the fines failed to ensure discipline, the authorities employed the rod, imprisoned students, or expelled them.

Students in turn resisted their masters through formal protests and through legal recourse (as the university students at St. Andrew's did in 1459 when they felt they had been unfairly scored on placement tests). Of course, most of the resistance that authorities met with from students had to do with regulations imposed on student social life, with the rules against, say, gaming, staying out past curfew, or consorting with immoral women.

Like modern-day university towns, medieval university towns had a complex relationship with the steadily growing student body: although students were a constant challenge to a town's authority and nighttime peacefulness and at times wrought havoc, they did bring money into the area. Students needed lodging, food, clothes, and supplies, and as the universities grew, so did the demand for such necessities; a decent-size university could thus produce a great deal of capital for a city. For the towns as for the officials trying to maintain control over students, an unfortunate consequence of a student presence was a proliferation of certain trades that catered to their unruliness, among them taverns and houses of ill repute. Although some student venues have evolved over the centuries, many have not; university towns throughout Europe are still notorious for their drinking and "entertainment" establishments. A fondness for unruliness in students in the United States is also a reliable source of income; in the 1970s and 1980s, for example, Daytona Beach, Florida, became famous for its wild "spring break" offerings for students (over the course of a few weeks the hotels, bars, and entertainment establishments in the little Florida coastal town generated huge revenues from students making the annual pilgrimage from as far away as Alaska to partake of the town's abundance of sun, surf, and wet T-shirt contests). Of course, the town itself would be left in disarray by summer, and eventually Daytona's residents endeavored to discourage students from coming, pressuring the city to clamp down on the students as much as possible when they did. A similar phenomenon occurs in Atlanta, Georgia, once a year when African-American students pour into the city for a spring break celebration called "Freaknik"; and here too, the residents have in recent years pressured city officials to control the riotous behavior as much as possible and so lessen the inevitable damage to property and people.

As in the twentieth century, the relatively small personal investment medieval students had in the communities in which they temporarily resided encouraged a lack of respect for property and local codes of social behavior. This observation applies of course to transgressions against real estate and behavioral norms, but also to the types of student political resistance that we are familiar with in the modern age; students who have little to lose materially or socially will take risks and will, upon occasion, transgress with force (especially when there are other students around to back them up).

In attempting to control student wantonness, the authorities of medieval universities were fighting battles not dissimilar to those in which the townspeople were engaged. In the late Middle Ages, the authority of the proctors in England extended well beyond their immediate charges; for instance, they had the power to arrest and expel prostitutes from the town, though such authoritarian acts were to some locals unpopular (and proctors were often attacked while arresting "lewd women" on the streets at curfew; violence over such incidents by both townies and angry students occurred frequently in Oxford and in other towns throughout the 1600s). Yet every time a crisis became great enough to warrant state involvement, the town was likely to suffer. By the seventeenth century, Oxford University officials had gained a tremendous amount of power over the town (this complicated the town-and-gown relationship, for the university officials who sometimes butted heads with town officials were also aligned with them in trying to control student behavior). The students, who were clearly the group that "needed controlling," soon recognized that they were a threat to the established order, and thus the power that students had, and increasingly asserted, was cast in terms of resistance to oppression, with all the justification and righteousness that such victimization predicates.

Yet we should note that the groups of students at European universities were only one of many medieval guilds wielding economic and physical power, and for a guild to riot, or for several guilds to join together to make demands on a town, was common; spontaneous guild riots in Europe continued well into the Enlightenment. And, conversely, guilds just as often would turn on one another. In his history of Oxford, Woods notes, for example, that in 1306 on the eve of St. John the Baptist's Day, Oxford tailors celebrated by singing and frolicking in the streets throughout the night. Irritated by the ruckus while trying to study, an enraged student grabbed a sword, ran into the street, and stabbed one of the tailors; this altercation evolved into a larger student-tailor skirmish in which the annoyed scholar was himself mortally wounded.

The histories of medieval universities are filled with violent incidents between groups of townsfolk, tradesmen, and scholars. Once the universities formed, students realized they need not be shy about exerting their power; in medieval Paris, for example, roving bands of armed students became such a problem that Parliament was forced to issue a specific set of police regulations directed at their suppression. Scotland, which had no university until 1413, made up for its relatively slow start on the town-and-gown front; incidents between St. Andrew's scholars and the local townspeople were quick to materialize, and by 1457 students were forbidden to carry arms at St. Andrew's due to the violence they inflicted on the locals and on each other.[17] Town-and-gown skirmishes and riots occurred in most, if not every, city hosting a university in medieval Europe, and university records detail the violence as it arose in Berlin, Vienna, Glasgow, and Madrid in later years.

Understanding the frequency of such extreme violence is somewhat difficult five hundred years later. Still, modern parallels do exist. A relatively recent example of "guild clashing" occurred in 1970 in the United States, when an antiwar demonstration held by students on Wall Street in New York City was set upon by construction workers chanting "All the way USA!" The hard-hat and work-boot contingent routed the students in a riot that left dozens of people wounded. When student groups, whether with other guilds or the general populace, begin cooperating and combining their forces, however, great power can be generated. Ultimately, this is what governments fear might happen when students agitate and why troops were used to violently suppress the French students forging links to labor in Paris in 1968 or the workers joining the students on Tiananmen Square in Beijing in 1989. Modern university protests, whether the relatively tame ones staged on campuses in developed nations or the political revolutions that occur in some developing nations, have their roots in these medieval university protests. When students organize, they are not solely defining themselves, they are reviewing their numbers and gauging their strength. So while a demonstration is an articulation of a specific stance, it is also a show of defiance, a show of force. Student actions—organizing, demonstrating, and even battling—have historical roots in the very founding of medieval universities, and it is important to realize that although modern acts of resistance can at times be more civil or subtle than, say, lopping off an opponent's arm with an ax, this subtlety does not alter their status as actions of a struggle for quantifiable power.

Through struggles and influential allies, European universities continued to gain strength and assets through the Middle Ages, and by the Renaissance they were relatively stable institutions, with buildings, endowments, rules, regulations, and, most importantly, social and political power. The value placed on knowledge in the Renaissance assured both the importance and the future power of universities, but also locked in place the contentious struggle to control this influence among university, state, and church officials, not to mention the students themselves. The rules and regulations determining appropriate student behavior were expanded and institutionalized, and more and more universities incorporated themselves, becoming stable professional institutions.[18] Indeed, university officials had a distinct advantage over their students in this grab for power insofar as they had comparatively long-lived relationships with the institutions and thus could develop complex strategies, institute changes to their advantage over time, and build on the work and gains of their forebears.

Digging among the Historical Roots of Student Resistance

The history of Western education is a history of power struggles, and student resistance is as old as the university itself; students developed and used their individual and collective power, defining themselves in relation to the societies and social institutions they fought against. Early universities particularly were political and economic organisms from their very conception. Because they created themselves as they grew, developed their roles as society developed, and defined and regulated their own forms and natures, they were often unstable, volatile creatures. The collectives did quickly realize, however, that when they were challenged, they generally grew in strength, at least after the dust cleared. (Ironically, medieval student tactics of provocation in the hope of future gains would resurface in the late twentieth century, only

reconfigured: students would provoke a violent response from governments in the presence of media to garner public support.) Having little
personal investment in the towns and societies in which they studied,
with a corresponding proclivity for transgression, medieval students
ensured that universities would not be peaceful organizations. The freedom from the opprobrium of family or familial community, combined
with class privilege and state political support, made students extremely
difficult for host towns and university officials to control; and when
students banded together, they could bring a substantial amount of
physical, political, or economic pressure to bear on a town, their masters, or competing guilds.

Throughout the Middle Ages universities grew in power, but in forming collectives that were volatile and often disruptive, students were
increasingly perceived as a threat in need of external control by both
towns and university officials and, eventually, the state; meanwhile, the
students perceived themselves as besieged by rules and regulations, the
victims of a variety of oppressive forces. Students saw their exercise
of power, then as today, as not aggression but resistance. Of course as
students gained privileges and rights, or as their perception of their
rights evolved, they were indeed often victims of oppression as states,
societies, and institutions sought to limit their activities or otherwise
control them. In any case the students' perception that they were resisting oppression hardened their nerves in the fights they waged for
their causes.

As universities evolved into more stable institutions in the Renaissance, with substantial assets and social power, the power of the students did not make gains relative to that of the administration, the
masters, or the incorporated institutions themselves. A student alone
was transient, generally self-concerned, and, compared to those running universities, "ignorant" of the history of universities and of the
power that students have historically held. It is no wonder that students
eventually came to view themselves as subject to oppressive institutional forces, for as universities evolved and amassed power through the
centuries, the vast majority of it was funneled to those with long-term
relationships with those institutions and, ultimately, to the institutions
themselves.

Knowing the history of early collectives of students and acts of student rebellion or resistance is important for contemporary campus activists for a variety of reasons; simply realizing that universities were established expressly for the accumulation of student power can even radically change a student's relationship with her colleagues, with the student body as a whole, and with the university to which she belongs.

The Student Body Inflamed

2

The University and the Reformation

As the Renaissance slowly swept northward through Europe, universities continued to blossom and thrive, fed by the increasing popularity of learning, interest in classical culture, and their own local power. Although educational systems developed unevenly, throughout Europe universities for the most part enjoyed unprecedented growth and power as the clerical influence on European societies began gradually to wane, and the power of secular rulers grew.[1] As more secular studies developed, the halls of academe became sites of political tension: articulate university professors publicly debated questions regarding theological and national politics. The medieval theologian John Wyclif (1320–84), an outspoken scholar at Oxford and an academic who openly advocated church reforms, took an antagonistic stance toward the papacy that would prove influential in England and Bohemia, helping to set the stage for Martin Luther and the Reformation.[2]

The joint influence of the Renaissance and Reformation, championing intellectual progress as they did, helped to open up Catholic theology to debate and criticism. Regional leaders within the Holy Roman Empire allowed for varying degrees of free speech, paving the way for Martin Luther, a professor of theology, to post his Ninety-five Theses at a church in Wittenberg on October 31, 1517. The wars between Protestants and Catholics throughout the sixteenth and seventeenth centuries were both physical and intellectual, and universities faced both internal and external political battles. Professors throughout Europe were examined on their religious beliefs, and their classes were monitored for appropriate ideas. Faculty sometimes divided over theological issues, and professors would often grow either obnoxiously vocal or cautiously silent, depending on the beliefs they professed, where they lived and taught, and who was locally in power. But although many universities saw changes in officials, programs, and scholars, the secular activities of universities were relatively unchanged by the theology wars.

By the sixteenth century, universities in Europe were relatively secure and stable institutions. Most of the universities survived the tremendous political upheavals rocking Europe, and in some measure influenced the changes taking place, at the very least providing forums where debates over state and clerical powers could occur; universities provided sanctuaries in which intellectuals could develop and test their ideas through both informal discussions and formal debates before risking them more publicly. The social and intellectual upheavals were, as they are today, invigorating to the atmospheres of universities that survived such turmoil, but, even so, advances in secular studies remained relatively moderate, for Protestant authorities, like Catholic authorities, remained highly skeptical of the sciences. Enrollment at universities momentarily declined in the sixteenth century as a result of the Reformation (parents were reluctant to pay for theological training after the priesthood was discredited), but the drop in student numbers was only a temporary dip in universities' inevitable growth, and soon after the Reformation enrollments were greater than ever. And as European states reconfigured their matrices of power, so did European universities, becoming hosts to theological and political struggles, or advocates of states in bids for increased local power. On the whole, however, it was masters and scholars who led the fights in theological or ideological resistance while students followed.

Student supporters often backed major intellectuals at universities. For example, when the Dominican indulgence hawker Johann Tetzel (whose high-pressure theological sales tactics were notorious at the time) responded to Luther's Ninety-five Theses by publishing his 106 anti-theses through the Frankfurt University Press, loyal students of Luther at Wittenberg held a demonstration in their teacher's support. The central feature of the demonstration was the burning of a great many anti-theses in a large pile.[3] But to say students were mostly supporters in professor-led causes, not leaders of causes themselves, does not mean they were not radical, or thoroughly committed; rather it was not yet students who were spotlighted as leaders of ideological resistance movements. When the public debate between John Eck of Ingolstadt University and Martin Luther from Wittenberg was held on the neutral ground of Leipzig University, students from both universities turned out in great force. Luther and the Wittenbergers arrived with an escort of two hundred student supporters armed with battle-axes; Eck, in turn, found security in the form of armed Leipzig constables. Displays such as students hefting battle-axes were a dramatic reminder that student power was potentially violent and destructive, but students were also wielding power in more subtle ways. Students made their greatest intellectual contribution, for example, by conveying the ideas of the Reformation to the illiterate, acting as missionaries, teaching the new ideas to peasants, thus spreading the movement through the countryside.

Avid support of university leaders and Reformation missionary work notwithstanding, student-generated unrest at European universities during the Reformation generally consisted of spontaneous riots, in which students or townspeople used one excuse or another to run amok. These disputes were commonplace in every major university town in England, Italy, Spain, Switzerland, Austria, and the various German states, as well as in other countries hosting relatively young universities.

Oxford University students were particularly unruly during the civil war, primarily because King Charles I turned the campus into his military headquarters and court while he attempted to wrest London away from the Parliamentarians. During his four-year residence in the university town, the king lived and held court at Christ Church; the law and logics schools were converted into granaries; and the New College Cloisters were converted into powder magazines. In fact, all the university buildings found new uses: the astronomy and music schools became uniform factories; Magdalen College Grove was turned into an artillery park; All Souls became an arsenal; Christ Church quadrangle was used to house livestock; and other buildings were transformed into cannon foundries, food stores, and apartments for aristocracy or military personnel. Students and scholars had to swear oaths of loyalty to

Charles, found themselves pressed into military service for part of the week, and were fined if they failed to show for duty. Charles also forced the university to lend him vast sums of money, as the occupation of Oxford strained the royal purse. The students, who were primarily royalists anyway, apparently made the most of the situation, brawling incessantly and learning secular lessons of a questionable nature under the tutelage of occupying soldiers; student nobles, who before wore the robes of scholars, took to wearing armor (until Charles was forced to flee Oxford, and scholarly robes once more became fashionable).[4]

The most visible and typical acts of European student resistance of the time occurred spontaneously, with little design or planning, and were generally directed at local townspeople, who may or may not have represented some political force the rioting students opposed. Oxford students attacked the mayor of Oxford in 1658, for example, pelting him and his attendants as they were proclaiming Richard Cromwell protector, but the hostilities had more to do with local politics than state politics. And since students of all sorts of political and theological persuasions attended universities, altercations between students and townies, who were likewise a heterogeneous mixture of persuasions, occurred more or less continuously. The Popish Plot catalyzed further anti-Catholic riots, and Woods notes that in 1683 the hostess of a local Oxford inn "fell into fits and died" after being "most strangely affrighted by 3 rude persons" from All Souls College who called her a "Popish bitch" and told her she deserved to have her throat cut; the incident sparked a large town-versus-gown mêlée.[5] Riots of this kind continued to break out across Europe well into the eighteenth century. But even if the reasons behind the riots were political, the riots themselves were primarily local power struggles.

Populated in large part by the second sons of landed gentry, universities continued to grow with state support throughout Europe, and although the student resistance occurring during the Reformation and after was similar to that of the Middle Ages, it was also transforming as certain material aspects of universities were changing. Students, for instance, could see that outspoken university intellectuals like Martin Luther could wield both tangible and intangible power, and some modeled their own aspirations on such iconoclastic examples.[6] Explicit school reforms demanded other changes as well. These most often occurred in primary and secondary institutions, but their popularity influenced reforms in higher education. Born in northern France, John Calvin too was an intellectual, a literary scholar (he published on Seneca's *De Clementia*), and a lawyer; during his exile (1538–41) for unorthodox views, he taught courses in religion at Johann Sturm's school in Strasbourg and experimented with a "work ethic" in the classroom. He later established an academy of higher learning, and his disciples spread his reforms throughout France, England, Scotland, Holland, and the American colonies, founding dozens of universities and Calvinist colleges. There was not much chance of student resistance at these institutions: Calvin believed children to be born into a state of sin, naturally prone to evil, and thus justifiably subjected to harsh corporal punishment for infringements of school regulations, so long as the student remained a student. A welcome antidote to Calvin, Comenius (John Amos Komensky), a Moravian who attended Heidelberg University, also influenced educational reform throughout Europe, but unlike Calvin, Comenius advocated the humane treatment of students and a school system accommodating all citizens, not merely the intellectual or aristocratic elite.

Advances in education were not limited to Protestant endeavors; in 1534 Ignatius Loyola founded the most formidable educational institution ever established by the Catholic Church, the Society of Jesus. Structured along the lines of the military, the Jesuits controlled the most organized and thorough system of secondary schools and colleges in the Western Christian world for over two centuries. The Jesuits had their rivals, particularly in French schools inspired by the ideas of René Descartes (1596–1650), himself a graduate of a Jesuit college.

As students became educated, skirmished with local townspeople or each other, and prepared themselves for public office, life as gentry, or intellectual careers, universities as entities grew in assets and political power. The groundwork for modern student rebellions continued to be laid: scholars and professors increasingly played key roles in societal and cultural changes; schools continued to proliferate and thrive; and the various seeds of dissension of the time entered institutions of higher learning. Universities were thus becoming not only powerful political or theological havens (for those professors who could remain in them) but sites where voices of dissension and reform were increasingly heard. During the Enlightenment, secular questioning would continue to make inroads in institutions where it was allowed, and by the close of the American and French revolutions, students across Europe and the Atlantic would have numerous models for leaders of ideological or political resistance movements.

Extending Social Control and the Breeding Grounds of Student Dissent

During the Enlightenment thousands of public and private schools of all levels appeared throughout Europe; in England, education extended even to the poor, and by 1714 tens of thousands of poverty-stricken children all over the country attended charity schools. These institutions were not simply philanthropic endeavors but a means of social control meant to foster a prescribed morality, a respect for the existing social order, and social discipline—instigated by the wealthy, who feared the lower classes and social unrest. In France, Germany, Italy, and Spain, hundreds of schools were likewise founded for students of all ages and classes, for not only was the attainment of knowledge generally thought to be a moral good, with the numbers of schools taken as an indication of a country's cultural "progress," but people in positions of power also realized the benefit of these institutions as vehicles of social control. Sunday schools were founded, for instance, in the 1780s in England as an excellent way to keep children, who were often in school or working the other days of the week, under control on the seventh (the idea caught on throughout Euope, and within seventy years millions of children would be attending them).[7] The rise in numbers of institutions of lower education had a tremendous effect on the universities of Europe as the numbers of students subsequently entering higher education rose dramatically; more universities simply had to be built, and those that already existed were soon overcrowded. The popularity of learning, however, did not of its own indicate educational progressiveness. During the Reformation and well into the Enlightenment, many established European universities did not want to change their curricula or methodologies too quickly, although they would consider and institute more gradual reforms; indeed, the Royal Society of London, the Académie des Sciences of Paris, and the Acadia del Cimento of Florence were all founded because universities were considered too conservative by progressive scientists, scholars, and theorists.

Educational institutions were not yet hotbeds of student radicalism, although intellectuals were sowing the seeds for future activity. In his *Treatises on Government* (1689–90) and *Toleration* (1690 and 1692), professor of philosophy John Locke formulated and developed the famous social contract theory of government, in which he asserted the "natural right" of subjects to rebel against an unjust ruler. The principle would be cited by American colonists in their argument for independence, and repeatedly revolutionaries, including student leaders, throughout the world would justify their actions by referring to Locke. Despite the strong theoretical foundations of Locke's contract, the evolution of student resistance awaited two things: a model for the radical student leader and the political reorganization of the student body.

Modernizing the Corps for Student Resistance: *Burschenschaften*

Since the Middle Ages, numbers have been essential to successful student action: a collective is a thing of power. And yet not until well after the turn of the nineteenth century did students consistently begin to use their numbers for explicitly political ends. The first students to do so effectively were German. In 1811 Friedrich Jahn instituted one of the more notable scholastic reforms that aided the evolution of organized student revolt in Berlin. The Turnverein was a nationalistic gymnastics program that endeavored to toughen students physically through gymnastics (students trained on the side horse and the vaulting horse) to fight against France. The program was quite popular and lasted through many generations of students. A number of Turnverein students would subsequently play a significant role in the 1848 Revolutions, and when those uprisings were defeated and the vanquished fled to other countries, they disseminated their zeal for student organizations.[8] Many Turnverein students stayed loyal, and the program itself evolved and grew within the German educational system. Its importance to future student organizations lies in its existence as a national organization to which many students belonged, and its emphasis on student power and nationalism (a trend that only continued to grow as a part of German education, culminating in the Hitler Youth and the Nazi schools of the 1930s).

German students re-realized collective power in the nineteenth century when they began forming their own organizations, *Burschenschaften,* in 1815 at the University of Jena, under the sponsorship of a grand duke who, notably, allowed free discussion in the universities within his territories. Stressing nationalism, political activism, and unification, the *Burschenschaften* appealed to students disgusted with the apathy and petty fighting within the university or who were otherwise dissatisfied with the conservatism of the German states. The *Burschenshaften* members' idealism and commitment to change was infectious, and soon *Burschenschaften* began appearing throughout Germany.[9] The Jena students were fully aware of their local power, which gave them the confidence to conceive of a great *Burschenschaften* reaching across the entire confederation of German states. And although the students held local gripes against their host city of Jena, they also enjoyed a tradition of solidarity and collective power unparalleled within the German states, and spearheaded a national organizational movement to expand their power.[10]

In October 1817, the Jena *Burschenschaften* led a large assembly attended by students from a variety of German states, where they praised Luther, the Reformation, and the Battle of Leipzig (in which troops from Austria, Prussia, and Russia had crushed Napoleon's army). While honoring the past, the students at the Wartburg meeting also discussed the future. Many of the students had recently returned home from the military campaign against France to find that although they had liberated the German states, they still faced university and state restrictions. The attending students held a march and burned symbols of tyranny, including a wig and the *Code Napoléon*; and over the few days of the meeting, various individuals called for nationalism and social reform, while others advocated radicalism.[11] Students also attended sermons and performed gymnastic exercises in the Wartburg market. The student event did not go unnoticed; the French Reign of Terror was still quite fresh in memory, and all over Europe intellectuals and politicians saw the meeting as a troubling sign, the birth of a potentially dangerous student movement.

Enthusiasm for *Burschenschaften* swept through Germany's universities during the year following the Wartburg meeting; on the anniversary of the festival, representatives from the individual groups met to form an umbrella organization, and in 1818 the Allgemeine Deutsche Burschenshaften was born, the first fully modern and extremely powerful student organization.[12]

The organization of the *Burschenschaften* is important as an express act of student resistance itself—not because the movement countered authority or any set of regulations (the *Burschenshaften* actually enjoyed the patronage of powerful figures) but because they were expressly political in nature, with a defined agenda. The *Burschenshaften* claimed to be organizations against oppression, political apathy, cynicism, conservativeness, and non-Christian values, and although they did not at first know exactly what they would do, they knew they should do something to effect social and political reform.[13] The members saw themselves as the bearers of the political future; and by their very nature, they distinguished themselves from the elitist dueling fraternities fashionable among wealthy German students, which were decidedly apolitical societies. In meeting at Wartburg, the students realized the power they had, and sensed the even greater power they could generate. Although they suspected they could use their power for reform, they were not yet aware of the complexities and intricacies of state politics, particularly of the economic forces at work in the confederation. In articulating a need for solidarity and a future for the German state that would differ radically from what currently existed, the students were reacting mostly to what they perceived as chronic social and political apathy.

Some of the groups forming at the time, however, were more specific in their goals than others. At the University of Giessen, a reactionary faction of the *Burschenschaften* known as the Schwarzen (the Blacks) formed. Their primary concern was patriotism and the establishment of a unified German state, which would exclude any citizens tainted with non-Aryan blood.[14] Carl Follen (1795–1840) led the Schwarzen, which supported unification through the overthrow of the leaders of the separate German states.[15] Follen's notoriety as a political radical soon forced him to move from Giessen to Jena, and he began a group of the Schwarzen there as well.

A volunteer during the 1814 War of National Liberation, the young Follen returned to civilian life to study theology at the University of Giessen, where he began his career as an organizer by forming literary clubs. Heavily influenced by philosopher Johann Gottlieb Fichte, Follen soon turned his attention to politics and rhetoric, articulating a platform for the regeneration of Germany. Follen's group of increasingly radical intellectuals believed that regeneration justified whatever means could achieve it, and their uniform mirrored their radical platform. As with any modern group of students seeking to define themselves publicly, the Schwarzen developed their own fashion: they grew their hair long, sported black velvet coats, and always carried a knife thrust into their belts.[16] Sensing trouble from the group, the university administration at Giessen outlawed the Schwarzen in 1817, which only served to radicalize the group even more. With the organization officially oppressed, Follen claimed the regeneration he envisioned could not come about through "proper channels." Where Follen led, the radical *Burschenschaften* increasingly followed; together they began exalting violence for Germany's sake, while their leader preached the virtues of the revolutionary martyr.

One impressionable student at Jena, Carl Sand (1795–1820), became particularly taken with Follen's message. A zealous member of the Schwarzen, Sand decided to assassinate August Kotzebue (1761–1819), a playwright and novelist known for criticizing the *Burschenschaften*. Sand ambushed Kotzebue in March 1819, fatally stabbing the writer. Captured, tried, and sentenced to death, the student activist was unceremoniously executed in May 1820.[17]

Follen's and Sand's actions had great impact on German universities, though not in forms the Schwarzen desired. Under the leadership of

Klemens Metternich, the German states clamped down on universities after the assassination, putting monitors in lecture rooms, eliminating freedom of the press, infiltrating student groups with government spies, and prosecuting or expelling anyone considered guilty of spreading sedition. The radicals on campus perceived this as more oppression and used it to fuel their drive toward terrorism.

Sand left a legacy for student reactionaries as well, and student radicals began a campaign of violence against public figures. The growing boldness of students resulted in Metternich's calling for a meeting of the heads of the separate German states to formulate means to thwart the brewing revolt. Representatives gathered in Bohemia in August 1819 to draft the Carlsbad Decrees, which suggested that the German Confederation censor university press, outlaw the *Burschenschaften,* and expel all dissidents from universities. The confederation set up an organization to identify radical organizations, and once the separate German states adopted the decrees, even moderately radical students found themselves actively oppressed.

They were not apathetic, however. Offshoots of the suppressed *Burschenschaften* formed at various universities, keeping the organizational movement alive, and in Göttingen in 1831, students rebelled against King Wilhelm, took up arms, and "liberated" Göttingen before quickly surrendering to advancing Hanoverian troops. Students also tried to liberate Heidelberg. By this time, efforts of oppression only fueled the rebelling students' passion for resistance. The following year, for example, a massive demonstration of students and workers occurred in Hambach, and tens of thousands of participants protested for German unification. But although the demonstration was a great show of force and of solidarity between students and workers, they could not generate a plan for unification; the confederation, however, retaliated with arrests and tighter restrictions on students.

Despite government efforts to suppress it, student unrest con tinued to blossom throughout Germany, and numerous conspiratorial student groups formed in response to the confederation's crackdown following the Hambach demonstration. In 1833 one such student group attempted to spark a revolution in Frankfurt by seizing federal buildings. But the attempted revolution was an abysmal failure; without organization, it lacked strength and public support, and the Prussian authorities immediately suppressed it. Of course, Prussian authorities became more repressive than ever as a result, but the German students already realized their strength, and by suppressing the student organizations, the various German governments gave the university activists a common enemy against which to fight.

In 1837 Ernst Augustus, the king of Hanover, ejected facuulty from the Georg August University in Göttingen when they criticized his recent suspension of Hanover's constitution. A large contingent of students immediately protested the firings with local demonstrations and protest marches and were suppressed. Although state troops attacked and scattered the students, the fires of revolution had been lit; flare-ups like the one in Hanover were individually stamped out, but a major conflagration was only a matter of time.

The early nineteenth-century acts of resistance in the German states ended disastrously for the individuals attempting to start rebellions, but they did show German university students the extent of their potential power, and that their governments feared that power. State troops' killing of students and governments' official imprisonment and execution of others gave both radical and moderate university students clearly defined enemies, along with undeniable proof of real oppression; students were no longer rallying for abstract freedoms but fighting for their lives. Forgotten was the extremism of the early terrorists that had provoked the crackdowns; the increased surveillance and ongoing suppression of even moderate groups were daily reminders to the students of their oppression. Thus the governments' continually harsher responses to growing student unrest delineated the issues at stake for the greater German studentry, and established that students were oppressed as a group. Although some students and groups supported the states and the confederation as they stood, the numbers of those who identified themselves as oppressed were on the rise. At the same time, the suppression of student groups and the increased surveillance in and constraints placed upon universities reinforced the notion that students were a viable threat to government, a power to be feared. In the face of governmental suppression, students throughout the German states were thus encouraged in their resistance by the fear they inspired, and they stepped up efforts to antagonize their governments.

Thus Carl Sand's actions, although self-destructive, did bring heavy suppression down on students in German universities, which eventually led to massive student unrest in the long run, aided by a complex network of increasingly volatile student groups. But even if the *Burschenshaften* articulated a nationalist agenda and promoted the unification of Germany, they could not form a viable plan for running a unified nation. Thus when they came, the 1848 revolutions were led by immature students without an understanding of real political power, their own political climate, or what might actually be involved in running state governments. They had, however, by the approach of midcentury, formed powerful student groups, and they succeeded in threatening their governments. Their own attempts at self-definition—their growing anti-Semitism, for example—clarified students' causes but also limited their numbers, and without the aid or support of the population at large, they never had a chance of instigating a full-scale revolt. In short, the early nineteenth-century German student groups were important because for the first time in Europe, students founded large nationalistic organizations focused on political reform; they organized and showed both themselves and their governments the potential political or military power students held when acting collectively, though they had yet to learn how to employ their power effectively.

Polish Conspiracies

As Europe watched the German student movement develop, the rise of the *Burschenschaften* encouraged students across the continent to organize as well, and at Breslau University in 1816, and later at many Polish universities, students began their own secret societies called Polonia, based on the ideals and organizational structures of Freemasonry.[18] The nationalistic Polonia began conspiring against Russia. Fearful of the growing student organization phenomenon (both in Poland and in the German states), the state government outlawed all such societies, effectively suppressing the public actions of radicals. The groups nevertheless continued to meet, discuss, and plan the overthrow of the Russian occupation, but they never successfully put their plans into action.

The Russian government continued its persecution of Polish student societies throughout the decade, cracking down on universities where students appeared to be capable of demonstrating, or where antioccupation literature materialized, increasing the state surveillance on campuses, and tightening the restrictions placed on students. Thus the Polish student conspiracies remained only that; the student lodges were eventually infiltrated and destroyed during the 1820s and the radical student leaders jailed or pressed into Russian military service long before they had the chance to act.

French Blanquism—The Fashionable Fight

While the bohemians were making the Left Bank of Paris the European center for alternative lifestyles through exhibitionist fashions, Louis-Auguste Blanqui began his radical career as a student revolutionary in 1827, and he continued it by organizing groups of students to plot against the French monarchy in the 1830s.[19] Blanqui's underground conspiracy groups attempted to start a revolution against France's government in 1839, and their leader was arrested and sentenced to a life term in prison. He would be freed following the 1848 revolution, only to be reimprisoned later for agitation, a pattern that would be repeated throughout the remainder of his life. A vocal extremist, Blanqui had great influence on radical French students; his revolutionary socialist ideas appealed greatly to liberal French students opposed to the monarchy. In 1868, a century before Paris would erupt in the greatest student uprising it has ever known, in which students violently clashed with police in an attempt to topple Charles de Gaulle's government, Blanqui wrote and distributed a manual for students engaging in urban warfare against the state. Thus, when the May riots of 1968 broke out, they did so in a cultural context that included historical precedents encouraging French student guerrilla tactics against police, fashionably theorized by the most prominent French student radical of the previous century and—at least theoretically—condoned within the university intellectual canon.

Early American Student Resistance, Antislavery Actions, and Nineteenth-Century Medievalism

The spirit of independence pervading the colonies prior to the American Revolution fed a growing student resistance movement at Harvard, culminating in a major confrontation between students and administration in 1768.[20] Students organized and demonstrated against administrative oppression and what they perceived as an overly parental system of university government. From 1765 to 1860 student resistance actions and uprisings consistently and often shook American campuses. Columbia, the University of North Carolina, Yale, the University of Georgia, the University of Virginia—all witnessed tremendous student turmoil at various times during the era, primarily due to extremely rigid university behavioral policies, strict rules against drinking, poor university food, and little student participation in government, combined with the strong sense of American liberty and personal independence among students, as well as the prevalence of violence and the justification for the use of force against oppression promoted by the advocates of the American Revolution.[21] Although many demonstrations included entire student bodies, especially on campuses in the South, most of the acts of student resistance occurring until just before the Civil War concerned local issues, particularly university governance (a great number of them were simply riots sparked by incidents such as rancid meat being served at a dining hall, an unruly party being broken up by school officials, or a student's punishment for an infraction).

By the mid-nineteenth century in the United States, however, student agitators were also involved in antislavery organizations at Amherst College, Bowdoin College, Dartmouth College, New York University, Oberlin College, the University of Illinois, and Williams College, among other universities and colleges.[22] At Lane Seminary in Cincinnati, Ohio, a group of over fifty antislavery students threatened to leave in protest over the administration's interference in their demonstrations for emancipation.[23] When the administration refused to allow the students to organize, they left the school to join colleagues at Oberlin. Although the threat of removal of a group of students from a town or college was the first formidable organized action of student resistance, developed in the Middle Ages, it takes a substantial number of students for such actions to have any real effect. Thus, although the student departures from Lane were a clear political statement, they accomplished little: the college lost some support over the demonstration and some revenues, but it also gained the willing departure of its most vocal critics.

Not all nineteenth-century actions of student resistance in the United States centered on the struggle for human rights or civil freedoms.[24] At Harvard, for example, students began wearing black Oxford-style mortarboards. In May 1842 an African-American local wearing a mock Oxford cap confronted a Harvard law student, who proceeded to assault the man. Days later, Harvard students attacked another townsman wearing a similar hat, and a series of skirmishes between townies and students occurred regarding the proper use of Oxford caps, mostly started by townies mocking the students' attire.[25]

In what can only be seen as a bad caricature of medieval European town-and-gown riots, several hundred Bostonians, many wearing mock mortarboards, attacked the university in late May. A group of armed students rose to repel the invaders, who withdrew after vandalizing the campus. Fortunately, the Oxford-cap-wearing fad died for students and bellicose townies alike soon after the confrontation.

The Modernization of Student Power and Rise of the Student Leader

The 1848 Student Revolts

After the 1848 French Revolution, King Louis-Philippe's abdication, and France's being proclaimed a republic, revolutions raged across Europe; student actors and actions played a significant role in many of them. Particularly significant to the history of student resistance were the revolutions occurring in the German states. Students, for instance, joined demonstrating workers in Berlin, calling on King Friedrich Wilhelm IV to establish a parliament and freedom of speech; the protest quickly turned into a general riot in which workers and students constructed barricades and manned them against advancing Prussian troops. In overrunning the barricades, the troops killed hundreds of protesters. Although many students gave their lives in street battles, students also contributed to the uprising by spreading revolutionary ideas and enlisting participants; they printed flyers and traveled throughout the city convincing workers to join the revolution. More workers were actually more politically radical than were the majority of university students at the time, although a small number of students were so extreme that they alienated even the most zealous of workers, thus jeopardizing the groups' collaborations.[1]

Uprisings such as the one at Berlin occurred throughout the German states. At Munich that year a liberal *Burschenschaften* spearheaded a widespread public condemnation of King Ludwig I of Bavaria, who had fomented resentment by instituting increasingly reactionary policies and through an embarrassing intrigue with Lola Montez, a South American dancer (Montez's scandal of the moment concerned her public exposure in a compromising situation wearing a student's cap, compounded by her continued patronage of the student group that the cap represented).[2] Under pressure of public outcry, civil unrest, and the dancer's sudden departure, Ludwig gave in to the demands of the students, allowing them to assemble representatives of the state and to organize a militia; he then abandoned the throne. Lola Montez ended up in Australia.

Meanwhile, over 1,000 student representatives met at Eisenach to discuss the possibilities of liberating the universities from the individual states and organizing them into a confederation; the move was intended to free students and faculty from oppression and regulation and to promote freedom of thinking and expression. After lengthy discussions, the representatives voted and agreed to form an umbrella government over all of the various universities, to demand more government funds, and to allow students to participate in university governments. The National Assembly, which was currently drafting a constitution for a unified Germany, listened to the resolutions of the Eisenach meeting but for the most part categorically dismissed the students' requests.

The revolutionaries, however, failed to achieve their goals for a *Grossdeutschland* in 1849 when the assembly could not adequately define the new Germany that they had hoped for, and the assembly had neither the organization nor the power to reform the German system of government.[3] Bismarck, who eventually succeeded in accomplishing what the 1848ers could not, blamed the failure of the prior attempts at unification on a lack of centralized power and the unwillingness of the assembly to make executive decisions effectively. The 1848 revolution did succeed, however, in conceptualizing a *Grossdeutschland,* even if it could not attain it. Students learned that if they could mobilize small groups effectively, they could muster massive blocks of organized power that could unite with groups of workers to topple governments. This lesson was not one that European universities or neighboring states would easily forget.

Testing the extent of their power, students at the University of Vienna drafted a petition demanding Emperor Ferdinand I grant citizens greater freedoms, such as freedom of speech; when they passed the document around the university in March 1848 for signatures, the general student reaction was immediate and overwhelming.[4] The students of

Vienna, like students all over Europe, had caught rebellion fever.[5] Ferdinand ignored the petition, and the students took to the streets of Vienna, where police, afraid of the size of the demonstration and the students' fury, opened fire on the protesters. The demonstration turned into a full-scale riot, and students constructed barricades across the streets while workers rushed to swell their ranks. Vienna police attempted to quell the rioting, but the students and workers had armed themselves and fought back vigorously. The police were quickly outnumbered.

Metternich, Austria's foreign minister, resigned, and by March 13 (only one day after the protest) it was clear that the students held the capital city. Forcing open the armory, the students armed themselves and organized into companies, forming a governing Academic Legion and electing a Committee of Safety.[6] Again, they presented their demands to Ferdinand I, who authorized the drafting of a new constitution. As the students rallied in the streets, government officials bent their heads over a new constitution, which the students subsequently rejected. The revolutionaries drafted and presented their own constitution to the government. The emperor fled the capital on May 17, and the government again sent troops against the Academic Legion, and again barricades were raised and battles ensued; once more the government troops were repelled.

The students controlling the city were not terrorizing it; on the contrary, they continued existing social services and even provided new ones; in return, citizens gave the Academic Legion their support. But the strain on the group was enormous, and the organization itself was rife with internal dissension and power struggles. By October the Academic Legion began disintegrating, and many of its leaders abandoned the student government over internal quarrels; relations between workers and students broke down. Sensing the time was right, on October 6 government troops struck suddenly and with extreme violence, and anarchy enveloped Vienna.

Troops under the command of various members of the aristocracy joined the struggle for control of the capital, and the fate of the uprising was sealed the moment they entered the contest. The Academic Legion attempted to fight the professional armies but was no match for experienced soldiers, and the city fell to the military by the end of October. The conquering armies smashed the Legion, which had devolved into chaos, and arrested all of the leaders that could be found. Ferdinand I abandoned the throne, and the new government rescinded the constitution the emperor had signed; the glorious student-led revolution of Vienna was a thing of history.

The student revolutionaries were incredibly effective at leading an uprising in Vienna, and for a brief time they assumed power over the capital. But what makes for a successful revolt does not necessarily make for a successful government, and the students found themselves ill prepared for the demands of rule. Indeed, they found they could neither control nor effectively negotiate with other political forces in their newly formed governmental committees, such as those of labor and the general public. This reveals much about the nature of student power—namely, that its survival is often contingent on its own formulation as resistance. When the immediate, monolithic threat subsides, and when those alliances with which they opposed that threat break apart, the students lose much, if not most, of their power; they may find themselves in new positions of power, but unless they can make the transition from student radicals to state politicos, their tenure in office will be brief. More often than not, when students do cause a coup d'état, as they repeatedly did in the twentieth century, they deliver a country into the hands of another powerful figure or group—one prepared to rule by force. What is surprising about the Vienna uprising is not that the students were able to overthrow a government, but that they managed to hold and to run the city for so long.

After the Revolution: European Studentry Regroups

Students were comparatively quiet after the 1848 revolutions, and although demonstrations and protests ignited sporadically in all of the European states, they were on the whole localized and of relatively minor import. Yet the students were not apathetic; on the contrary, even though the various 1848 revolutions brought disaster to student agitators and existing organizations, they also united students in political causes and defined a role for them in European political and ideological struggles. Students continued to organize afterward, especially in Germany, forming groups, associations, and associations of associations—a significant factor in the coming political events of the early twentieth century. In Germany informal apolitical groups dedicated to reading and studies began forming in the 1850s; these groups were significant because they connected individuals who would otherwise not associate with one another. The sheer number and variety of German student organizations was impressive. One group, Wingolf, an anti-Semitic Protestant national organization that condemned German dueling fraternities and amorality among university students, formed in 1852. Another, the Kosener Verband, a dueling fraternity that eventually incorporated all other dueling fraternities, organized in 1855 (the organization lasted until 1935). Many other organizations formed in the second half of the nineteenth century, including the Roman Catholic Kartell-Verband, the anti-Semitic Verein Deutscher Studentin (organized in 1880), the Freie Wissenschaftliche Vereinigung (organized to counter the Verein Deutscher Studentin in 1881), the Kartell-Convent (an anti-anti-Semitic organization of Jewish student groups formed in 1896), and Finkenschaft (founded in 1896), an antifraternity association of students whose members were previously not part of any student organization but who wanted the support of other self-motivated, solitary students.

The student-organization fever spread through other countries as well. Sweden had its Verdandi (begun in 1882), a student society dedicated to radical liberalism, as well as its Heimdal (founded in 1891), an association seeking to preserve Swedish student conservatism and tradition. In France the first apolitical secular organization, the Association Générale des Étudiants, formed in 1877, and by 1900 every university town in France boasted at least one chapter. And Great Britain saw the birth of the Students' Representative Council, organized in 1884 at Edinburgh. All over Europe, students joined organizations—some political in nature, others expressly apolitical—and many of these organizations joined forces to form associations of organizations, so that by the twentieth century European universities were the sites of complex networks of interrelated student groups.

Major demonstrations and student conflicts remained sporadic, localized, and relatively weak affairs, however, although they occasionally occurred. On April 10, 1865, Spanish troops fired on students demonstrating against the dismissal of a Madrid University professor; nine students were killed and dozens wounded in what became a symbol of state oppression. The violence generated popular support for the students, and served as a harbinger of the 1868 Spanish Revolution. In England, extreme violence broke out in Oxford in 1867 during the traditional commemoration of Guy Fawkes Night (November 5). The anniversary turned violent when townspeople, angered over unfair market prices, rampaged through the town and over university grounds, whereupon the university turned loose its student cadets, who promptly exacerbated the situation, turning the confrontation into a bloody urban war. And during the Dreyfus trial (1898), students at the University of Paris and other French universities vehemently battled both the police and each other, though because the student population divided over the issue, they for the most part expended their energies upon one another.[7]

Student Conflicts on Non-European Grounds

By the latter half of the nineteenth century, European imperialism had exported Western education throughout the world. European-style universities served both as social control and to validate the culture of the imperialists. From Mexico to China, from India to Peru, colonial powers had imported their educational systems along with other aspects of their culture. The final domination and "educating" of Africa did not come until 1880, ostensibly for humanitarian reasons (to end slave trading, to open the continent to other forms of trade, and, of course, to spread Christianity). Exporting Western-style universities was extensive and globally pervasive, though in many cases the results were fusions of local existing educational systems and practices with the European university models. Following the subsequent liberation from imperialism that occurred in many colonial nations during the last decades of the nineteenth century and throughout the twentieth century, however, many of the hybrid educational institutions and systems, albeit modified, remained in place.

China, for example, had a long history of both advanced education and concomitant student resistance efforts. By the first century B.C.E. students were already launching large-scale demonstrations; one of the earliest massive incidents recorded protested the sentencing of an official during the Han dynasty, and thousands of students participated in the demonstration. The ancient Chinese educational system was geared to produce altruistic leaders who would strive to improve society, and this tradition would later combine with Western discourses romanticizing student leaders to play key roles in modern Chinese student resistance. For instance, one ancient Chinese philosopher, Mencius (372–319 B.C.E.), propounded the fundamental right of the subjects of any state to rebel against an unjust ruler (just as John Locke would argue in England over one thousand years later).[8] Students listened and took the philosopher at his word. During the Sung dynasty (960–1279), students and citizens demonstrated for the government reforms. In 1126 one such protest got out of hand and turned into a riot that left a number of the emperor's retinue dead. Although a few protesters were summarily arrested and executed, the emperor also capitulated to some of the demands for reforms in an effort to end the protests.

The willingness of the emperor to negotiate with the students marked a crucial moment in the history of Chinese student protest because it signaled that students had enough power to intimidate the government and to affect state policy; the emperor's capitulation also indicated the beginning of more complex student-government power relations and the realization by subsequent Chinese governments that unruly students must be dealt with through the exercise of decisive state power. Of course Chinese students and scholars during the Sung dynasty were much different than those inhabiting Chinese universities today, as they were groomed to be scholar-elite officials, helping to guide and guard the state, and they did so successfully for centuries, until imperialism and the complexities of the modern world made the educational system in China obsolete.[9] The traditional Chinese scholar was clearly outmoded by the time of the Opium War (1839–42), after which modern Western-style public universities took root in China (the first was founded in Beijing in 1898)[10] in an attempt to modernize the country. In 1905 the traditional examinations (which covered Chinese classics and resulted in appointments to state positions) were officially abolished.

With the influx of European-style universities into the Middle East and East Asia came European-style student protests. In 1876 students frustrated with their government in Turkey went on strike in Istanbul. Armed, Turkish students insisted that religious leaders be removed from state power; surprisingly, the state capitulated and ejected the leaders. A decade later students launched another protest against their government, this time in an effort to topple it; although the popular 1896 revolt failed, the attempt elicited greater enthusiasm for the activist students, notably among military students.[11]

In India the Students' Congress organized as a political association backing the Indian National Congress Party (after India gained independence, however, the National Congress dismantled the Students' Congress, which was perceived, by then, as a potential political rival). In 1890 the Indian Muslim Student Union formed, and shortly thereafter, the Bombay Students' Brotherhood (which was open to female members) organized at Bombay University to promote political causes, attacking, for instance, the caste system and debating the political future of Indian women.[12]

In the United States, abolitionist student groups continued to form in the North and the Midwest prior to 1865, but their actions were often countered by proslavery fraternities. In the North both antiwar and proslavery sentiment ran high. Just prior to and during the Civil War, abolitionist student groups formed in many northern schools, but the achievements of such groups were relatively limited and for the most part localized. After the war and increasingly as the new century approached, issues of whether black people should aspire to white middle-class status and assimilate or develop racial pride and follow a separatist agenda had students agitating at black colleges throughout the United States.[13] Following an 1885 ruling by a Baltimore judge that a law barring black people from Maryland's legal profession was unconstitutional, two black students, Harry Sythe Cummings and Charles W.

Johnson, entered and integrated the University of Maryland's law school in 1887. Even though the two students finished their studies with distinction, the law school once again excluded black people in 1890 following a series of white anti-integration protests on campus.[14]

Radical Russians: The Student Assassins

In the fifty years following the 1848 student uprisings in Europe, the most volatile student revolts occurred not in Europe, Africa, or the Americas but in Russia. Education had spread very quickly through Russia, leading to the equally quickly increasing rise in student groups and the government's merciless suppression of all student demonstrations. In many ways, compared to their European counterparts, Russian students were centuries behind in their use of collective power, but once they realized the extent of their potential leverage, they quickly made up for their relatively slow start.

Russian universities developed later than their European counterparts in large part due to the Mongol conquest in the thirteenth century. With Mongols controlling Russia for approximately two centuries, Russia's educational system was obliterated. So, even long after the ouster of the Mongols, most of Russia's citizens remained largely illiterate; the few institutions of higher education eventually established were devoted exclusively to military training or to the rigorous development of mathematical skills. Severe handicaps to the development of comprehensive universities—mainly the scarcity of teachers and the reluctance of the nobility to send their children to public institutions where they might mix with children of lower classes—remained effective well into the nineteenth century, despite efforts, especially by Peter the Great and by Catherine the Great, to rectify them.[15]

Only after Alexander I assumed control in the nineteenth century was a viable Russian university system organized; the tsar reformed the educational system when he divided Russia into six separate states, each of which held a separate university. To the list of three universities already existing at Moscow, Dorpat, and Vilna, Alexander I added three new institutions at Kazan, Kharkov, and Petersburg, and to offset the scarcity of Russian teachers, he enlisted foreign professors who taught their courses in Latin.[16] The nobility countered such progressiveness by sub-sidizing their own schools, which taught fashionable modern European languages and lessons in fencing, dancing, and etiquette. Russian students at both public universities and private schools, however, were soon also schooled in European liberalism and modern intellectual trends, and were given doses of European political history.[17]

Following the Napoleonic wars, and soured on European fashions, Alexander I turned extremely religious and conservative, and decided to restrict the educational influx of liberalism and the potential threat of nationalism surfacing among university students. The tsar clamped down on the Russian universities, forbidding anything that even smelled of activism or political reformism. After Alexander's death in 1825, his successor, Nicholas I, continued the restrictive measures his forebear placed on higher education, but he also had greater plans for higher education. Nicholas recognized in the fledgling Russian school system a means of controlling the nation's youth; mandating a conservative curriculum stressing loyalty to the dynasty, the tsar turned education into a state tool for fulfilling social predestination based on class. University students were uniformed, and inspectors observed and reported on the political orientation of individual students and professors. Government spies lurked in classrooms and in dormitories. Predictably, university students did not appreciate the sudden imposition of the new antiliberalism, but they could do little about it; unorganized and lacking both historical precedents for uprisings and numbers, they had little choice but to leave or to don their uniforms and go to class. In spite of the strictness, Russia's universities and educational system continued to grow.

Student resistance did not occur on any sizable scale in Russia until the 1860s. Presaged by growing student unrest (specifically, a limited protest against police brutality in Moscow in 1857, and a general student strike in Kharkov the following year protesting the viciousness of local police) and fueled by increases in restrictions placed upon all students by the state, massive student protests exploded in St. Petersburg and Moscow in the 1860s. A sizable number of students at St. Petersburg University gathered in 1861 to protest against the public silencing of a professor by local officials; they were brutally dispersed. Two weeks later students gathered again in St. Petersburg, where they were set upon by Cossacks. This brought more students into the streets in new waves of protest. Responding to the escalation in student activism, Tsar Alexander II backed a university statute denying students the right to organize and raised tuition—a clear message to the students that acts of resistance would incur penalties. Compounding these restrictions were others imposed by a new minister of education who, following the tsar's lead, not only further increased the price of university tuition (making an education prohibitive for a number of "fringe" students) but also implemented stricter regulations, described in a handbook that all university students were forced to read and to sign.

A large number of students at St. Petersburg who depended upon student aid to offset the cost of their education were suddenly threatened with removal from school, and the mandated signing of a regulation handbook was categorically disliked by all university students. Thus provoked and for the first time united in a protest against state regulations, the St. Petersburg students convened and decided to act as a unified body. Students forced their way into a university building to hold their first resistance meeting. The university responded to the students' audacious action—of breaking into a university building—by subsequently locking all students out of the university. Massed, but prevented from gaining entrance to the school, the students marched through St. Petersburg and began a strike. Instead of attending classes on the following day, students held a rally, which local police violently suppressed. The day after, even greater numbers of students rallied, but this time soldiers appeared; together with the police they beat and arrested hundreds of protesters. The students continued their boycott of classes, and the student strike eventually led to the university closing until the fall of 1863. The cost of the resistance was high, however; although most of the students arrested were released following the demonstrations, many of the leaders were exiled.

The St. Petersburg strike set a precedent for other disgruntled students to follow. Moscow university students immediately held a strike of their own, for example, though troops attacked the protesters and quickly dispersed them. In 1863, the state authorized measures to preempt further student dissension: regulations restored to the universities their pre-1861 autonomy, but at the same time outlawed student groups and assemblies (women activists were also targeted in the new statute; for example, it prohibited women from attending university lectures). But contrary to its intended purpose, the statute fostered more resentment than ever, and student groups that were subsequently forced to operate covertly became more extreme in their stances and their proposed actions. Student resistance was clearly on the rise, and the government's reactionary attempts to curb it through acts of negative reinforcement only exacerbated the situation.

Students met government suppression with strikes, demonstrations, and the formation of an active student counterculture that promoted liberalism and nationalism: students all over Russia vocally disparaged the state and began wearing the color blue to signal their solidarity. Russia was relatively isolated, but its students were not unaware of the European revolutions of 1848. Nor were they ignorant of the role students played in those uprisings; many envied the freedoms their European counterparts enjoyed. Additionally, Russian university professors had imported the concepts and ideals of both the Enlightenment and romanticism, and were teaching a generation about contemporary social movements.

In 1862 officials arrested Moscow university students for giving outlawed publications to peasants, but prison sentences gave the students time to compose more pamphlets, which called for immediate, violent revolution, the people's appropriation of industry, and the equal distribution of wealth. Printed outside Moscow and then passed throughout the city and the neighboring countryside, the pamphlets had immediate effects: fires were set in government buildings, and state property was vandalized; the state blamed the publications and attempted to eradicate them and the dissidents. The state's reaction only furthered the cohesion of student opposition groups.[18]

By 1865 Moscow students dedicated to revolution had banded together in secret groups that conspired to wreak havoc on the government. Deciding he would assassinate Tsar Alexander II in 1866, one such student conspirator, Dmitri Karakosov, journeyed to St. Petersburg (after the university had dropped him for not paying his fees), where he publicly distributed pamphlets heralding his intended upcoming regicide.[19] In April of 1866, as Alexander II toured the Summer Garden, Karakozov took up a position in a crowd and waited for the tsar to pass. When Alexander did, Karakozov stepped forward with a pistol, fired, and missed. The would-be assassin was quickly arrested, along with his student associates, whom he implicated. The student radical hanged in September. Karakozov's actions provoked a statewide crackdown on students in which police arrested hundreds of suspected radicals, relentlessly persecuted university liberals, and spied on university students' private lives.

Defeated and for a while purged from the universities, student activists turned away from university politics to focus instead on educating Russia's peasantry. Students organized local revolutionary groups that printed and disseminated socialist literature in an effort to prime the peasants and workers for revolution. The government tried to stamp out such revolutionary fires wherever they started, and for most of its early history, the Russian student movements played a dangerous game of survival; students formed groups, which the state would identify, infiltrate, and destroy, and any students surviving the raids would then reorganize new groups. For example, in 1871 Mark Natanson, leader of the socialist Natanson Group, was arrested and exiled for distributing illegal materials, but the organization's surviving members reformed to become the Chaikovsky Group, taking the name of its new leader. One of the group, Sofya Perovskaya, would eventually be implicated in the assassination of Alexander II and hanged in 1881.[20] The overwhelming and relentless suppression of small student organizations by the government effectively precluded any large-scale student organizations from forming in Russia in the last half of the nineteenth century, but ironically, illegal student societies became immensely popular and thrived in Russia's universities—the rage of both the politically as well as the fashionably minded. When students did publicly protest, however, they took great risks—if apprehended at a demonstration students faced the likelihood of arrest, imprisonment, labor camps, or deportation, after facing a line of charging Cossacks.

This relentless suppression had long-term effects for radical student causes and direct bearing on the coming revolution. Barred from articulating their interests within the university or the larger political sphere, students turned to the masses for an audience, aligning themselves with workers and with peasants. The masses did not always greet such an alliance favorably, but significantly, the categorical separation and violent antagonism that generally characterized the relations between European students and European peasants did not develop in Russia. The students focused on bringing socialism to the Russian peasants, and by the mid-1870s hundreds of university activists were in the fields preaching to rural laborers. Although the farmers did not appreciate the students' efforts as much as the students would have liked, importantly, the state recognized the two groups as an aligned, mutual threat.

The Land and Freedom group was one such organization that presumed an alliance between students and peasants. Mark Natanson, audaciously reappearing after his 1871 deportation, started the student group in 1876 in St. Petersburg, stating that the goals of the organization were to redistribute Russia's lands fairly. In December of 1876, the group marched and publicly called for open revolt. Of course, they were mercilessly attacked by police.

Most of the protests the organization planned over the next few years met with disaster, though the police habit of attacking everyone present at demonstrations, including innocent bystanders, only increased the solidarity of students and commoners in opposition to state authority. Confronted by such severe suppression, radicals turned to terrorism, and assassinations or assassination attempts became rather commonplace in Russia during the 1870s and '80s. University officials, police captains, state officials, and especially tsars—all were fair game for the extremist Russian student radical.

Student radicals were not operating in a vacuum, however; they were part of a revolutionary culture that promoted sacrificing oneself to a cause, one popularized in literature romanticizing alienation and venerating student martyrdom. Books such as Ivan Sergeyevich Turgenev's *Virgin Soil* and Sergei Mikhailovich Kravchinski's *Career of a Nihilist* (1889) only added to a well-developed Russian student counterculture that enjoyed its own fashions: men wore their hair long and women wore their hair short; both displayed a penchant for anything

and everything blue as long as it fit the nineteenth-century Russian ana-
logue to twentieth-century American grunge fashion. They were also
extremely vulgar in speech and propounded sexual license.[21]

Land and Freedom began to fall apart when its members divided over
the controversial turn to terrorism, but one of its proterrorist factions
stood firm by their goals and in 1879 planted a bomb under the tracks
over which a train carrying Alexander II from Odessa to Moscow would
pass. The bomb refused to ignite, however, and the tsar's train passed
safely; but at the opposite end of the rail, other members of the group
frantically dug a tunnel from a rented apartment in Moscow to another
spot on the tracks. The excavation completed, the group packed the end
of the tunnel with dynamite and lit a fuse as the tsar's train approached.
Once again the intended victim's train sped safely over the dynamite, but
this time the explosion destroyed the train following, with the tsar's
attendants and guards on board. Determined but ineffectual, more like
protagonists of a bad slapstick film than radical terrorists, the determined assassin student groups unsuccessfully tried to blow up the tsar a
few more times but succeeded only in killing bystanders.

They made a final attempt in 1881, and on this occasion the assassins
included backup strategies in case mines planted along the tsar's route
failed to kill him: they were to throw hand bombs at the tsar's personal
car and then charge with pistols. The death squad consisted of Ignaty
Grinevitsky, Nikolai Rysakov, and Ivan Yemelyanov; a fourth member,
Timofey Mikhailov, lost his nerve and withdrew his membership from
the conspiracy group just before the attack. Two women from the terrorist group, Vera Figner and Sofya Perovskaya, also helped plan the
assault. On March 1, the group exploded their bomb as the tsar passed
over it, and this time the tsar's car was actually hit, although the tsar
himself was unhurt. A Cossack was killed and a small boy was badly
wounded by the blast, however, and when Alexander emerged from his
car, Grinevitsky threw his grenade, which exploded at the tsar's feet.
Evacuated from the scene but mortally wounded, Alexander soon died.
All four of the men, Perovskaya, and another woman, Gesya Helfman,
were arrested, tried, and condemned to death, and all hanged. After
the assassination, police intensely suppressed the young radicals of
Russia, but militant students refused to surrender, making bombs and

assassinating more state officials (in 1882, for example, a group killed General Strelnikov).[22]

Over the next few years the cycle of student violence, government repression, and violent student retaliation continued, and the state continued to treat workers and students equally brutally. On the anniversary of the assassination of Alexander II in 1887, three members of a student group with grenades were arrested on the Nevsky Prospekt, where they were hoping the tsar might pass. The arrested students gave up the group's entire membership list, and five of the group, including Alexander Ulyanov, were hanged (the other members were sentenced to prison terms). Police also arrested and imprisoned the brother of Ulyanov, along with other students suspected of being radicals. Upon their release, they were expelled by their university at Kazan. Ulyanov's brother would afterward assume his martyred brother's revolutionary spirit and a new name: Vladimir Ilyich Lenin.

Serious student resistance in Russia for most of the last half of the nineteenth century was primarily a terrorist cat-and-mouse game, with the violent suppression of relatively small student protests fostering student political extremism and assassinations, which in turn fed the state's fear of student radicals and provoked harsh government reactions whenever even small student organizations and demonstrations surfaced. Limited protests and local demonstrations occurred from time to time, but the state immediately and decisively squashed any fledgling revolutionary act. Not until the eve of the new century did the Russian state begin to encounter widespread and organized mass student resistance.

Student unruliness within Russian university lecture halls sharply increased in the 1890s, as students increasingly perceived professors as aligned with university officials and viewed both as agents of the state. It was not uncommon in the 1890s for professors' lectures to be drowned out by catcalls from the attending students. Additionally, the illegal student societies were beginning to work together in a network. In 1891, in an unprecedented show of interuniversity student support, Moscow students went on strike to protest the police treatment of students at St. Petersburg; Cossacks attacked the Moscow students, and hundreds of students were afterward imprisoned or exiled. Another large action occurred in 1896, when students demonstrated in Moscow to commemorate those killed in the Khodynka stampede; once again Cossacks brutally attacked the participants, jailing hundreds of students. As a result of such suppression, demonstrations by university students increased in size and scope, and in turn the government stepped up its policy of quelling them by force. Demonstrations and violence escalated on both sides. In 1897 Maria Fedoyseyevna Vetrova, a student held at the Fortress of Peter and Paul on suspicion of operating an illegal press, martyred herself by dousing herself with oil and setting herself on fire; her funeral brought thousands of students together to march in solidarity. Protesters commemorated Vetrova in Kiev and Kharkov, where they were attacked by police.[23]

In February 1899 students called a series of massive national strikes after mounted, whip-bearing Cossacks charged student demonstrators at St. Petersburg University. Their demand was straightforward: students would not attend classes until police were forbidden to harm Russian students. The strikes began at St. Petersburg, but within a few weeks, thousands of students at a dozen universities had joined the protests. The strikes wavered but continued for most of the month of March, with the organizers of the steadily weakening action claiming victory in having challenged the oppressive state. The University of St. Petersburg retaliated by suspending all students and making them seek readmission in a process that would weed out the activists; angry, the students called more strikes.

But this time, the state reacted with overwhelming force: Cossacks attacked St. Petersburg University on March 31 and arrested hundreds of students. Moscow University expelled close to a thousand students, and protesters at the other institutions suffered as well. In a critical blunder of magnitude, student activists organized an emergency national conference with representatives from all the universities and institutions of higher learning; allowing the conference members to assemble, the police fell upon them and in a single swoop arrested all those leaders of the student strike who, up until that moment, had remained at large.

Russian students suffered greatly in striking, but although their gains were largely intangible, they realized that with collective solidarity and a central, popular issue, they could conceivably mobilize against the state.[24] The immediate losses were overwhelming: student deaths, mass expulsions from the universities, deportations, prison terms, and the implementation of further restrictive measures (students henceforth caught in disruptive behavior were to be conscripted into the military). Still, the Russian strikes also clearly defined students—all Russian students—as objects of state oppression; and after the general strike and its suppression, students could see the possibility of a national student movement, driven by a student-specific ideology, gloriously resisting the oppression of the autocrats. Students of revolutionary tactics also learned more practical lessons from the 1899 strike and its resolution. One was that rallying around popular issues with wide support avoids dividing the collective, which ultimately holds the source of student power; another was that never, even in desperate situations, should actively suppressed students put all of their political eggs in a single basket.

Although many students agitated, went on strikes, and assassinated officials or otherwise spread chaos and terror, the general studentry of Russia's universities could not effectively launch a mass movement against tsarist oppression in the first decades of the twentieth century. It would be up to workers and peasants to lead the revolt against Tsar Nicholas II in the spring of 1917, bringing an end to tsarist rule in Russia; and it would be Lenin's Bolsheviks who subsequently toppled Kerensky's subsequent provisional government. Lenin, who as a youth admired student leaders such as his own brother and Ivan Platonovitch Kaliaev, came to see student radicals as unstable and student movements as untrustworthy of carrying through a greater cause. Indeed, when the Bolshevik Revolution finally occurred, liberal students were left on the sidelines and even fell before the masses as victims; those joining in (largely members or supporters of the Social Revolutionaries) were reactionary leftists soon to discover that the popular causes to which they had ascribed had little use for intellectuals or respect for individual rights or independent thought, and could be just as totalitarian and terrorist as the system previously in power.

Although Russian studentry organized quickly once the universities were established, they were only rarely effective as a political force; kept isolated or limited to small groups, student activists and agitators repeatedly resorted to terrorist tactics that rarely sparked social change. The state's stranglehold on student resistance remained secure largely because universities had been developed from the top down, as institutions controlled by a powerful and largely uncompromising state. Unlike their European models, which often began as student collectives, Russian universities lacked precedents for effective acts of student resistance or the structures for accomplishing them. Students also faced overwhelming odds against a brutal and well-equipped police force that successfully kept individuals from organizing large collectives. The sole political recourse available to radicals—acts of individual terrorism—only served to feed the state's fears and caused it to tighten its grip on universities. The state itself as an organism of power was not greatly hurt by such individual acts of assassinations; tsars and ministers were replaced easily enough. Radical students themselves adopted the public roles of idealists, extremists, martyrs, and assassins and so—for a variety of reasons both within and beyond their control—did not join the greater revolutionary causes as rational or moral leaders seeking the realization of a better or more just society. In short, Russian student leaders of the era were on the whole great provocateurs, even great revolutionaries, but rightly perceived by the masses and the state as interested more in revolutions or revolutionary ideals than in the commitment to see a revolution through or concerned with the everyday realities of what a revolution might practically entail.

Success, Sabers, and Sacrifice, 1900–1919

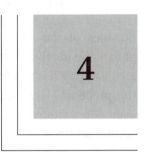

4

The Global Proliferation of Student Power

While students at Moscow and St. Petersburg were attempting, generally unsuccessfully, to launch a massive student campaign against institutional and state repression, students in the West were generating tremendous activist momentum, and student resistance energies continued to increase at a relatively stable pace in twentieth-century Europe. A fever for student organizations and demonstrations proliferated throughout the rest of the world in the first two decades of the twentieth century, however; Germany continued to lead the world in the production, upgrading, and networking of student organizations, although China ran a close second, and even surpassed Germany in exercises of direct action. The rage for student activism spread to a number of developing countries, including Argentina, Chile, Bosnia-Herzegovina, and Hungary. Philosophies advocating liberalism, the rights of the masses, and just revolts against political tyranny were used by students to legitimate struggles from China to Peru.

Students increasingly turned to terrorist measures, especially in Eastern Europe, in part because of the suppression of student political organizations but also due to the escalation in the production of cultural myths glorifying extremist student radicals. Indeed, a member of a radical Bosnian student group with a predilection for the radical Russian student martyr literature of Leonid Andreyev and the moody discontentedness of Fyodor Dostoyevsky and Miroslav Krleza struck the match that ignited World War I. Most student actions were far less violent than the assassinations occurring in Eastern Europe and Russia yet still had tremendous social effects, such as the student-led educational reform movements in Latin America. During these years student groups began to form truly international confederations as well. In short, the first decades of the twentieth century witnessed a hitherto unparalleled global rise in student activist activity, and while the weapons and strategies used by the modern students were for the most part developed in the preceding century, they also employed new tactics to new effects; even when students in different cultures and political contexts relied on similar strategies, they garnered radically different results.

European Students Continue to Organize

Student organizations continued to flourish in Germany after the turn of the century, and many students belonged to at least one organization or fraternity, and generally several. Seeking more power, smaller student groups aligned themselves under larger umbrella groups, and thus German studentry continued to develop a complex network of organizations, all seeking to define themselves individually and generate more power collectively. Since anti-Semitism and anti-Catholicism permeated many of the fraternities and elite student groups, threatened Jewish and Catholic students often sought security in liberal and antiexclusionary organizations, which quickly began forming to protect the interests of groups that were quickly becoming marginalized or disenfranchised. Other organizations formed to promote socialism, extreme nationalism, virulent racism, nonpartisanship, pure academics, or a folksy "Germanness"; student groups appeared in a myriad of varieties and with as many different agendas.

The fashion for organizations extended off campus to German youth, who between the ages of twelve and nineteen could belong to organizations such as the Deutscher Pfadfinderbund or the Wandervogel, an enormous organization of provincewide groups.[1] The prevalence of the German student and youth movements during the first few decades of the twentieth century suggested that the youth of the country were gripped in a need for self-definition and self-determination and desperately yearned for organizations that would give them a sense of collective power.[2] Although the formation of a group is itself a political action, the student groups of Germany during this time were not actively promoting reform or revolution as they had half a decade earlier; they primarily sought self-definition and busied themselves with organizing—often, it is true, in opposition to other groups. Of course the groups, or *Bunde,* served as appendages of social control as well, as long as the participants did not challenge society or the state. After World War I, a new cohesiveness characterized the relations between various youth and student groups, but the cooperation was generally based on patriotism rather than on revolt.[3] This is not to say that some groups did not seek revolution. Returning from military service in World War I, for example, Ernst Toller enrolled at the University of Munich and began agitating for revolution among his colleagues and local workers. The charismatic Toller organized and effectively sparked a local revolution in April 1919, with students and workers joining forces to "liberate" Munich. Forcefully taking control of Munich's government, the revolutionaries established a socialist Bavarian Republic in Munich. Troops immediately attacked and overwhelmed the revolutionaries and arrested the new republic's leader. In general, however, Germany's studentry was heading in a different direction than Toller's idealistic socialism. (Toller was incarcerated from 1919 to 1924; when freed he traveled to the United States, where he worked on his autobiography.)[4]

Other European countries witnessed the rage for organizing as well, though not nearly to the extent that Germany did. In France the Union Nationale des Etudiants de France (UNEF) was formed in Lille in May 1907. Initially, and for many years, UNEF remained weak and apolitical, but following World War I, membership increased dramatically and the group's numbers climbed, largely due to the jump in student enrollment at universities and the organization's increasing focus on student concerns and the quality of student life. In Great Britain, town-and-gown clashes continued at universities, and a number of student groups organized; but most of the organizing in the country occurred among preuniversity youth, who flocked to organizations such as the Boy Scouts (founded in 1907) or the Wolf Cubs (1916). A rage for organizing students and preuniversity youth swept through most other European nations, which all witnessed a significant rise in the number of such organizations and group memberships.

The organizations of European students, and youth, during the first decades of the twentieth century defined and mobilized large numbers of people; just as significant, though, are their objects of resistance, which tended to be other groups, not their universities or state governments. Their respective governments thus could look on the numbers of students mobilizing and not be immediately threatened by them; unlike their Russian counterparts, European students would be permitted to continue to organize and mobilize, to define themselves, and to grow in numbers and power. And as they did, they increasingly both shaped public opinion of them and influenced popular culture.

Russian Terrorism: The Suppression Continues, 1900–1919

In Russia, however, the student resistance scene continued to be dominated by strikes, suppression, and retaliation. In December 1900, students at Kiev were again striking, in this instance over the imprisonment and expulsion of student leaders. Cossacks, supported by several companies of professional soldiers, encircled and captured the protesters, and under the new regulations regarding the treatment of students convicted of disorderliness, over a quarter of the prisoners found themselves members of the Russian army. A poorly attended protest staged by the convicted students' colleagues followed the sentencing, resulting in yet more bodies for the Russian army. No further protests immediately occurred. The government's no-diplomacy policy thus effectively silenced organized student protest in Russia, although it also fostered individual extremist actions.[5]

Tensions rose between students and their universities and government; large protests, such as one in Kazan (March 1901) and another in Moscow (February 1902), sporadically erupted, but the government reacted in each case with immediate, crushing force. Responding to the Kazan demonstration, for example, Cossacks herded over one thousand protesters up against the front of the city cathedral before charging into the crowd with drawn sabers. Students captured by Cossacks at the demonstration at Moscow one year later were imprisoned or expelled from the university, and many found themselves in Siberia. Forced to seek other means of protesting, radical students turned to solitary acts of violence, thus completing the destructive cycle in which student protests were followed by violent government suppression, which provoked assassination attempts that led to arrests and executions—subsequently followed by another round of student protests.[6]

Unrest and violent suppression were not limited to universities, of course, though militant students were quick to join in any and all revolutionary activities; in January 1905, for example, Cossacks and soldiers brutally crushed peaceful demonstrators at the Winter Palace in the "Bloody Sunday Massacre."[7] In response, students all over Russia united in a strike, and Russia's institutions of higher education were closed by the students. Student agitation extended to private academies as well. Workers were striking at the same time throughout Russia, and when Russia suffered major losses to the Japanese in the Russo-Japanese War, the threat of a popular revolution loomed on the horizon. Besieged on several fronts at once, the state agreed to limited education reforms to placate the students, including granting the university autonomy and the students the right to organize and form political groups. The measures appeared to work, for the students subsequently ended the nationwide strike, but they did so primarily to use the universities and their new freedoms to organize and to further the growing revolutionary cause.

Holding political meetings on campus, which after the government concessions the police did not disrupt, students invited workers to attend and together they massed thousands of participants.[8] In October 1905 railroad workers called a general strike, and other workers, including state employees, joined in. Students continued to agitate and went on strike at many institutions throughout Russia.

Yet the government was not alone in its fight against the students and workers; angered by the chaos and the disruption caused by Russia's various strikes, mobs of conservatives believed the students to be responsible for the general labor strike crippling the nation, and guilds put under financial distress by the country's chaos invaded universities throughout the empire (students plotting a revolution ironically had to be protected by police when angry contingents of local businessmen attacked them). Responding to the chaos sweeping the nation, the tsar closed all universities, and in a surprising move, instead of suppression he agreed to give new freedoms to the students and to the masses: the October Manifesto allowed major government reforms and promised state representation for the hitherto unrepresented classes. Counter-reform riots immediately erupted, but it appeared for the moment that the leftists had won.[9]

Russia's universities finally reopened in 1906—once it appeared safe to do so—allowing women and Jews to attend, and student enrollment soared. The student revolutionaries were elated, and quickly turned their political attentions to academic and institutional issues; but in dividing themselves from the general population and Russia's workers in their new academic campaigns, they set themselves up to be conquered by their institutions and government. In a series of repressive measures, which included the expulsion of women and Jews from the universities and the revoking of students' right to organize, the state clamped down on the students.[10] Radical students retaliated with terrorist activities; Maria Spiridonova, for example, assassinated a military commandant in 1906.[11] Searching for a popular issue that would revitalize the student movement, students at massive memorial services for Leo Tolstoy tried to start a popular crusade for civil rights, but the effort failed, and police silenced the protesting students. Meanwhile, the state continued to rescind privileges granted by the October Manifesto. In 1911 the state boldly infringed on recently granted university autonomy by prohibiting student organizations on campus and mandating that police be used should students attempt to demonstrate. Students in St. Petersburg called a strike that soon spread to universities throughout Russia. This time students gained some outside support, with flimited support from workers after students and faculty were arrested for taking a stand against the state's assault on university autonomy; the damage done to the reputation of Russia's universities and their professional credibility fostered a smattering of middle-class outrage, but the student strike failed to provoke support or change. The students had once again isolated their concerns from those of the masses, and that insularity was their undoing.

A Bosnian Student's Action Sparks a World War

The century's turn witnessed students in Belgrade and Vienna reading the literature of revolution—Andreyev, Bakunin, Kropotkin, Ibsen, and

Herzen—and soon saw Slavic Bosnians publicly condemning the Austro-Hungarian domination of Bosnia. Heavily influenced by the Russian student terrorists, inspired by the Russian Revolution of 1905, and greatly angered by the annexation of Bosnia-Herzegovina to Austria-Hungary in 1908, many Bosnian students formed their own terrorist groups or abandoned universities outright to join militaristic revolutionary organizations such as the infamous Black Hand, founded in 1911 with a mixed membership of students, soldiers, and workers.[12]

As in turn-of-the-century Russia, student terrorism was the order of the day, and between 1910 and 1914 Bosnian students attempted to assassinate a number of Austrian officials. Imprisoned by the state or committing suicide to avoid capture, assassin students became martyrs to their fellow student terrorists, their sacrifices exalted in pamphlets and posters. As in Russia in previous decades, the state immediately suppressed all acts of student defiance, and in response Bosnian students increased their efforts—the more militant students retaliated against police suppression of demonstrations with a campaign of terror. After activism started heating up at Bosnian universities in January 1912, students in Zagreb seized a university building, barricaded it, and raised a flag of defiance; it took police, armed with sabers, two days to recapture the hall. That same year students demonstrated against the government in Sarajevo, and police troops called to disperse them opened fire with rifles. Demonstrations and violence broke out on campuses all over Bosnia. As police violence increased, so too did the militancy of the students. At a demonstration at which hundreds of students openly burned a Hungarian flag, a student activist leader and a member of the Black Hand was wounded when saber-wielding troops charged the protesters. Wearing a bandage stained with his own blood, Gavrilo Princip incited students in a strike the following day that spread from Zagreb across the rest of Bosnia. Troops suppressed the various demonstrations, though massive numbers of students engaged troops in pitched battles. The Austro-Hungarian troops, much like their Russian counterparts at the time, were relentless in suppressing student protests, and as a result student activists in Bosnia increasingly resorted to Russian-style student terrorism. In March the government closed all Croat-Serb schools, but the students continued to meet and to agitate off campus.

Students grew bolder. Even though they faced brutal suppression, more and more, they would appear in the streets protesting occupation. Assassination attempts, bombings, and acts of arson increased as well, and student terrorists made numerous attempts on the lives of the governor of Croatia, Count Cujav, and other state and military officials. In 1914 Princip (an avid fan of Kropotkin, Dostoyevsky, and Krleza) and a small group of Black Hand members attacked Franz Ferdinand as his caravan toured Sarajevo on June 28; one of the students tossed a grenade that destroyed the car immediately behind Ferdinand's, and in the ensuing chaos, Ferdinand's driver turned down a side street. Princip, who just happened to be close by, decided to act and shot both Ferdinand and the archduchess. The student was immediately mobbed by police. In custody the young assassin tried to eat a tablet of cyanide but failed; he was tried for treason with his comrades, but as they were all too young to be legally executed, they each received the maximum prison sentence for their crime.[13]

Austria-Hungary blamed Serbia for the assassination and on July 28, 1914, declared war; Russia, Serbia's ally, interceded on Serbia's behalf, and so began a chain reaction that provoked Germany, Great Britain, France, Italy, and the European powers to enter into the conflict. During the World War, student activism in all of the concerned countries fell off sharply, as the war effort drew the nations' youth into the conflict and absorbed most political and popular attention. Princip and his student allies may not have been responsible for the war, but their terrorist actions, cogs in a machine of repression and desperate reprisals, precipitated the conflict.

Radical Reforms in China and the Power of Protest

The first decades of the twentieth century were also filled with turmoil for China. An embarrassing defeat by the Japanese in 1895 allowed Chinese reformers the opportunity to voice their opinions publicly, and in 1898 a wave of revolutionary fever surged through the country, closely followed in 1900 by a sweeping reactionary movement. In an effort to modernize and Westernize at the turn of the twentieth century, China had sent students to foreign countries, primarily Japan, to study—though Japan was not particularly eager for an influx of Chinese students and restricted their activities and freedoms severely. Back on the mainland, an imperial edict abolished the 2,000-year-old exam system for students in China, but Chinese youth did not think reforms were happening quickly enough. Frustrated by the restrictions on them in Japan, and just as frustrated by the China they returned to, students began organizing, and in 1906 they formed a nationwide federation of students from all of the provinces of China, which promoted substantial political and cultural reforms. Arguing for a government parliament, increased educational opportunities, and the adoption of a single language, the organization published its views in pamphlets and newspapers, and although the federation soon fell apart, it was the beginning attempt at national organization in modern China.

As young intellectuals pushed for cultural, educational, and political reform, the revolutions of 1911 and 1913 successfully swept away the last of China's traditional educational system and ended the Manchu dynasty. During Sun Yat-sen's provisional presidency of the Chinese Republic and Yüan Shih-k'ai's subsequent inept tenure, newspapers and journals promoting further reforms or wholesale Westernization appeared that championed democracy, liberalism, and technology, and derided the "backwardness" of Confucianism and China's aristocracy. Many of these directly appealed to Chinese students for a complete cultural revolution and greatly influenced the future development of the May Fourth Movement by inspiring the formation of many student groups throughout China, one of which was formed under the auspices of a young Mao Zedong. [14]

A series of incidents led up to the 1919 May Fourth Movement. In 1915 Japan presented demands to Yüan Shih-k'ai, the president of the new republic, to which he submitted. The demands called for the appointment of Japanese officials to oversee China's government, military, and police, and gave Japan dominance over a number of Chinese territories. Angry students held demonstrations all over China, but Chinese police suppressed the student protests.

Many students fiercely opposed the presence of the Japanese in China; forming groups, they agitated for cultural reform and for resistance to Japanese imperialism, many of them publishing their opinions in pamphlets and journals. Most of China's students and much of the general public felt their own government was betraying them by simply handing China over to Japanese control after China's government allowed Japan to station troops in Manchuria and Mongolia. In May 1918, demonstrating students marched to the president's office in Beijing in protest. Student demonstrations occurred in all of the other major cities as well. Such demonstrations ended not in police violence but with government representatives trying to satisfy students with promises. The students returned to their studies but did not cease their criticisms of the government's submission to Japan.

Major student unrest burst out in the May Fourth Movement, beginning with demonstrations at Beijing University in 1919; like previous demonstrations, but much larger, the May Fourth actions protested against the Japanese domination of China. Following the Paris Peace Conference after World War I, students were stunned and outraged to discover that the victors gave Japan control of Shandong province rather than returning control of the region to China. On the morning of May 4, students began a telegram campaign to appeal to institutions and organizations throughout China as well as to others outside the country, to protest the decision of the Paris Peace Conference granting Japan control over Chinese provinces.

That afternoon thousands of students converged on the Square of Heavenly Peace in Beijing. After demonstrating for some time on the square, the students marched along a previously announced route, while police watched but did not interfere, until the students tried to march through the area of Beijing that housed foreign ministers. Blocked from proceeding, the students angrily attacked and burned the home of a Chinese official identified as a Japanese sympathizer. Police interceded and attacked the students.

Student group representatives met on May 5 and formed a student organization uniting both university and secondary school students. The students continued to demonstrate in Beijing, and in cities such as Nanjing and Shanghai, students marched to show solidarity. Several thousand students demonstrating in Shanghai were supported in their protests by thousands of workers and residents.[15] In a move that showed the backbone the students were calling for—though directed at the students rather than at Japan—the government ordered out the troops and viciously suppressed the demonstrators in Beijing, beating and arresting hundreds of students. Thoroughly outraged, the Beijing students declared a general strike on May 19 that was soon joined by students attending major universities and many secondary institutions in China. The government reacted by declaring Beijing under martial law and cracking down on students all over China as well. Prompted by the student strike, the workers and merchants of Shanghai instituted their own strikes, forcing the Chinese government to free the arrested and imprisoned students and to reject the pro-Japanese provisions outlined in the Treaty of Versailles, for a time blocking further Japanese imperialism. The victorious students called off the strikes, but they continued to boycott Japanese goods.[16]

The success of the May Fourth Movement empowered students and incited them to further agitate and join student groups, and many organizations formed immediately after the movement's victory.[17] One of the more significant new organizations on the scene was the National Student Association, a group that attempted to organize national student resistance actions. Riding a wave of generational enthusiasm, Chinese students advocated complete cultural and political reformation for their nation, increased Westernization, a national Communist Party, and stronger ties with Russia.

The importance of the May Fourth Movement in China's history cannot be stressed too much; it marked a turning point for the country, a moment at which the nation's traditional values and cultures and its existing political and philosophical structures were largely abandoned as China looked to the West for ideas and materials. The student-led movement united students, workers, merchants, and much of the general urban public in an effort to create a new China with a modern and reinvigorated Chinese culture.

Radical Reforms in Latin America

One of the few accurate generalizations that can be made about Latin America as a whole is that the area became a hotbed of student activism and resistance in the early decades of the twentieth century. Latin

American countries have always differed radically from one another culturally, linguistically, politically, and socially, and their educational systems differ as well; yet the influence of students and their movements has crossed many of the region's national borders. Many of the countries—including Peru, Argentina, Ecuador, and Mexico—already had by the twentieth century a history of local student activism, but it was after the turn of the century that student resistance in Latin America became a powerful, major force that had to be reckoned with by individual states.

One high-profile group, the Federación de Estudiantes de Chile, or FECH, arose in 1906 from a protest by Santiago students at the University of Chile, angered at their lack of local standing and power—local officials received more credit and better public treatment than the students, who had recently helped to stop an epidemic. In 1918 the government of Chile permitted FECH to incorporate, and the following year it began working with workers' unions. In 1920 it brought together hundreds of representatives from schools across the country to formulate an agenda and to plan strategies to agitate for socialism and social reform in Chile. Demonstrations and the appearance of student political publications soon followed. Although Chile's studentry rushed to join, FECH was neither embraced nor ignored by the general population of Chile; yet in the wake of protests against Chile's aggression toward Peru in 1920, members of the organization were harassed by right-wing youth. Following Argentina's student uprising and the major university reforms garnered in the neighboring state in 1918, FECH attempted to follow suit, but the union simply could not generate popular interest and thus had limited impact on the Chilean educational system, though it encouraged student involvement in politics both in Chile and neighboring nations. The federation fell apart in the early 1920s, but was later revived and eventually led an active life agitating for social and political reforms in Chile.[18]

Ecuador saw notable student involvement in politics in 1907, when university students marched in Quito to protest election violations and the president of Ecuador's unscrupulous business transactions. Quito police violently attacked the protesters, killing several and injuring many more, but students continued to demonstrate for government reforms. Student agitation and the violent government suppression of student demonstrations were not unique to Ecuador and Chile. Brazil, Peru, Paraguay, Bolivia, and other countries all saw increasing student activism and violent state retaliation in the first two decades of the twentieth century. The International Congress of American Students took place in Uruguay in 1909; representatives from Argentina, Brazil, Chile, Ecuador, Peru, Uruguay, Paraguay, and Bolivia attended as they debated university and state reforms in all of their countries. The students agreed on the necessity of student involvement in university decision making and on the need for major university reforms, and that an international congress of students should continue to meet annually. This congress initiated a dialogue among students of the different Latin American nations and established a consensus regarding important political reforms.

The student reform movement soared in Argentina. In March of 1918, University of Córdoba students went on strike, claiming they would hold out until their demands, which included student participation in university government, were met. When university officials ignored them, the student Comité Pro-Reforma retaliated by orchestrating a large public demonstration at the end of the month. University officials responded by shutting down the university. Deadlocked, with neither side willing to make concessions, representatives of the students and of the universities appealed to the minister of education, who agreed to a formal investigation of the problem—on the stipulation that the strike end and the university reopen. The investigation held the Córdoba university responsible for the problems. President Hipolito Irigoyen followed the advice of the investigation committee and signed reforms into effect in May. Elated, students rejoiced, but they also continued to organize to make sure the proposed reforms were followed.[19]

Elections were held one month later for the rector of the University of Córdoba, and when the students' favorite lost, they began to protest again, occupying the university. Students all over Argentina voiced solidarity with the demonstrators in Córdoba; popular figures in the public media followed suit, and the students' reforms suddenly exploded into a major political issue. In July, a congress of students representing Argentina's universities met and drafted a document accusing the universities of being archaic and corrupt houses of nepotism, sanctuaries for the mediocre and the ignorant. The congress characterized students as pure, heroic, uncorrupted; if at times violent, it held, they were so for idealistic reasons. The students also called for university autonomy, the opening of the universities to all classes of citizens, and increased student representation.

Although the new rector resigned, the university remained closed for months. Frustrated at government indifference, a group of students occupied university buildings yet again, and again they appealed to the minister of education for help. Police and government troops retook the university and arrested the students, and while provoked by their actions, Minister of Education José Salinas nevertheless investigated the students' complaints, and urged the president to accede to the student reforms. In October 1918, President Irigoyen did so almost categorically. The students clearly were dedicated to reform and willing to face armed government troops in order to achieve it, but their success hinged on the willing ear of Salinas and on his influence with Irigoyen. Argentina's universities did need drastic reforms, and by going to desperate measures—without resorting to violence or explicitly challenging the government or Irigoyen politically—the students were able to negotiate some remarkable changes.

The Argentinean university reform movement was a complete success, not only radically changing the nature of higher education in Argentina but also influencing many other Latin American student movements. At the University of San Marcos in Lima, Peru, for instance, students encouraged by the success of the Argentinean student reforms went on strike in 1919 for reforms to their own university system. After months of strikes by students and workers, Peru's government granted the requested reforms, which included student participation in university government, curricular reforms, and the separation of church and higher education. An organization leading the Peruvian student resistance actions, the Federación de Estudiantes de Perú, joined in an alliance with the Federación Universitaria Argentina in 1920 to generate the Alianza Popular Revolucionara Americana, or Aprista, political party.

The Argentinean movement serves as a textbook example of effective student resistance. It began with the founding around a central issue of an organization that used a variety of strategies to heighten public awareness and to marshal public support, including holding rallies and marches, disseminating publications, and releasing manifestos. It demanded and held the attention of national and international media. The movement then opened diplomatic channels with state officials, and student representatives sat down with university administrators in official arbitration meetings. When talks broke down, students resorted to the occupation of buildings, not to vandalize, but to focus public and media attention on their plight. Thus, the group successfully turned academic interests into national political issues. Its success also hinged on the fact that it posed no direct challenge to Irigoyen or the state, and that the state did not perceive it as a threat and suppress it, as other Latin American governments had done with student activists. The end result was the complete reform of the university system of Argentina: universities became autonomous institutions; student representatives were included in all university decisions, including the hiring of faculty; the university entrance policies were democratized, and financial assistance programs instituted; and students could design their own programs of study, select what courses they would take, and attend universities free of charge. Most significantly, the doors to the universities were opened to Argentina's lower classes.

The reforms achieved by the students in Argentina were desired by students in nations throughout Latin America, and the movement caught on in Chile, Cuba, Ecuador, and Mexico; eventually a total of eighteen countries joined Argentina in adopting all or part of the Argentinean students' reforms. Of course the power of Argentina's studentry depended to a great extent on the president of Argentina's indulgence. He was willing to listen to the grievances of the students. Irigoyen's 1922 successor, Máximo Marvelo de Alvear, however, attempted to destroy the progress made by the students in 1918, violently suppressing the liberal Argentinean student movement.

Student Resistance around the World

Many other countries witnessed student groups forming and agitating, but none saw the scale of student resistance or agitation that occurred in China, Latin America, Bosnia, and Russia at the turn of the century. Japan had its share of student activism during the century's first decades; a number of Chinese student organizations protested in Tokyo against Japanese imperialism before returning as a block to join the students in China in May 1919. But Japanese student organizations formed and demonstrated as well. Japanese workers and students began founding unions in 1918, and a national organization for Japanese students, Shinjin-kai, was also founded that year. It promoted social liberalism, publishing a newspaper called *Democracy*, and led in national organization efforts up until the early 1920s, when it was supplanted by the Gyominkai.[20]

Minor organizations promoting political activity but espousing no particular ideology, such as the Cosmopolitan Clubs or the Intercollegiate Civic League, formed in the United States in the first decades of the twentieth century. The most visible and notorious student organizations in the States were those actively promoting socialism, and universities in California and Wisconsin were the first to host socialist student groups. But the first student socialist organization of any size, the Intercollegiate Socialist Society, formed in New York. With Jack London as president and Upton Sinclair as vice president, the group fostered the formation of socialist study groups at universities across North America and published a newspaper called *Intercollegiate Socialist* (changed to *Socialist Review* in 1919). By 1916 the society boasted chapters at dozens of U.S. colleges and universities, but within two years—by the end of World War I—the organization was for all practical purposes dead, a victim of relentless attacks by the U.S. public, which mistakenly conflated the student group with the Socialist Party.[21]

Other student groups were more typical targets of American middle-class hostility. The Young Intellectuals, a group that advocated sexual license and actively supported socialism and feminism, was a prototype for many of the radical organizations that would inhabit universities later in the century. Other radical organizations of the time, which had agenda very different from the Young Intellectuals, included the Collegiate Anti-Militarism League (begun in 1915 at Columbia) and the Intercollegiate Liberal League for centrists on the student political spectrum (started in 1919). But by the end of the first decade of the twentieth century, U.S. student activists had a bad reputation with the nation's public. Outrageous declarations by groups such as the Young Intellectuals and actions such as the defiance of state-imposed emergency health quarantine during a smallpox epidemic by activists at the University of Nevada, Reno, in 1902 outraged many U.S. citizens and encouraged a popular perception that student activists were irresponsible and dangerous.[22] While a craze for youth organizations swept across North America, as in Britain, it was largely confined to preuniversity youth, who flocked to organizations such as Woodcraft Indians, Boy Scouts of America, Girls Scouts, and Camp Fire Girls. The proliferation of youth movements was important for university student movements; it both contextualized them and to some extent normalized their existence to the public. These organizations also prepared youth for working in student organizations in universities.

The first decades of the new century also witnessed the rise of international student organizations, such as the Socialist Youth International (organized in 1907) and the apolitical Confédération International des Etudiants (originally begun in Strasbourg in 1919 to unite students of the Allied powers), which the League of Nations would acknowledge in 1937 as the global representative for students.

In the first two decades of the twentieth century, student organizations proliferated around the world. Student resistance caused a revolution in Munich, led to reforms in educational systems in Latin America, aided the modernization of China, and touched off a series of events leading to a world war. The strategies employed by students varied greatly. Russia and Bosnia were caught in a brutal cycle of violence—student demonstrations were violently and effectively suppressed, forcing extremists to resort to terrorism and assassinations, which caused more suppression, demonstrations, and violence. The acts of terrorism were also an indication of the desperation of student activists, and indeed Russian and Bosnian students could not launch a major student movement because of their governments' zero-tolerance policy. By contrast, students were able to unite and achieve significant results in China and in many Latin American countries: in the former because they were able to tap other sources of power—namely, workers—against an unpopular government, and in the latter by organizing and forcing their criticisms on university systems and not directly challenging state authority. In both instances, the students were able to pitch their concerns to the general public and garner popular support. In any case, students across the globe realized the power of the collective and joined or formed organizations in unprecedented numbers. Their power and limitations were felt and realized by many governments, and many future political leaders. But the establishment of schools and youth organizations—often an explicit means of social control— came with a significant risk, one that would be acutely realized in the decade to come.

Reform and Terrorism in the 1920s and 1930s

5

Revolutions in Latin America

Students continued to organize throughout Latin America in the 1920s and 1930s. Even though the flagship of Latin American student resistance in Argentina had sunk by 1919, the revolutionary wake it generated swept over its neighboring nations. In 1922, and again in 1924, Colombian students inspired by the reform movement in Argentina held national conferences and formed the Federación de Estudiantes Colombianos, an extremely active, if relatively ineffectual, political organization. The Colombian federation used tactics similar to those employed by the Argentine students, but because the students lacked public support and the Colombian government was willing to use force against them, the group achieved little. In May 1923 students from the University of San Marcos at Lima protested against Peruvian president Augusto Leguía's autocratic policies. Again, suppression was swift and violent; the Peruvian police fell on the demonstrators, killing two protesters. After the suppression, Leguía shut down the university and deported the leaders of the demonstrations. Led by pariah Victor Raúl Haya de la Torre, a new group, the Alianza Popular Revolucionara Americana, or APRA, movement (members of which were known as Apristas), spread through Latin America calling for unity and solidarity across all Latin American nations, and among all of its peoples and classes. The Apristas were anti-imperialists and revolutionary socialists whose goals of social reform and nationalism of industry heavily influenced many national Latin American student organizations.[1]

Inspired by the success of the students in Argentina, students in Venezuela also began their own movement for reforms. President Juan Vincente Gómez ruled the country with an iron fist, prohibiting both demonstrations and student organizations from university campuses. In

February 1928 students openly registered their disapproval of Gómez with a week of loud, riotous demonstrations; originally organized as a cultural celebration by the Federación de Estudiantes de Venezuela (a politically progressive student group), the protests quickly grew in size and intensity, and their focus shifted from highlights of Venezuelan culture to a critique of the dictator. Although students caught by police were arrested and imprisoned, they continued to plan future actions, and upon their release they began demonstrating again, attempting to incite a general revolution, going so far as to attack the Caracas military base and Gómez's palace. But the Tyrant of the Andes had earned his moniker, and the student-led revolution was doomed; the military feared Gómez more than students or their generals, so troops quelled the rebellion, arrested many of the demonstrators, and deported the students' leaders. (One of these, Rómulo Betancourt, would eventually return to rule Venezuela.) The student federation itself was suppressed by Gómez and forced to go underground, but on February 14, 1936, it resurfaced with a vengeance against Gómez's political heir, Eleázar López Contreras. In a violent protest students stormed the residences of Venezuelan officials, vandalizing them and attacking whomever they could find on the premises. Police troops called out to restore order were excessively violent and opened fire on the rioters, leaving a great number wounded or dead. Yet the new dictator was watching events carefully; fearing that the student uprising might spark something larger, López subsequently restructured Venezuela's educational system and some social systems, including health care.[2]

A general air of revolution hung over Latin America in the early twentieth century, but the individual student-led reform movements in Central and South America were often radically different from one another in scope, goals, and efficacy. In Argentina in September 1930, for example, thousands of students demonstrating in Buenos Aires against President Hipólito Irigoyen, the Argentinean president who had listened to students a decade earlier, were attacked by police armed with guns and clubs. The direct challenge to Irigoyen could not be ignored by the government, but the police violence turned the public's favor toward the students, and as a result of public pressure Irigoyen resigned. The next day, the army, supported by the demonstrating students, took possession of the government. Having claimed responsibility for the coup, the students suddenly found themselves political bedfellows with the right-wing military. The generals who took over the government subsequently refused to relinquish control, and the Argentinean students learned an important lesson: although instrumental in felling an unpopular leader, they were politically weak when left without a specific force against which to fight (in this case, once Irigoyen was gone). Thus Argentina's student-led revolt followed what was already becoming a typical twentieth-century pattern: students goading the government into violence that the media covered, and which subsequently brought massive public support behind the students. But following another pattern in the history of student resistance, once the Argentinean students' opposition fell, they found they were ill equipped to rule.[3]

Heady with the anticipation of revolution, students from all over Latin America met in Mexico in 1931 to form the first Latin American Student Congress, which further spread the seeds of discontent, and allowed the students to experience a certain amount of international solidarity. Students at the congress railed against dictatorships, praised democracies, and advocated democratic social reforms, and they also shared strategies for effectively holding demonstrations and strikes, disseminating revolutionary information, and constructing boycotts. Throughout the next decade, students would continue to strike and demonstrate for political and social reforms, and the threat of revolution remained strong in various countries across the continent, but the heyday of effective, large-scale Latin American student action had for the time passed. And yet the mythology of the Argentinean student resistance had only just begun; entering the discourses of Latin American student activism and student power, the Argentinean reform movement would serve as a future model for student resistance in Latin American countries for years to come.[4]

Student Struggles in China

In response to the May Fourth movement, localized Communist organizations began to form throughout China in 1920, and in 1921 representatives of a number of these small groups met to form the Chinese

Communist Party in Shanghai.[5] One of the representatives, Mao Zedong, soon emerged as a leader, and he welcomed students to the organization; a great many accepted his invitation. The Guomindang government, which was itself increasingly becoming Leninist, also enlisted students in the process of reforming China, and during the mid-1920s, the two parties appeared on peaceful terms, if not actually allied in mutual reform efforts. Near Canton, Chiang Kai-shek began training a Guomindang military elite at the Whampoa Military Academy, and students from all over China swelled its ranks, yearning for nationalism, national revolution, and a future Chinese military power.

Meanwhile other Chinese students joined with workers to clash against imperialist organizations, Chinese police, and foreign soldiers in a series of violent protests. In February 1925 Chinese workers went on strike at a Japanese-owned textile mill in Shanghai, eventually inducing workers at other Japanese-owned factories to join them. Students from the University of Shanghai aided the workers in their demonstrations and helped spread the strikes to other factories. Factory officials and strikers negotiated a settlement, and workers returned to the factories in a few weeks; in May unhappy workers called another strike, and in protests that month a worker was shot and killed in a confrontation between Chinese strikers and Japanese overseers. Students supporting the workers immediately responded by organizing a large demonstration against foreign imperialism and holding a memorial service for the worker, which thousands of people attended. Police arrested a number of student leaders following the service.[6]

By the afternoon of May 30 the situation at the police headquarters holding the arrested students was extremely tense; hundreds of students marched through the streets of Shanghai before stopping before the police station shouting for the jailed students' release. Armed police under the command of a British officer met the angry students in front of the station, and his troops were given the command to fire on the angry crowd. They slew ten students outright and wounded many more. Outraged at the violence, students and workers marched again the following day, along the same route, and were again brutally attacked by police. More students were killed.

The violence united students, workers, and residents, and over the next four months, in what became known as the May Thirtieth Movement, students and workers in Shanghai went on strike and declared boycotts on imperialist goods; their principal goal was to halt production in foreign-owned factories, but they also wanted increased civil rights, social reforms, higher wages, and better working conditions. Uprisings elsewhere in the country suggested that China was on the verge of a revolution. In June 1925 the cadets from Whampoa Military Academy publicly marched to demonstrate against the massacre of the May Thirtieth protesters, only to be shot by British machine guns. Following the killings, nationalist fever among Chinese youth hit its highest point; students and youth flocked to national or anti-imperialist organizations, including the Guomindang and the Chinese Communist Party.[7] Foreign factories in Shanghai were shut down for months, and the strikes finally ended in September when the Shanghai workers' union agreed to negotiate with the imperialists. Although the structures governing Shanghai trade and labor remained relatively unchanged by the strikes, the May Thirtieth Movement united Chinese students, merchants, and workers all over the country in anti-imperialist sentiment and actions (many foreign goods continued to be boycotted long after the strikes ended, for example), induced many individuals to join unions, and generally heightened the political fervor consuming China. Hitherto apolitical students were radicalized by the event, and it brought thousands of new members to the Guomindang and to the Chinese Communist Party.[8]

Activist students continued to demonstrate against foreign imperialism, but they were met with brutal suppression from either foreign troops or police hired by Chinese officials. In March 1926, for example, anti-imperialist demonstrators in Beijing consisting mostly of university students were brutally gunned down by the mercenary troops of a Beijing politico. Nearly fifty protesters were killed. Similar incidents of violence occurring throughout China spurred more and more supporters to the Guomindang and to the Chinese Communist Party, the two major nationalistic groups; as these two groups individually increased in power, they began to compete with one another, and in 1927 Chiang

Kai-shek, the leader of the Guomindang, ordered the purification of the state, purging Communists from the government and universities. Communist teachers were expelled or executed, as were many radical students; for example, the party sentenced to death Communist members of China's National Student Association. Students were subsequently forbidden to form unions or hold mass demonstrations; the Guomindang government proclaimed that students were to study and do nothing else. But although Communism was publicly attacked, and Communists were purged from the government and hounded out of the universities, the Communist Party nevertheless remained a strong force in China.

Students on the whole in China, however, were politically driven by nationalism; as the Guomindang government based in Nanking was at that moment in history the only organization with the potential power to challenge the imperial powers, China's studentry generally backed the government.[9] Chiang Kai-shek realized the power that students could generate and skillfully encouraged their anti-imperialist anger at the Japanese. In May 1928, for example, the Guomindang military battled in Tsinan against mercenary soldiers and Japanese troops "officially" there to maintain the peace; using the Japanese presence to incite China's studentry, the Guomindang profited by the students' subsequent protests against the Japanese and a national student boycott of Japanese products. Yet as the student movement increased in strength, the Guomindang became alarmed by its power—especially since many student groups had Communist leanings. Rather than suppressing student activism, however, the Guomindang government began to work closely with student leaders, allowing protests and strikes but diplomatically ensuring that the student protests remained legal and controlled, and of course directed at Japan. The national government thus marshaled the students' power.[10]

The Japanese invaded Manchuria in September 1931, and thousands of students across China protested, calling for immediate action; students in Shanghai wanted to form student militias. Chiang Kai-shek encouraged the students on the one hand, letting them demonstrate and organize into volunteer militia led and trained by members of the Guomindang, but on the other he failed to move against the Japanese.

As his first concern was in eliminating the Communist threat in China, the leader of the Guomindang played a delicate game of appeasement between the unruly at home and foreign aggression while purging the country of Communists. When a group of students angered at the invasion of Manchuria attacked a foreign official in Nanjing, for example, Chiang Kai-shek voiced disapproval of the students' actions and in the same breath claimed the government would repel the invaders, knowing at the time that China was unprepared to resist the Japanese. When it became clear to the Chinese students that the Guomindang government was not going to fight the Japanese in Manchuria—that, instead, it was taking a conciliatory stance with the invaders—the students began to defy the Guomindang government openly. By December students in Shanghai and Nanjing were striking in an effort to force the government to address the invasion, but they protested in vain. The government simply would not face down Japan. Frustrated at China's continued submission to Japan, thousands of anti-Guomindang students rampaged through the streets of Beijing, destroying government offices and battling with police; Beijing police violently quelled the riot and arrested the leaders of the demonstration. Police forces across China brutally suppressed subsequent demonstrations and effectively destroyed the student movement.[11]

As the Red Army retreated from its base in South China, fearing Chiang Kai-shek's Guomindang forces, in 1935 students gathered in Beijing yet again, in the largest demonstration the city had yet seen: protesting new Japanese movements in Mongolia and Chiang Kai-shek's inaction, thousands of students marched on December 9, demanding government action and an end to the Guomindang and Chinese Communist Party hostilities, arguing for a truce so that a united opposition to the Japanese could be launched. The Guomindang police roughly suppressed the demonstrators, but the brutal actions also provoked a wider protest. One week later, thousands of striking students again took to the streets and instituted a boycott on all Japanese goods. For some time the students in the streets repelled city police and Guomindang troops, though many demonstrators were severely beaten. The Guomindang again used the student uprisings as leverage in dealing with the Japanese (they claimed the citizenry of China was on the brink of revolt and would not stand for the Japan's new demands), but this time, to the government's dismay, the student movement threat was real. It had gained public support, spreading to over a dozen major cities, and ignited scores of sympathetic demonstrations. Because it garnered massive public support, the December Ninth Movement successfully forestalled the creation of a new northern province, which Japan would control, and inhibited further acts of Japanese imperialism, radicalizing students while spreading disillusionment with the Guomindang, thereby increasing the popularity of the Chinese Communist Party as a political alternative.[12]

Lu Ts'ui, a student at the Tsinghau University in Beijing, was one of the student heroes of the December Ninth Movement, personally leading thousands of Tsinghau students on a December 16 antiimperialist march to Sunchih Gate in Beijing. Blocked by the closed gate and a unit of police, Lu Ts'ui herself dived under the gate and attempted to unlock it from within; the police inside the gate beat her in front of the gathered students and then jailed her within the compound. Her followers held a strike before the gate until she was released that evening. Appearing at the gate opposite the striking students, she dove under the gate again and, flanked by the demonstrators, marched back to the university. On their way back, they were attacked by police with clubs. The notoriety of Lu Ts'ui and the Tsinghau University protesters swept across China and inspired students to protest, but their actions came with great costs. In mid-February armed police troops launched an unprovoked attack on Tsinghau University; surprisingly, they were repelled by students. The police were forced to retreat, and the students erected defensive barricades. Trying to enter the university to arrest specific students for political dissent, university officials and a small contingent of policemen were captured by the students and held hostage; that night hundreds of police troops, supported by companies of the Guomindang army, invaded the university, but the dissidents they sought, including Lu Ts'ui, had by then escaped. The Guomindang attacked the university once more in February but were again unsuccessful in capturing Lu Ts'ui and other Tsinghau University radicals. This time she fled to Paris, where she became a member of the Chinese Communist Party; she continued to organize, to agitate, and to work for a Communist revolution in China. Although exiled, Lu Ts'ui remained an inspiration to the students of China and was mythologized by students for generations to come.[13]

The last major actions of student resistance before the oncoming war with Japan, which subsequently absorbed most of the political students' energies, involved a desperate act in which Chiang Kai-shek was captured by members of the Northeast Army. The leader had encouraged student veterans of the December 9 uprising to join his troops, and hundreds of these students formed companies in his army. Criticized by Chiang Kai-shek for sheltering revolutionaries, the army commander retaliated; on December 12 he and a contingent of soldiers and student-soldiers captured Chiang Kai-shek. Although radical students and members of the Chinese Communist Party supported an immediate government takeover, the Guomindang, backed by a large right-wing student movement, pressured for Chiang Kai-shek's return, and even Mao Zedong publicly backed Chiang's return to freedom. In the hope of uniting the factions vying for power in China, the president was released on December 25 (and the renegade commander was himself arrested). Disillusioned, the veteran students of the December Ninth Movement abandoned their ties to the army, left the universities, and headed north to find the Red Army.[14]

Attacking Imperialism in the East

Following the Versailles Treaty, imperialist Japan's reach extended over Korea, as well as much of China, and anti-Japanese sentiment ran high among politically oriented students in Korea in the 1920s. Their hostility erupted in a few notable acts of student resistance. On June 10, 1926, thousands of students in Seoul joined a larger demonstration during the funeral of Korean emperor Sunjong. During the demonstration, a group of students hoisted the illegal Korean flag and began chanting anti-Japanese slogans; police arrived on the scene and attacked the protesters, dispersing the demonstrators and arresting those students they could catch. For the next few years, university students held localized demonstrations and strikes protesting their treatment by Japanese in Korean schools. In 1929 conflict broke out between Korean and Japanese students at public schools in Kwanju, Korea, over Japanese students' racism and sexism, which was primarily leveled at female Korean students. The initial conflict immediately expanded, and Kwanju's schools split along national lines, becoming battlegrounds for violence. The student battles raged throughout the city, and when Korean students were arrested for the disturbance, colleges and secondary schools all over Korea erupted in violence. Tens of thousands of students, many of them angry women, participated in the uprisings, which shook the nation for almost six months, but although the riots united Korean studentry in anti-imperialist actions, the students had neither the organizational infrastructure nor the leadership to develop an effective student movement; that is, they generated tremendous power but could neither sustain nor control it. The most lasting outcomes of the riots were lengthy prison sentences for hundreds of students.[15]

Student rebellions troubled imperial Japan abroad, and they also challenged the Japanese government at home. Following World War I, a barrage of new ideas and ideologies—including socialism and democracy—invaded the island nation. The war had exacerbated the rifts between the social classes in Japan by accelerating industrialization and capitalism within the country, and that division, combined with the influx of foreign notions of social progress, threatened the nation's social and civil order. The government of Japan attempted to stamp out social progess and labor and student unrest. Socialist, democratic, or Communist organizations were perceived as a real threat to national security and were forcibly suppressed. This did not stop students from agitating, however. In 1921 the Gyominkai formed at Waseda University and came under immediate attack by the Japanese government. The following year Tokyo University saw the formation of the Gakusei Rengo-kai, a national umbrella organization uniting a number of student groups. Having witnessed the student uprisings in its imperial territories, the Japanese government feared student unrest at home and so jailed members of the Gakusei Rengo-kai in the attempt to disband the organization, which had not yet staged any major incidents, although many of its members advocated radicalism and direct action. As students rushed to form and join organizations and agitate, the state grew concerned and outlawed student groups in 1928. The Gakusei Rengo-kai continued to meet illegally, but by the end of the decade government suppression finally succeeded in dismantling the umbrella federation and its constituent organizations. The government of Japan was often challenged in minor acts of student resistance during the 1920s and 1930s, but Japanese students rarely held large-scale protests during these decades. There were a few minor successes: for example, a 1923 student demonstration blocked the formation of a government-fostered proto-military student group at Waseda University. But for the most part, the progressive organizations were matched in number and strength by ultranationalistic, militaristic, and elitist student groups, although unflinching governmental suppression hammered the final nails in their coffins.[16]

The common denominator of acts of student resistance in the East in the 1920s and '30s was anti-imperialism. In Indonesia, which would later host some of the most important acts of student resistance in the world's history, students relentlessly pushed for independence from Dutch control in the early 1920s. Indonesian students formed political organizations that advocated Indonesian self-rule, and significantly, when Indonesia finally achieved independence in 1945, many of the leaders of these student groups became leaders in the new government. Organizations pressing for independence within Indonesia, such as the powerful Indonesian Communist Party, or PKI, also formed student affiliates that began resistance efforts. And the man who would be the first president of the independent Indonesia in 1945, Sukarno, began his political career as a resisting student in the early 1920s as well, helping to start an organization in 1926 that advocated nationalism and condemned Western imperialism. In 1927 Sukarno founded the organization that would evolve into the Indonesian National Party, and he orchestrated the union of Indonesia's various parties to resist Dutch rule. Jailed in 1929 by Dutch police and incarcerated for a year, Sukarno nevertheless remained at the head of the resistance movement, organizing and agitating for Indonesian freedom (from both inside and outside prison, and even after being deported). Indonesia saw independence at the conclusion of World War II.[17]

Students in India and Burma also protested against imperial power, though their venom was directed at British colonialism. A major

Burmese act of student resistance took place in December 1920; a large-scale student strike, backed by the general public, protested university entrance qualifications. The students took the opportunity to call for reforms of the entire educational system; although largely unsuccessful, the action united the Burmese studentry in a cause, establishing student groups as powerful structures. Another major demonstration by Burmese students occurred in 1936 at the University of Rangoon, when students went on strike for educational reforms and voiced opposition to imperial Britain. Two student leaders of the strike would later become powerful men in Burmese politics. Thakin Nu, the head of the University of Rangoon Student Union, along with Aung San, the union's secretary, were both arrested and imprisoned after the strike. Thakin Nu (later known as U Nu) would be arrested by the British for treason in 1940, but after his release during World War II and Burma's eventual independence in 1948, he became the nation's prime minister. Aung San helped form the All-Burma Students' Union following the strike and then joined a radical Burmese nationalist organization and fought against the occupation. Hunted by the British for anti-imperialist actions, Aung San escaped to Japan but returned with the Japanese invasion in 1941 to organize an Indonesian army against the British; too politically savvy not to realize that the Japanese would never free Burma once they controlled it, he instead mobilized his resistance forces against the Japanese invaders. Following World War II he successfully petitioned the British for granting Burmese independence in 1948. It is likely that Aung San, a Burmese national hero, would have been elected leader of independent Burma instead of U Nu had he not been assassinated in 1947 by a competing politician.

Imperial Britain ran into tremendous student resistance in India in the early 1920s when students across India flocked to Mohandas Gandhi's Non-Cooperation Movement. The first All-India College Students' Conference met in Nagpur in 1920 and agreed to strike at universities receiving state money. When the Indian National Congress advocated boycotting institutions in 1921, students throughout India greeted the call by striking at their respective schools, blocking classroom entrances to prevent nonstriking students from attending them. The strikes successfully politicized the universities and unified India's studentry, although the majority of Non-Cooperation supporters subsequently left their universities in the name of the cause. In 1927 student organizations amassed thousands of participants in demonstrations for educational reforms; and again in 1936, tens of thousands of participants led by a variety of student organizations protested an English language requirement for matriculation into Indian universities.[18] Students also formulated a widely popular charter in 1936 that demanded free speech, the right to organize, and the same privileges for student organizations that labor and trade guilds enjoyed. The charter was extremely important to subsequent Indian organizations in defining student reform goals. In 1936 the All-India Students' Federation formed, advocating nationalism and independence, and the organization attempted to mobilize and steer a national Indian student movement; they also held an annual conference that met in conjunction with the Indian National Conference. By 1940 the federation claimed tens of thousands of members, yet that same year, the organization fractured over hostilities between the socialist and Communist factions.[19] But even as some student groups agitated for nationalism and Indian independence, others, such as the All-India Muslim Students' Federation, fought for a separate and independent Muslim state.

Students, both native and foreign, protested against empire in England as well. In 1925, for example, Lapido Solanke organized the West African Students' Union, which sought West African independence from Britain. After establishing the union's international headquarters, which coordinated demonstrations and information dispersal, in London, Solanke went to Africa, where he spread the organization throughout the West African states.[20]

German Student Resistance between the Wars: The Perverting Power of Fascism

Nationalism characterized the German student movements of the 1920s and '30s, but unlike those occurring in Asia, they were generally not drives for democracy or liberalism or against imperialism, but for a kind of elitist, jingoistic conservatism.[21] In 1919 the Deutsche Studentenschaft formed as a federation of university student unions. Though the

Studentenschaft was democratic at its inception, it also adopted the stance that the German peoples should be united. In order to achieve its *grossdeutsch* principle, the organization attempted to accommodate both the democratic views of German members and the anti-Semitic sentiments of Austrian and Sudetenland students; in its first years it effectively united developing student movements, and it successfully instituted programs that offered financial and social assistance to students in need. But run-ins with authorities of the individual German states and the increased popularity of the National Socialist student groups weakened the Deutsche Studentenschaft's power; in an effort to retain membership, its leaders increasingly adopted right-wing stances on issues, eventually giving control of the union to Nazi students. Thus the Deutsche Studentenschaft, which began as a democratic organization in 1919, was by 1933 orchestrating book burnings at German universities.[22]

Of course numerous leftist groups existed and actually fought against increasingly fascist popular German ideologies, but theirs was a losing battle; the trend to the right in German universities was the outgrowth of larger political and cultural movements, not the seed. Many students returning to their studies from service in World War I, or entering them for the first time just after the war, were disillusioned with the government and the attitudes of the generation controlling their society. They displayed their resentment in their very clothes: students dressed plainly, in antibourgeois, antifashion fashions; the more radical students sported paramilitary accessories that included arm ribbons, daggers, and even revolvers.[23] Violence became commonplace on university grounds and even within classrooms, especially as the right-wing students gained strength. Students fought with one another, and leftist, liberal, and Jewish professors increasingly faced harassment and threats in the early 1930s.

Of course, the German student organization that eclipsed all of the others between the world wars was the Nationalsozialistischer Deutscher Studentbund (National Socialist German Student Group), a branch of the Nazi Party. Organized at the University of Munich in 1926, the group began its existence catering to the concerns of poorer students unaffiliated with the elite student Korps or political organizations on campus; it was far from extremist at its inception, espousing academic freedom and free speech and hiding fascist ideology behind intellectual and philosophical arguments. The Nazi Party supplied funds for the organization, and the group produced a student journal, and members began wearing starched brown-shirt uniforms and paramilitary accessories.

Baldur von Shirach assumed control of the group in 1928 and began a highly effective campaign targeted at extending membership to a wide variety of students. His membership drive tactics were simple and extremely effective: to appeal to the intellectual interests of university students he organized lecture series, workshops on National Socialism, and discussion groups that debated Nazi ideals.[24] These educational events investigated Nazi ideas within the contexts of the various academic disciplines—political science, art, literature, anthropology—and sought to build a greater understanding of theoretical aspects of Nazism. Under Shirach, the National Socialist German Student Group endeavored to reach the poor students, the disenfranchised students, and the sons and daughters of laborers, as well as the rich, the elite, and the members of the various fraternities and groups. In a brilliant sleight-of-hand maneuver, Shirach transformed the Nazi organization into an intellectual champion for conservatives, nationalists, reformists, community supporters, and free-speech activists, and then he turned the students who joined into Nazis.

As the popularity of the group increased, members in good standing found themselves in powerful positions on student councils, in local student organizations, and in the national Deutsche Studentenschaft. When leftist organizations and liberal students and professors finally recognized their precarious position in the early 1930s, it was too late to save themselves. For example, the Studentischer Verbandedienst organized in 1932 against Nazi student members in the Deutsche Studentenschaft; they correctly anticipated that they were trying to take over the student council, the only other major student organization and the union's only competitor.[25] Liberal student groups held anti-Nazi demonstrations and rallies, but the resistance actions began too late to gain the momentum or the support they needed: pro-Nazi groups, backed by the student union or by the party, simply and violently disrupted protests, and university officials chose not to interfere with student conflicts. Although opposition to the Nazi ideology on campus increased substantially in 1932 as the fascist threat loomed large, Hitler's rise to power in 1933 reinforced the authority and power of the National Socialist German Student Group; within a few years it was the only viable student organization on German campuses.

The Nazis were able to capture the student organizations in Germany because although the majority of politically active German students in the 1920s and '30s were generally nationalistic and "pro-Germany," the student resistance actions they promoted were antiliberal and undemocratic. Only a limited number of radical activists realized, most belatedly, that the students enchanted with nationalism and power had also embraced fascism. National Socialist students rose to positions of power in student organizations throughout Germany by exploiting the political climate already existing on campus grounds. Intellectually and patriotically framed as an organized resistance against the corruption of German idealism, of the German people, and of German nationalism, and one that championed academic freedom—all under the guise of intellectualism—the Nazi student union spread through the universities with blinding speed. Anti-Nazi resistance movements began too late to be effective, and were both physically overpowered and tactically overmatched by their opponents. Acts of Nazi-condoned student resistance, such as book burnings and violent rallies, were a tremendous symbol of the terrible implications of student fascism, and they were also clearly exercises of student power—they defined the acting students' beliefs and agenda, illustrated what the students were both morally and legally capable of, and inspired fear in those whom the students opposed. Inasmuch as these student actions amassed and exercised power, they were extremely effective.

Radical Student Actions in Europe

In hindsight it is perhaps ironic that during the years between the world wars French universities also witnessed a rise in right-wing and fascist student organizations and actions.[26] The Etudiants Action Française, a reactionary organization and part of the larger Action Française movement that had been a dominant player in the Parisian political scene for over a decade, increased its actions of resistance against what it perceived as oppressive liberalism and republicanism in the 1920s and '30s. Already infamous for tactics such as aggressively interrupting the lectures of liberal professors and even assaulting them in their classrooms, the Etudiants Action Française launched a campaign against the Sorbonne in 1921, in which members strategically interrupted classes through actions called *chahuts*, or "unruly disturbances."[27] Opposed by liberal students and socialist student organizations, they were nevertheless successful in their actions because their goals were simply disruption; they were also quite popular, repeatedly elected to key positions, even presidencies, of universitywide organizations such as the Association Générale des Etudiants. The Union Nationale des Etudiants de France (UNEF) did not interfere with the warring university groups because of its declared nonpolitical stance; UNEF perceived such student actions as part of larger political movements, and indeed students of various political persuasions often violently battled each other both on and off campus.[28] Even so, right-wing students were extremely effective in sabotaging the transmission of liberalism.

In 1925, for example, the Etudiants Action Française identified political and Masonic corruption as the reason why the Paris Faculty of Law hired Georges Scelle as a professor, and they began a riot each time he attempted to lecture; though police quelled the disturbance in every case, unruly students became such a problem that eventually the minister of education closed the Faculty of Law. Led by members of the Etudiants Action Française, the Association Générale proclaimed a strike against the law school, catalyzing a general strike that spread to universities beyond Paris; eventually Scelle resigned.[29] Like their forebears during the trials following the French Revolution, students used primitive but highly effective mob tactics to shout down and intimidate the accused. Even Premier Edouard Herriot, the liberal Socialist Democrat, suffered such treatment in 1925 by members of the Etudiants Action Française when he tried to speak at an awards ceremony at the Lycée Louis le Grand. Herriot's government eventually fell to social unrest in December of 1932; the Etudiants Action Française were again on the scene, participating in Herriot's downfall by beginning riots on the Left Bank that blossomed into a mob of tens of thousands. Over the next four years the right-wing students continued a program of inciting anarchy on the Left Bank, until both the Action Française and the Etudiants Action Française were outlawed in 1936.[30]

England also witnessed unsettling student actions in the 1930s. In February 1933 members of the conservative and elite Oxford student union shocked the country by taking a pledge of pacifism a few days after Hitler became Germany's chancellor. Alumni, the government, and the general public harshly criticized the pledge, condemning the union, which reacted to the hostilities and criticisms by voting against participation in any national conflict. Other university unions—including the one at Cambridge—followed suit, also taking the Oxford Pledge. Stunned and horrified, the general public excoriated students in the press and on the streets; articles denouncing the Oxford-led pacifism and decrying its dangers appeared in American papers as well, not foreseeing that American students were close behind their colleagues overseas in taking a pacifist stance.

Student Movements in the United States: The Activist Explosion

Although many groups formed in the United States and protested in the nineteenth century, U.S. student actions remained relatively localized and fairly conservative in their aspirations until the twentieth century.[31] Students in the United States began organizing national efforts in earnest in the 1920s, with the National Student Forum leading the way. The forum attracted liberal, politically motivated students from dozens of universities and colleges; its program centered on liberal education, and it sponsored conferences addressing current issues, including national and international politics, education, democracy, and feminism. Its publication, *New Student,* found a wide audience and for almost a decade disseminated information and articles on student issues (in 1929 *New Student* folded after a great number of forum members abandoned the organization to join more powerful socialist organizations).

In 1926 the nationalization of student organizations took a great leap forward with the formation of the National Student Federation, an umbrella organization joining hundreds of student governments at universities and colleges throughout the nation; within a few years it boasted almost half a million members. The federation linked students across the country through a political network that could pass information and concerns to its constituents rapidly, provide local student representatives with issues and models and means to address them, nationally unite students within a political forum, and serve as a national representative of American student interests, giving students a voice or at least the perception of a voice on the national political scene. In the 1930s, one of the more illustrious presidents of the federation, Edward R. Murrow, began a radio show entitled *University on the Air* to raise student awareness of national and international political affairs. Although activists within the federation pushed through programs and publications that the federation would sponsor, the federation itself was rife with apathy and avoided taking stances on issues. The federation promoted awareness and political involvement but would only commit to positions on academic issues; that said, the organization allowed for those who were political activists, both liberal and conservative alike, to network and to rally together on a national scale.[32] Thus the first hurdle to launching effective student resistance on a national level—organizing and establishing a political infrastructure—was well under way in the United States by the 1930s.[33]

Other national organizations soon followed, including the leftist National Student League, originally begun as a response to City College of New York president Frederick Robinson's efforts to ban a pro-Communist, radical student journal. Students successfully demonstrated against Robinson's attack on the magazine and its editors, whom he had dismissed; following public protests the students were reinstated and the school's board affirmed the students' rights to publish their views. After the protests, the demonstrating students formed the league, which focused on fostering leftist activities on campuses across the nation. Promoting student activism as a solution to institutional and social problems and outlining methods for achieving results, the league's popularity grew quickly throughout the nation, in large part due to the widespread distribution of their new journal, *Student Review*. The National Student League entered the national spotlight in 1932 after local officials derailed a demonstration it had planned to aid miners holding a strike in Kentucky. The strike between impoverished miners and coal company authorities had already turned violent (a mercenary security force hired by a coal company had, for instance, used clubs and guns against strikers), and the National Student League thought a humanitarian aid mission was in order. In March 1932, buses filled with student volunteers from northern universities and colleges—including Columbia, Hunter College, the University of Wisconsin, Harvard, and Smith College—left New York for Kentucky. Armed local deputies stopped the caravan of students in Kentucky, viciously beating some, then escorting them back to Tennessee. The students were denied entrance into the coal conflict, but the police violence and civil rights infringements garnered public support for the students and the miners. It also raised the league's national profile and subsequently brought in many new members.[34]

In April 1932 the league was in the news again for sponsoring a mass demonstration in New York City to protest the expulsion of the student editor of the *Columbia Spectator*, who had accused the school's food service of corruption. (Often critical of the university's administration, the paper had long been a thorn in the school's side, attacking among other things, the school's privileging of sports over academics.) An overwhelming majority of the university's students supported a league-organized strike, which began on April 6. The strikers were successful: on April 20, the university reinstated Harris and investigated the food service.

Quick to come to the aid of students through tactics designed to gain the public's attention, the National Student League led a number of creative protests. In October 1932 the League became involved in a City College of New York demonstration after President Frederick Robinson called police to disperse a group of students protesting his dismissal of a faculty member for the teacher's ties to the Communist Party. At a gathering of over one thousand students, the league held a public trial for Robinson and convicted him of censorship. Furious, Robinson suspended the students responsible. In 1933 the league again targeted Robinson in another demonstration after he—armed with an umbrella—physically assaulted students picketing an ROTC ceremony. This time students attracted media attention by forming an umbrella march through the streets of New York in which chanting demonstrators carried umbrellas—symbols of oppression—and others hoisted a massive umbrella. Both creative actions garnered media interest, which helped bring public attention and public support. The following year, another "trial" was held for Robinson, this time for violating academic freedom by suspending demonstrators and the Student Council of City College after a riot broke out during a college-sponsored assembly honoring a visiting student group of Italian fascists. Instead of welcoming the visiting students at the assembly, during his turn at the microphone a Student Council member who also belonged to the National Student League voiced his personal views on Italian fascism, which were, to say the least, unfavorable. Before he had time to elaborate on these views, he was attacked on stage by the school's Italian club; this in turn brought the entire assembly into the fray, which quickly escalated into a massive riot. The National Student League held demonstrations following the event and sought Robinson's removal from office. Almost all of the suspended students were subsequently expelled. Not to be intimidated, the demonstrators expanded their protest and took it to the streets of New York. Such acts brought media attention again to the students of City College, and more importantly, public and alumni support, exerting tremendous pressure on the school's board, which ultimately replaced Robinson and reinstated the students.

Encouraged by these successes and those of the Columbia strike, the National Student League joined the Student League for Industrial Democracy (SLID) in a national student strike for peace in 1934; in April over 20,000 students at universities across the United States boycotted their classes for one hour in the largest student protest the country had ever seen.[35] Striking students spent their time taking the pacifist Oxford Pledge. A similar strike was held the next year, and this time the action claimed over 150,000 participants, with large numbers of them at Columbia and Berkeley. That same year the National Student League and the Student League for Industrial Democracy created the American Student Union, which boasted close to 200,000 members;[36] they called a peace demonstration again in 1936, and 300,000 students (a significant proportion of which attended U.S. universities) joined the strike, the largest resistance action by the nation's studentry up until then. Although impressive, the act was in vain, as the country was soon pulled into the conflict.[37]

Before putting aside their ideological differences and joining with the Communist-oriented National Student League, the socialist Student League for Industrial Democracy was already a well-established coalition of activist students, founded as a part of the League for Industrial Democracy. Since 1932 SLID had been a conspicuous organization on many campuses, attracting vocal leftists and socialists and promoting active participation in political and government issues. It published a journal to encourage student activism and to elicit new members, though its membership in the American Student Union lasted only six years; the union fragmented in 1941 after the United States entered the war.[38] Beleaguered by antisocialist sentiments, SLID nevertheless continued to operate, though in an increasingly impoverished state; not until it changed its name in 1960 to the Students for a Democratic Society and became a champion of civil rights did the organization began to grow again in membership and power.[39]

Political organizations with student wings active on campuses during the years between the world wars included the Young Peoples' Socialist League and the Young Communist League, though both were relatively slow to begin organizing and recruiting members on university and college campuses. The American Youth Congress also had a strong university and college student contingent, and was even able to carry its liberal, antiwar sentiments to President Roosevelt through the offices of Eleanor Roosevelt, an early and avid supporter. Like many others in the United States, the Roosevelts soured on the group in the late 1930s, however, when many of its leaders were publicly exposed as Communists.

During the Great Depression, U.S. students organized and protested for more general economic and social reforms as well. Local student cooperatives boomed on campuses throughout the nation in response to increases in the cost of room and board and the scarcity of funds. In 1937 students from the University of California formed a labor board to help students who were struggling financially. Finding that students at the Berkeley campus were underpaid by their employers, the board developed a set of working conditions and wages appropriate for students and effectively instituted student boycotts against employers who refused to comply. During the depression, students also carried their demands to the president in the first major march on the White House in U.S. history; in 1937 thousands of students and youths, many representing national organizations, demonstrated for three days in the nation's capital to focus public and government attention on the plight of America's impoverished youth.

Finally, 1937 also witnessed the formation of the Southern Negro Youth Congress in Richmond, Virginia. The student congress concerned itself with issues of racial equality both on and off campus, staging strikes and boycotts and establishing education cultural programs.[40]

6

Student Militancy and Warfare, 1940–1959

The Radical Reformation of European Activism during and after World War II

World War II radically changed the nature and appearance of student organizations on European campuses, the effective strategies of resistance available to European student populations, and the existing student movements themselves. The war drew a tremendous number of students from universities throughout Europe directly into the conflict and purged schools of their activists; international issues and their implications for home overshadowed other domestic concerns, including education; and in many cases universities and colleges simply closed down for the duration of the conflict. But although the war eclipsed or rendered moot many student issues, groups, and actions, students throughout Europe not directly involved in combat continued to agitate and work for causes, which in most cases concerned liberation or imperial conquest. By the end of the war students would find the world a very different place, with new political allegiances and new political threats.

Most German students remaining in German universities did not publicly oppose Nazism going into World War II. The Nazi government literally annihilated student resistance and opposition movements during the war.[1] Directly involved or implicated in Nazism and by extension the Holocaust, students in the Federal Republic of Germany avoided ideological causes and charismatic leaders for decades after the war's close; skepticism, more than any other trait, characterized the West German student populations of the late 1940s and 1950s. Since the German Democratic Republic was under the ideological stamp of Communism after the war, its population, already defeated and exhausted, had little energy to protest against the new powers controlling it.

In 1948, however, one significant event occurred that would have lasting effects on West German student politics: the creation of the Freie Universität Berlin (Berlin Free University), established to demonstrate to the world the academic and political freedoms available to citizens in the West. In 1947 students in West Berlin demonstrated for the founding of a school based on democratic principles; the drive for the establishment of the university gained momentum after the Soviet crackdown on East Berlin's Humbolt University. Originally, the organization of the Free University was unique, as students and professors related more as colleagues than as members of a traditional university hierarchy, though in the 1950s this changed. Notably, as the gap between students and professors widened, students became more vocal and more radical in their politics, a trend that would lead to demonstrations, agitation, and violence on the Free University campus in the 1960s.

Student actions increased in West Germany in the late 1950s, at first in response to the Federal Republic of Germany's acceptance of NATO and the integration of West Germany into the Western bloc, and subsequently when the United States moved to install nuclear weapons in Germany. Yet the level of activism in West Germany increased very slowly during the 1950s, as German studentry still suffered from the cultural and political effects of World War II, manifested in a general aversion to public demonstrations of political idealism.

During World War II and the occupation, of course, most politically active French university students were absorbed by France's larger struggles, joining the Resistance movement or various political organizations working against, or in some cases for, the Vichy government. The university system itself, however, remained relatively stable during the occupation, though enrollment figures for colleges and universities in France dropped during those years. By 1943 enrollment was at a new high.[2]

Anti-Vichy or anti-Nazi protests that took place during the occupation were immediately and brutally suppressed. On November 11, 1940, for example, a group of students marched to the Arc de Triomphe in the first student demonstration against the occupation. Police troops attacked the students, killing about one hundred of them; many of those surviving the attack were arrested and deported to work camps in

Germany. As far as the Vichy or Nazi government was concerned, demonstrations against the occupation amounted to participation in the Resistance, and were treated as such. Students inclined to fight the occupation generally left the universities for the Resistance anyway or participated covertly, and the majority of students remaining, who were tacitly cooperating with or more openly supportive of the Vichy government, were obviously not the disruptive type.

The Union Nationale des Etudiants de France survived the occupation, because it did not fight it; the union fared well for a while, but after the war's end, its former relationship with the Vichy government severely hurt its popularity and its clout as a postwar representative of French studentry. In 1946, after the liberation, the union was taken over by students who were active in or had otherwise supported the Resistance, and they turned the union into an activist organization promoting organized student resistance for both student and social issues. In subsequent years the union successfully held strikes and won victories for students, including reductions in tuition, as well as the institution of more government grants and increased student services.[3] But in the first half of the 1950s, many students became disenchanted with the left, which increasingly focused on abstract political issues. In general, French students were becoming more interested in material matters; and the rise of the Cold War, the growing unpopularity of Communism and Communists (many of the leftist political activists at the time were Communist), and Charles de Gaulle's own systematic efforts to undermine French student power—all took their toll on the leftists. Some student groups remained active, such as the Union Nationale des Etudiants de France, but the majority of the students were apolitical and uninterested in acts of resistance, as had been the previous generation of students who stayed at universities during the occupation.

In 1954, however, the Algerian fight for independence gave new fire to both the left in general and student activists in particular. In 1956, the Union Générale des Etudiants Musulmans Algériens was organized in Paris because such unions were illegal in Algeria, though the organization began operating in both France and Algeria, openly advocating independence. The French government responded by jailing Muslim students in both countries. In Algeria, students from the University of Algiers flocked to the Front de Liberation Nationale to participate in the struggle for liberation. Resisting the French government, union students successfully staged university and high school strikes and boycotts in Algeria, and began putting pressure on the French government by spreading unflattering information about the French occupation of Algeria internationally through ties to outside student groups. The occupation government responded brutally—arresting, imprisoning, and even torturing members of the student organization. Persecuted in Algeria and in France, the Union Générale sought refuge in Switzerland. The organization survived French suppression, but it could not survive Algeria's 1962 independence and subsequent civil conflict; factionalism ravaged the group, and in 1963 it was reorganized as the Union Nationale des Etudiants Algériens.[4]

In France, the Union Nationale des Etudiants de France (UNEF) supported Algerian independence and demonstrated along with the Union Générale des Etudiantes Musulmans Algériens publicly. When the Algerian struggle with France ended in 1962, the student left in France was once again bereft of a cause; with its means for generating, organizing, and using power ill suited to the new and relatively apolitical university environment, UNEF's prominence again began to decline.

During the postwar years, student political resistance in England primarily concerned nuclear disarmament. In April 1958 hundreds of students participated in a fifty-mile march from Aldermaston to Trafalgar Square held to protest nuclear arms. The Emergency Committee for Direct Action against Nuclear War, which Bertrand Russell cofounded, organized the 1958 march, and the Campaign for Nuclear Disarmament oversaw another the following year; the 1959 march drew thousands of participants. Within a few years the annual march would swell to over fifty thousand protesters. Similar demonstrations spread throughout England and to other European countries. As the anti-nuclear arms movement carried into the 1960s, student activists began employing strategies of civil disobedience in England to draw attention to the issue.

Postwar Student Resistance in Eastern Europe: Attack and Counterattack

Hungary hosted one of the most notorious actions of national student resistance in Eastern Europe during the immediate postwar era, an event that eventually led to the 1956 Revolution. In 1953, facing the imminence of a revolt against the unpopular Hungarian dictator Mátyás Rákosi (who brutally executed thousands of political dissidents), the Russian government removed Rákosi, supplanting him with a more progressive leader, Imre Nagy. Nagy not only immediately released tens of thousands of prisoners imprisoned under Rákosi's government, he also began to take steps to liberalize Hungary, including allowing free speech. More threatened by Nagy than by the grumblings of Hungarians, the Russian government put Rákosi back in charge in 1955. But the respite from the hated leader inspired students to agitate.

In 1956 university students formed the Petöfi Circle, named after a poet and Hungarian cultural icon who gave his life repelling the Russians a century earlier; the group quickly grew in popularity, and its membership soared, largely due to its demonstrations for free speech and its teach-ins. Amid growing social unrest, the Petöfi Circle continued to agitate and to demonstrate (often against Rákosi), and the Russians replaced the dictator again, this time with the equally disliked Ernö Gero, who allowed a public memorial service for László Rajk (a national figure executed years before by Rákosi). To Gero's surprise, hundreds of thousands of Hungarians participated. Hungarian university students capitalized on the display of general popular unrest by organizing a national revolt, hoping for a smooth, relatively peaceful revolution. Students in Budapest drafted a set of demands that included free general elections, numerous social and economic reforms, freedom of speech, and a complete Soviet military withdrawal; in October 1956, thousands of students gathered to endorse the demands and plan a protest march. They began a city-wide campaign to elicit public support. The students' organizing and timing paid off.

On the day of the march thousands of students were joined by hundreds of thousands of laborers, merchants, and sympathizers in a demonstration through Budapest before assembling on Parliament Square. Gero publicly attacked the demonstration over the radio, and when a group of students protested outside the station where Gero was broadcasting his condemnation, Gero's personal police guards began shooting into the crowd. Hungarian military troops suddenly appeared, but instead of joining the police and attacking the crowd, they equipped the students with guns, and together the troops and the students began shooting at Gero's police.

Hungary almost instantaneously erupted in revolution as the general population joined the students in fighting Soviet police. Fearing more Hungarian troops would side with the rioters, Soviet commanders locked them in their quarters, but the soldiers passed their arms to those outside who could fight. When Soviet troops in tanks tried to enter Budapest, Hungarian soldiers and rebels throwing Molotov cocktails stopped them. One tank battalion sent to secure the central military barracks for the Soviet-backed government promptly defected to the opposition. By October 28 the Soviet military had been successfully repelled in Budapest by thousands of rebels armed with captured Soviet weapons and homemade gasoline bombs.

Laborers throughout Hungary went on strike to support the revolutionaries—most of whom were youths—and the European press overwhelmingly supported the revolution. By the end of the month the newly released Nagy declared Hungary's withdrawal from the Warsaw Pact. But just when the revolution looked as though it would succeed, the Soviet military captured the commander of the renegade tank battalion during peace talks, and the following day a reinforced Soviet military attacked Budapest, overwhelming the organized resistance and reclaiming the streets of the city. While revolutionaries continued the fight with guerrilla tactics, Nagy and his cabinet took sanctuary in the Budapest Yugoslav embassy. The Soviets tricked Nagy into leaving the embassy, however, and he soon joined thousands of other prisoners of the state executed for the attempted revolution. To rid the area of young rebels who continued resistance efforts on their own, the Soviets deported thousands of children and teenagers to Russian work camps and prisons, where many served terms until they were old enough to be legally put to death. The majority of the thousands of rebels killed or wounded by Russian soldiers during the revolution and the thousands imprisoned afterward were in their teens and twenties. Hundreds of thousands of refugees, those lucky enough to escape, evaded Soviet ire by fleeing to Western Europe.[5]

Although the Soviets brutally smashed the revolution, the attempt had tremendous importance to students within Soviet-occupied Eastern Europe, both because it brought government suppression upon university organizations throughout Eastern Europe and because it served to show young revolutionaries the potential they had to challenge Soviet oppression. To the careful watchers in the West, it was the first significant crack in the Soviet occupation of Eastern Europe.[6]

Poland had its own share of student resistance during the Cold War—though the nation did not witness any events as spectacular as those in neighboring Hungary. The Warsaw Riots of 1957 began in October when students from the Warsaw Polytechnic Institute, gathered in the capital to demonstrate against the government's suppression of a journal, were attacked by baton-wielding police. Arming themselves with sticks and throwing bottles and bricks, the students resisted the police onslaught for several hours before finally retreating. Twice as many students from the institute gathered the following afternoon in a peaceful meeting with a member of the government, but when they attempted to leave the conference, they discovered police troops again waiting for them; the police attacked, and the resulting mêlée raged until nightfall. The riot spread beyond the university, and over the next few days, police and government officials found themselves assaulted throughout Warsaw by roaming mobs of teenagers, students, and laborers. Deciding the situation was out of hand, the students backed off and tried to distinguish their organized actions from the terror in the streets, suing the government for peace. The government accepted the overture, but the student leaders involved in the early stages of the protest were arrested and imprisoned.[7]

Student Power in Postwar Asia

Students in Japan began organizing local groups after World War II in an effort to secure affordable food and materials for others who were struggling to survive in the wake of the nation's surrender. In 1946 representatives from many Japanese universities formed a national student union to unite Japanese students, to help them formalize their local concerns, and to organize individual university unions and self-governing organizations. Students at Tokyo University established a student government in 1947, and when the university officially recognized the organization as representative of the student body, students enrolled at other Japanese schools followed suit, forming their own student governments. Nonetheless, the Japanese government clearly remained in control of Japan's universities. In 1948 the government dramatically increased tuition at all Japanese universities; the action impelled the recently formed local university student governments into their first union in June 1948 and caused them to begin larger and more organized protests, such as bringing petitions before the Japanese Diet and staging a series of national strikes.

Many attempts at uniting the student associations occurred over the next few months, but not until the fall of 1948 did Japanese students form the organization that would allow them to resist both Japanese and occupational authorities effectively. The Zen Nihon Gakusei Jichi-kai Sorengo, or Zengakuren, was a well-organized national federation started by the union of student government associations, whose stated mission was to protect students and student freedoms from occupation reform efforts, to promote democracy, and to ensure students' economic and material security. In its first few months of operation, Zengakuren attracted hundreds of thousands of members. The national student organization efforts alarmed government authorities, and in October the government of Japan began efforts to hamstring student political organizations. Meanwhile the Zengakuren was hammering out its own national agenda of university reform, which included an autonomous and freely elected governing committee to oversee Japan's universities. When the Japanese Diet ignored the students and began to consider repressive reforms in 1949, the Zengakuren called for a national strike, which, enacted by hundreds of thousands of students, lasted for a month. The Japanese government dropped the ministry's suggested reforms, and the Zengakuren's membership soared.[8]

In 1950 Japan's government began efforts to rid the university system of Communists, and again the Zengakuren led another series of strikes; this time too the students' organization's efforts succeeded. As the Cold War developed and the Japanese government, motivated by U.S.-led interests, became increasingly anti-Communist, the Zengakuren leadership began to align itself with the Communist Party, sparking dissension in its ranks and major rifts in the organization. Over the next few years, Zengakuren's membership and wieldable power radically declined as more and more factions within the group pursued their own interests. Sensing its own demise, the organization backed away from its support of the Communists in the mid-1950s, promoting student welfare instead, though in 1957 the Zengakuren joined in a number of student and worker protests against a U.S. military base close to Tokyo, bringing thousands of activists to a series of demonstrations. A number of students and workers were arrested during the protests. The arrests were important for the cause, however, because at the eventual trial the judge announced not only that the arrests were illegal but that the original Security Treaty between Japan and the U.S. itself was unconstitutional under Japanese law.

The declaration of unconstitutionality anticipated a revised treaty already in the works, which had already inspired opposition among many student and social groups, including the Zengakuren students, Japanese socialist organizations, and numerous trade unions. All of these had large but peaceful demonstrations against the treaty, which the government quietly ignored. Frustrated by the ineffectiveness of the protests, in November 1959 a group of about one thousand students opposing the treaty took matters into their own hands, attacking the Tokyo Diet House; tens of thousands of demonstrators massed outside while almost a half a million more joined in protesting the treaty nationwide. Over the next few months, as the Diet considered the new treaty, students led numerous demonstrations and forcefully occupied a number of government buildings in addition to the Diet House. Police were relatively restrained in their dealings with the protesters, controlling and arresting them, but showing little violence. In June, thousands of students again amassed to march against Japan's expected endorsement of the treaty; while one part of the group invaded and occupied the local police station, the rest again occupied the Diet House.[9] Police attempted to disperse both groups of students, and they resorted to violence. The conflict escalated after a student was killed, and the ensuing riot did not end until the following day. Police brutally attacked the students and eventually drove them off. Undeterred, three hundred thousand people protested against the government and police brutality at the Diet House two days later. Tokyo students subsequently called for a national strike and held further protests against the government. Japan's government adopted the new security treaty, but in the face of such opposition Japan's prime minister stepped down.

Student turmoil troubled the mainland as well. During the war years Chinese students, along with the rest of the country's citizens, suffered greatly; malnourishment and tuberculosis plagued city residents and peasants alike. Those students who were not in the mountains with Mao Zedong's Communists generally supported Chiang Kai-shek's fight against the Japanese. Kept at their desks during the fighting, however, the students were frustrated in their desires to express their nationalism, and by the end of the war most had become cynical or apathetic about the government's policies and programs.[10] When hostilities resumed between Mao's Communists and the Guomindang forces, most students remained uninvolved, although they were increasingly drawn to Mao's camp. In 1947 thousands of students from many universities in Nanjing and Shanghai, unhappy with China's ongoing internal conflict and the economic inflation caused by it, protested in Nanjing, calling for an end to the twenty-year civil war between the Guomindang and the Communists.[11] Police troops attacked the marchers, severely injuring many and arresting hundreds of students. The attack triggered demonstrations in cities throughout China, which provoked further police attacks and arrests. Within a few months, police arrested over ten thousand students in Beijing, Nanjing, Shanghai, and other cities.[12] In the face of fierce governmental oppression, the students aligned themselves with the Communists; thus when Mao's army swept south, the leader found students aiding his momentum. With the establishment of the People's Republic of China after the 1949 revolution, student resistance again disappeared from the public theater. The Chinese Communist Party secured complete control of China's universities, and the majority of students were either publicly supportive of, or apathetic about, that control.[13]

Seven years later, however, students were again holding local strikes and protesting government policies; in an effort to accommodate the students' growing need to express themselves, and thereby to defuse the growing dissension in the universities, Mao tried to win student support in 1957 with his "Hundred Flowers" speech (supposedly embracing as many different social viewpoints), henceforth allowing students a measure of freedom of expression. The students at Beijing University repaid his generosity by plastering the walls of the university with posters decrying the policies of the Chinese Communist Party and calling for democracy, university reforms, private enterprise, and westernization. The government forcibly countered what it feared could become a larger movement, arresting hundreds of Beijing students and deporting them to work camps. Communist Party educators were subsequently placed in universities throughout China, and for the next two years students attended mandatory courses on proper politics and expression of political ideas. Recognizing the perils of loosening its firm grip on student resistance, China's government returned to a zero-tolerance policy toward student rebellion.

Students in countries throughout Asia were also organizing and resisting authorities in various ways in the post–World War II years,[14] but Japan and China clearly illustrate the different effects of student resistance. On the one hand, Japanese students were extremely effective at organizing, strategizing, and demonstrating, and they had great impact on national opinion and their federal government; on the other, Chinese students were generally not major players in national politics at the time (although many students participated in the 1949 revolution, they played only a supporting role in the final episode of the civil war). And once the Communists came to power in China, dissenting student voices were effectively silenced; China's new government knew how to suppress the threat of student opposition.

The Rise and Decline of Student Resistance in India

For decades, Indian student activists had followed the nonviolent efforts of leaders such as Mohandas Gandhi and Jawaharlal Nehru, and although colleges and universities were still elitist institutions, their student body by 1940 was highly politicized. As students became more and more concerned with national and international politics, they responded more energetically to the independence movement—either for or against it. In 1940 the All India Students' Federation separated into two groups: Communists (who supported the British in their military efforts against Germany, which had invaded Russia) and socialists, who with the Gandhians were actively working for the Indian nationalist cause and opposed British imperialism. The latter eventually abandoned the federation to form the All India Students' Congress.[15]

On August 8, 1942, the Indian National Congress, led by Gandhi and Nehru, resolved that Indians should resist the British in any and every nonviolent way imaginable; and India, they declared, would not support the Allies in the world war until British forces left the country. Unwilling to allow Gandhi and Nehru to agitate, British authorities jailed both men and a number of their supporters the following day, sparking off nonviolent protests throughout the country. In spite of the pacifist nature of the demonstrations, the government met the resistance with violence, dispersing the demonstrators with clubs and guns. Students retaliated with violence of their own, and student strikes closed many colleges and universities; many stayed shut for months. Students held demonstrations and boycotts nationwide, and they also distributed illegal pamphlets calling for independence and aired subversive speeches on underground radio broadcasts. More impetuous than most of Gandhi's followers, they more easily turned to violence, bombing communication and transportation systems, torching government buildings, and physically resisting police. In the years leading up to India's independence, university authorities ejected unruly students, and police beat and arrested thousands, but these oppressive acts only galvanized student support for independence and made many students more extreme in their actions. Yet as independence loomed closer, and the National Congress made more concessions to the British to achieve freedom for the nation, students grew upset over the congress's conciliatory measures, and their enthusiasm for the independence movement as it existed declined.[16]

After independence, many of the student organizations in India simply disintegrated. Without the ideologically unifying cause of liberation, politically motivated students fell to infighting, many considering the statehood India achieved as compromised. By 1947 students began to look more to their own individual futures than to the nation's, and careerism began to dominate many of the formerly political organizations. Students continued to participate in large student organizations that relied heavily on the financial support of various political factions within India or on international support from the Soviet Union or the West. Although such support was crucial to the groups' continued existence, it generally worked against wider student appeal. By 1960 the majority of students at India's universities and colleges were indifferent to politics. What little student resistance occurred generally concerned student political factionalism or local educational reform issues.

African Student Resistance: Student Power Meets Political Power

Student resistance played widely different roles and had a variety of impacts on governments and societies in the individual African nations, but the actions were similar in their legacies for individuals, in that often the leaders of student political organizations became key national leaders; the lessons in power politics that student activists learned in university conflicts served them well in their postacademic careers.[17] Kwame Nkrumah, the first president of independent Ghana, is a case in point. Nkrumah was very active in politics when he studied in the United States; he attended Lincoln University and the University of Pennsylvania, and was involved with the African Student Organization, quickly rising in its ranks to the office of president. He continued his studies and his political interests in London and served as vice president of the West African Students' Union, an organization concerned about the region's political future. In 1947 Nkrumah moved from England to the Gold Coast, where, using the lessons he'd learned in the African

Student Organization in the United States and in the West African Students' Union in London, he organized a political party and initiated an independence movement in Ghana. By 1952, Nkrumah was prime minister, an office he held through Ghana's independence in 1957. He became its first president in 1960.[18]

Nkrumah was obviously invested in the future of Ghana and colonial states in general, but he was also clearly self-serving. Once in power, the former student activist had little tolerance for dissension among Ghana's studentry. His Convention People's Party held an iron grip on Ghana, effectively controlling all aspects of the government, as well as the press. In 1958 a student organization called the National Union of Ghana Students organized and eventually took Nkrumah's policies to task; but when the group attempted to demonstrate over the following years, police suppressed them, and they were unable to launch any successful resistance to Nkrumah's government. The union disintegrated by 1965, re-forming only after the president's regime fell in a military takeover in 1966.

Nkrumah's understanding of student resistance and power relations helped him become an important international political leader, but many African students took less prominent roads, fighting not for personal achievement so much as in wider ideological battles. In South Africa two student organizations battled one another over issues of apartheid. The National Union of South African Students advocated integration, while the right-wing Afrikaner Student League, founded in 1948 in opposition to the union, supported segregation. That same year, the conservative Nationalist Party won national elections and subsequently instituted apartheid, which the National Union of South African Students only weakly opposed.

The Afrikaner Student League (which came into being as a coalition between two organizations: one, a pro-Nazi organization, and the other, the Federation of White South African Students), fully supported apartheid and actively worked toward the segregation of universities; by defining itself as patriotic, against the leftist and "unpatriotic" National Union, the Afrikaner Student League was able to gain government support and to increase its student membership dramatically until it was clearly the most powerful student representative in South Africa. By the mid-1950s, the government was instituting racist educational policies and attempting to segregate South Africa's universities. The National Union of South African Students subsequently rose in defiance of the government's apartheid efforts, and began demonstrations and strikes to protest segregation, but the group was too weak to have any significant political impact, even on the campuses at which its organizations were based.[19]

During the 1940s and '50s, student unions organized and began local and national resistance efforts in many African nations—Algeria, the Congo, Kenya, Rhodesia. In 1956 the National Union of Nigerian Students formed, for example, demonstrating for government and social reforms. Organization and unity among African studentry from nations across the continent also became a cause, and in 1958 the first Pan-African Student Conference met at Kampala.

U.S. Student Activism and the Cold War: Warding Off the Chill

Compared to the 1930s, the level of student resistance in the United States in the 1940s and '50s was negligible. As World War II progressed and increasingly disturbing revelations of both Nazi and Japanese war atrocities were made public in the American press, the conflict evolved into a moral battle, and the antiwar and pacifist student resistance movements from the 1930s began to disappear. Prowar student organizations, such as the Student Defenders of Democracy and the Student League of America, formed relatively early and backed U.S. involvement in the conflict, and as the country became further invested in the anti-Axis effort, their numbers significantly increased.[20]

Following the Allies' victory, most patriotic groups disbanded or transformed into anti-Communist organizations, and Communist and socialist student movements came under fire by both conservative and liberal student organizations. The United States Student Assembly, for example, which was expressly anti-Communist, united many smaller groups in patriotic efforts and in the aid to and reconstruction of countries suffering from the devastation of the war. Other groups, such as the Socialist Youth League, tried to establish or promote "untainted" forms of socialism or Communism in the United States, but like the American

Youth League, which vocally advocated Communism, it was attacked by patriotic "American" organizations "resisting" the red tide.[21] By the late 1940s, Communist and socialist student groups were not only being condemned by other student groups for anti-American subversiveness but also faced a barrage of criticism from the House Un-American Activities Committee. The Young Progressives of America (which supported Henry Wallace), the Labor Youth League (a Communist organization that attacked American capitalism), and the United World Federalists (which agitated for the formation of a single world government) are just three of many organizations that could not survive the Cold War climate in America in the late 1940s and '50s.[22]

McCarthyism did not go unchallenged, however; in 1951 university students formed the American Association of University Students for Academic Freedom, which agitated for more freedoms on American college campuses, and explicitly combated reforms spawned by the purveyors of the red scare. Other groups also concerned themselves with student rights and university policies, although they often found themselves virulently attacked by student opposition groups. The National Student Association, which was originally established in 1947, ratified a Student Bill of Rights, took a stance against racism and sexism, and in the 1950s endeavored to work internationally with other representative student organizations. Right-wing student groups targeted the National Student Association as a left-wing, Communist threat and sought its destruction through tactics, including demonstrations and the harassment of individual association members. Politically the most significant student group agitating in the United States in the 1950s, the Students for Democratic Action fought for civil rights and for academic freedom. The highly political organization demonstrated for its causes and lobbied for aid for the rebuilding of European nations.

Although student groups were active during the U.S. involvement in World War II and afterward, in general the 1940s and '50s saw a great decline in U.S. student resistance actions and in liberalism; student, social, and governmental hostilities severely weakened leftist and Communist-affiliated groups while other organizations, such as the Campus Crusade for Christ, thrived. There were some notable exceptions to the trend of declining leftist student activism, however; the student wing of SANE, the National Committee for a Sane Nuclear Policy, organized in 1958, had representative groups on the majority of U.S. campuses in the years immediately after, and staged demonstrations and rallies against the development of nuclear arms. On the Berkeley campus of the University of California, students created SLATE, a political campaign to depose right-wing students from their student government offices; the campaign failed but, nevertheless, successfully spotlighted issues of student discrimination and civil liberties on the Berkeley and other California campuses. SLATE members also joined in the growing civil rights campaign by boycotting and demonstrating against local merchants, and in 1960 they protested the operations of the House Un-American Activities Committee in San Francisco. One other liberal organization, the massive pacifist Student Peace Union, had its start in Chicago in 1959; in the '60s it would stage large protests for pacifism in Washington, D.C., and aid the antiwar effort.

Another student organization, the Congress of Racial Equity, or CORE, formed in 1942 at the Chicago Theological Seminary. Under the guidance of activists such as James Farmer, the organization devoted itself to developing nonviolent means for protesting racial injustice, and in 1947 CORE members successfully staged sit-ins at segregated restaurants. The once tiny organization quickly grew, and throughout the next three decades members continued to demonstrate effectively against local merchants and public institutions, both in Chicago and in other U.S. cities. Farmer, who was also involved with the Student League for Industrial Democracy in the 1950s, helped link CORE to other student organizations, but CORE rapidly outgrew its own student membership, becoming one of the greater forces in the American civil rights movement of the 1950s and '60s. Farmer would be elected the group's director in 1961, a post he would hold for the next five years and from which he would launch the Freedom Rider bus station integration campaign throughout the South, forcing transportation stations to comply with federal integration laws.

Students were also fighting to desegregate universities throughout the United States; in 1945, for example, students at Washington University joined forces with civil rights organizations and forced the St.

Louis school to integrate its medical school and school of social work in 1946–47. Activists eventually forced the University of Washington to integrate fully in 1952.[23] Although the Supreme Court's 1954 *Brown v. Board of Education* decision opened the road to the desegregation of the South's universities, they remained essentially segregated for the remainder of the decade.

Like many European countries, the United States was also taken to task in the 1940s and '50s for colonialism; in 1946 the majority of students at the University of Puerto Rico at Río Piedras went on strike after U.S. president Harry S. Truman blocked the island's attempt to legislate Spanish as the primary language of Puerto Rico's schools. The strike raised the issue's public profile, and the measure to make Spanish the primary educational language passed two years later. And when Pedro Albizu Campos, who had been tried at the beginning of the decade and found guilty of organizing a revolution against the United States, was freed in 1947, students at the University of Puerto Rico greeted his release with anti-U.S. demonstrations. When the administration suspended some of the students and barred Campos from the campus, students protested by taking control of university buildings. After police reestablished order at the university, the administration outlawed campus organizations. Puerto Rican students again lit a torch for independence by forming a University Federation for the Independence of Puerto Rico, which ever since has fought for liberation, university autonomy, student rights, and increased academic freedoms.[24]

Latin America: Student Resistance Erupts with a Vengeance

Unlike the United States, Latin America surged with student activism in the 1940s and '50s, much of it violent. Students in Cuba, for example, played a major role in the downfall of dictator Fulgencio Batista. Shortly after Batista's rise in 1952, students at the University of Havana began agitating against him in protests orchestrated by the Federación Estudiantil Universitaria, a federation of student organizations. Police responded to the protests with violence, killing one student in 1953. The federation retaliated by mandating a general strike, the first of many to occur throughout the following years. Meanwhile, students continued to demonstrate and to endure subsequent police beatings to protest again, in a vicious cycle that is all too familiar in the history of student resistance. In 1956 the president of the Federación Estudiantil Universitaria, José Echeverría, became head of the covert Directorio Revolucionario, a group that advocated revolution by any means, including assassination. In October 1956 members of the Directorio shot and killed Batista's chief of military intelligence as he and other military leaders were leaving a club in Havana with their wives and escorts; a second officer and his wife were wounded in the attack.

The following month a student, Frank Pais, led a group of Castro supporters and members of the July Twenty-Sixth Movement (so named after the date of Castro's first revolution attempt) in an attempt to take the town of Santiago; the attack was supposed to happen at the same time as Castro's own forceful landing and return from Mexico, where he had assembled a small but trained and equipped military. Although Castro's boat had trouble negotiating the waters off Cuba, delaying his arrival until after the attack, the students and July Twenty-Sixers managed to capture government buildings in Santiago as well as a prison. Without Castro's support, however, the rebels were forced to retreat into the hills, where they eventually linked up with Castro's forces, but they returned in sorties to destroy more government facilities before Batista's troops could reassert full control over Santiago. Pais was killed in Santiago, but his efforts brought many students to Castro's support.

In March 1957 the Directorio went directly after Batista, breaking into his palace, where they fought an intense gun battle with guards. While palace guards were in the process of killing a dozen Directorio assassins, Echeverría and others were forcing their way into a radio station to commandeer the airwaves. Echeverría did not survive the night, and those of his colleagues who could not escape from Cuba were tracked down over the following weeks and arrested. Anti-Batista resistance resurfaced in 1959 when revolutionaries and students acted in concert with returning expatriates to violently seize government, communication, and police facilities in Havana and Santiago. Castro's forces finally overwhelmed Batista's. Following the revolution, the students resistance movement withered in Cuba.[25]

Student resistance actions rocked other countries as well. The União Nacional des Etudantes was a major force on Brazilian campuses in the 1940s and '50s, staging demonstrations both on and off university grounds; its concerns included university reforms, social reforms, and opposition to U.S. imperialism. The union garnered international notoriety in 1956 when workers and students demonstrated against government-mandated public transit increases in Rio. After the protesters froze Rio's traffic with street demonstrations, Brazilian troops were unleashed on them. Riots erupted in Rio, and protests broke out on campuses all over the country. The União Metropolitana des Etudantes of Rio, which was also involved in the actions, started a general student strike, and students at universities throughout Brazil joined the protest against the government's use of force. In a surprising move, Brazil's president negotiated with the leaders of the students and the workers involved in the Rio protests and agreed to lower rates. Despite subsequent efforts by Brazil's government to control student organizations, student groups became increasingly politically active, attacking U.S. colonialism, striking for extreme educational reforms, and agitating for reforms in neighboring countries. However, the efficacy of student actions, such as those in Rio, depended to a large extent on gaining non-student support.[26]

Student actions in Latin America led to reforms and to revolution, but not all of those actions, or even the revolutions to which they led, were characterized by violence. For example, students at San Carlos University in Guatemala were successful at setting the stage for the peaceful revolution of 1944, which toppled the government of Jorge Ubico Casteñeda. Students initiated the sequence of events that would lead to the government's collapse when they organized and asked the dictator general for university reforms; the government initially indulged the students, showing some interest in their concerns, but when the students subsequently criticized Ubico's government, it responded by declaring martial law. The students retaliated with a strike and held a massive march in San Carlos. Police did not interfere until dark, when they fell on the students caught in the streets. The government brought in the military, who succeeded in killing a resident and wounding others. Once again students called a strike, which was joined by workers and merchants and effectively shut down San Carlos and other major cities in Guatemala. Faced with a national uprising, Ubico stepped down. The country's troubles were not over, however, and within the year students and a faction of the military overthrew the corrupt provisional government that had replaced Ubico.[27]

Student resistance successfully toppled several other repressive governments in Latin America during the 1950s as well. In the spring of 1957 students demonstrated throughout Colombia against President Gustavo Rojas Pinilla after he made an attempt to get himself illegally appointed for another term; the protests led to a national strike by students, merchants, and workers, and Pinilla's ultimate flight to the United States after the Colombian army moved against him. The following year Venezuelan students had their turn to lead a revolution. A decade earlier, Marcos Pérez Jiménez had seized control of Venezuela, instituting a militaristic campaign of violence that included assassinations of public dissidents and the suppression of all opposition political activity. When students protested at Venezuela's universities, he closed them. In 1955 students formed covert organizations whose purpose was to plot the downfall of Jiménez; such groups were not alone, but joined by other interested parties, including military factions. In January 1958, defectors in the military attacked Jiménez's palace, initiating a military coup, but the coup itself never materialized. Two weeks later, however, Caracas university students marching en masse against the corrupt regime found support in the city's frustrated workers; the demonstration swelled rapidly, and laborers disaffected with the government joined the uprising. When the military tried to intervene, protesters armed with bricks, guns, and Molotov cocktails manned street barricades, effectively repulsing the soldiers. Support for what could clearly be a revolution grew outside of Caracas, and Jiménez found himself attacked on numerous fronts. Even the navy defected, and ships off Caracas threatened to begin bombing areas held by the government. Armed students and defecting troops finally overran the military police protecting

Jiménez, who subsequently abandoned Venezuela. The revolutionaries won, but within the year, they were again manning barricades to protect Venezuela's fledgling government from military overthrow. The students, joined for a second time by workers of Caracas, repelled the attack and successfully defended their government.[28]

Student uprisings in other Latin American countries were less effective, and often only provoked fierce government oppression. In financially strapped Paraguay, for example, President Alfredo Stroessner slightly loosened his repressive grip on the country in 1959 in the face of growing public resentment, claiming he would allow freedom of the press and allow open elections. The following month, however, when he tried to raise public transportation rates, students from the National University decided to test their new liberties by demonstrating; the protest, however, soon grew into a destructive riot. Fearing further challenges to his authority, Stroessner took away the freedoms he'd previously granted and removed dangerous students and faculty from Paraguay's universities. The student resistance movement in Paraguay simply could not withstand the suppression, and student activism died on campuses across the country.[29]

Other acts of student resistance achieved specific limited results in highly repressive states. In 1945 Argentina was suffering under the heavy hand of its own military government, and in risky demonstrations against the government's attack on university autonomy, students at the University of Buenos Aires, the Littoral University, and La Plata University captured and occupied campus buildings, though police sorties eventually overwhelmed and captured the students. Nonetheless, the protesters succeeded in securing future university autonomy.[30] Students at Buenos Aires achieved results again in June 1951 after they boycotted class for the release of Ernesto Mario Bravo, an activist student who had been arrested and jailed by Juan Péron's police. Surprisingly, Bravo was freed and the students resumed their studies. Buenos Aires students were demonstrating yet again in 1956—this time for the removal of an education minister, who was promoting the establishment of private universities. Students once again captured, and then barricaded themselves into, university buildings, held public marches, and went on strike—measures that put enough pressure on the minister to force him from office.[31] During the 1950s Argentina's activist students thus achieved limited successes; but the cohesiveness of the student movement subsequently fell prey to factionalism as organizations began to break away to pursue their own political agendas at the close of the decade.

International Student Groups and the Cold War

Student concerns and organizations crossed national boundaries, and an international union of students was established in 1946 in Prague. Although it had been formed by representatives from seventeen nations from around the globe, representing, for the most part, nations that had opposed the Axis powers, the group suffered during the Cold War. By 1950 the representatives from most Western nations had withdrawn from the organization. In spite of the loss of its anti-Communist members, the organization continued to survive and even to flourish. Students from Western bloc countries formed their own international student organization in Stockholm in 1950, and asserted a nonpolitical agenda focusing on international educational issues. Both groups attracted many new members well into the 1960s.

Student resistance dropped off dramatically in Europe, Russia, and the United States during the 1940s, primarily because the political activists in many of the countries had directly entered the war or simply because the studentry, like the general public, was exhausted. As the Cold War escalated, however, so did the level of student resistance. A new generation of students occupied the universities and began to agitate against Communism and McCarthyism, against nuclear weapons, against imperialism, and for civil rights.

But if the war and its outcome exhausted the students in some nations, it only inflamed student activists in others: students played a key role in a revolution in Hungary and fought imperialism in Japan, India, China, and numerous African nations. In Cuba, in Guatemala, in Colombia, in Venezuela, in Ghana, in India, and in China, student resistance efforts led or aided the toppling of governments during the 1940s and '50s. As student organizations proliferated around the world, they generated collectives of power on an unprecedented scale, and as communication systems evolved and students of different nations increasingly exchanged information, ideology, and tactics, their awareness of their potential power grew and their tactics became more sophisticated. By the 1960s, students all over the world were again organizing on an unprecedented scale, and within a decade student resistance would erupt on an almost global scale.

7 | Student Resistance in the 1960s

South Korea: The Fires of Revolt

Although South Korean students have traditionally lacked the complex networks of large-scale student organizations that characterized other Asian countries, which helped students marshal and focus national student power, they nevertheless managed to generate enough power to topple their government in 1960, after Syngman Rhee, the South Korean president, forced his subordinates to orchestrate his reelection. Prior to Syngman Rhee's reelection, repression and frustration characterized the political climates of universities: students could only demonstrate in support of the president's policies, which they were increasingly frustrated with, especially as the economy of South Korea languished in the 1950s. The ballot-box stuffing was the final straw for students who were already disillusioned with the government. Their protests after the election results were announced led to a police crackdown, which catalyzed more demonstrations and further police attacks. For over a month students protested and battled police. In mid-April, massive numbers of students from the University of Korea at Seoul began a major uprising against the government; the students set fire to police buildings, ransacked the residences of prominent politicians, and filled city streets with angry crowds. Their goal: to remove all unpopular officials, including Syngman Rhee, from government positions. The students would not be deterred, resisting all efforts by Seoul police to disperse them, and while students and police struggled for the upper hand in the streets, the city's general population supported what was looking more and more like a national rebellion.

Ordered to suppress the student demonstration at all costs, the South Korean Army prepared to crush the protesters late in April but ignored government officials when the commands to attack came; within a week the troops, along with their tanks and armored vehicles, had fallen into rank with the students, training their weapons on the government buildings instead. South Korea's military had joined the students in demanding the president's resignation and a new election. Syngman Rhee fled the country, and students closely monitored South Korea's legislature, which began forming the structure for the nation's new Republic. The student-led, military-backed revolt had succeeded, and for a while students continued to influence their local and national governments through the sheer size of street protests. Once South Korea appeared to be safely on the path toward liberalization and modernization, the students lost their unifying cause and fell victim to infighting and careerism. By the end of October 1960 they could not mobilize for any cause with size or force, and six months later, in May 1961, South Korea's embryonic republic fell to a military coup backed by the United States. Once the new government seized control of South Korea, it immediately banned student groups and organizations and arrested and imprisoned all but the most conservative leaders of student groups, allowing only apolitical student government associations to exist.[1] Over the next few years, students slowly found their political voice again, but they never recovered the unity or power they had exhibited in the revolution of April 19, 1960.[2]

Japanese Students Continue to Organize

As South Korean national student organizations disintegrated during the country's brief republic, so too did Japan's massive student federation, Zengakuren, in the early 1960s. The federation that had organized and successfully directed the nation's student interests, forcing the Japanese government to amend both domestic and foreign policy in the 1940s and '50s, fell prey to infighting, splitting along political ideologies in the early 1960s. Dozens of groups within the larger organization realigned themselves, most commonly uniting socialist- or Communist-oriented associations.[3]

Students continued to battle authorities in the 1960s both inside and outside university walls, though their protests often led to counterattacks by other students. For example, early in 1966, a group of liberal students at Waseda University protesting for residency in a newly completed university building as well as university reforms was attacked by conservative students. The university had repeatedly denied protesting students' demands, and a large group of Waseda students opposing the demonstrators decided to take matters into their own hands. A full-scale riot consumed the building. Thousands of police forcefully removed all of the students from the building. Over the next few months, protesting students tried to capture the building several times, only to be harassed by competing groups until they all were dispersed by the police, who grew increasingly violent in their handling of the students. The demonstrations achieved little (most students were indifferent about the concerns of the striking students), but they did create a substantial amount of turbulence at Waseda and other campuses as protests over university reforms and police brutality spread.

Factionalism dampened the efficacy of small-scale protests in Japan, but it was not strong enough to neutralize movements centered around greater concerns. Students banded together, for example, to resist U.S. imperialism in Southeast Asia and Japanese government cooperation in these efforts. Students became alarmed in October 1967 when Japan's prime minister intended to tour Southeast Asia, a trip that was popularly seen as a condoning of U.S. operations in the region. In October thousands of students, many of them Zengakuren, wearing plastic helmets and sporting wooden sticks, descended on the airport at Haneda to physically block the prime minister's departure. While many more of their colleagues traveled on to the airport to form the blockade, a group of over one thousand club-wielding demonstrators took a stand at a train station where the official's train would have to pass. Similarly outfitted but much better trained police troops arrived at the station and charged the demonstrators; the police routed the students, who could not resist their onslought. Informed beforehand of a student army riding the trains to the airport, police troops had also set up defensive positions there. They wedged police cars across entrance bridges and surmounted them with fire hoses. Students equipped with clubs and Molotov cocktails stormed the barricades nevertheless, but were repeatedly repulsed by the hoses and phalanxes of police in full riot gear.

Occupied with overcoming the barricades before them, the students failed to detect riot police moving into position behind them on the bridges; the flanking troops, also in full riot gear and wielding batons and shields, stormed the students on the bridges from behind. Trapped between the police forces that relentlessly pushed toward the center of the bridges from both ends, the students panicked, and many were seriously injured in the chaos. Live reports broadcasting descriptions of the battle and the news of student deaths electrified Tokyo's students, and many rushed to join the fray. Students, workers siding with students, news teams, and police—all eager to participate in one way or another in the struggle—packed trains arriving from Tokyo. The fighting on the bridges continued, and the police forces that had flanked the students found themselves attacked by arriving students and workers, who themselves came under attack by arriving police reinforcements. The police finally overcame the masses of protesters, but hundreds of students, workers, and police were wounded before the conflict ended. Prime Minister Sato Eisaku was not, however, deterred from his travel plans.

The trains were again overflowing with bright plastic helmets in November, the morning of Sato's planned flight to Washington, but thousands of forewarned Japanese police troops in full riot gear smashed the student forces as they came off the trains. Unlike the earlier airport battle, this incident left many more students wounded than police. Sato departed with little hindrance. Two years later, a similar uprising would again occur, but radical students attempting to block the prime minister's visit to Washington would have no chance of successfully storming the airport as the sheer number of police troops at the facility was prohibitive; they decided instead to take control of the train stations en route to the airport, and thus deny Sato's access to his plane. The night before the prime minister's trip, they laid siege to the stations, and while the battles at the stations were intense, with students hurling rocks, bottles, and gasoline bombs and fighting hand to hand with the police, the students could not match the well-trained troops, whose numbers alone (tens of thousands of police had assembled) guaranteed the protesters' defeat. Troops arrested thousands of demonstrators, and Sato's trip was only temporarily delayed.[4]

The Cultural Revolution and the Dissolution of Dissidence in China

China also witnessed a great deal of anti-U.S. sentiment among university students in the 1960s, but the attitude was only part of a larger, public anti-imperialist sentiment; state-supported xenophobia played a key role in the internal political wrestling gripping China's government. The Chinese Communist Party split in the early 1960s between Mao's supporters and enemies, and in 1966 Mao Zedong enlisted China's youth in a fight to purge not only the government but the entire nation of his political adversaries; the stated object of the enterprise was the destruction of all bourgeois and anti-Communist elements and materials in Chinese culture and society. To ensure the continuance of his political program, Mao tapped into the power of China's ideologically minded youth, creating the Red Guards as the means for securing a Maoist future. Closing the country's schools and enlisting tens of millions of young people, including university students, in the Red Guards and arming them each with a little red book of his quotations, Mao turned them loose on China to search for and to annihilate offensive cultural artifacts and to arrest enemies of the people (which included many Communist Party officials, businessmen, professors, and students—anyone remotely suspected of resisting Maoism). Red Guard units roamed freely in cities and over rural China throughout 1966 and 1967, with official license to identify and strike down anything and anyone offensive to the party. Living off the indigenous population, unruly and enthusiastic about destroying all prerevolutionary culture—including public and private libraries, museums, and all manner of historical or cultural collections—and sanctified in their mission by the state, the Red Guards soon provoked the hostility of the general populace, as well as of party officials, for not only did they violently disrupt the lives of everyone they descended upon, but in their zeal they also attacked important members of China's industries, and even state officials. Almost immediately upon inception, the Red Guards caused tremendous anxiety, and their efforts cost hundreds of thousands—some estimate, millions—of lives.[5] By the end of 1967, with the country tiring of them and their mission of destruction well accomplished, they were officially disbanded; the schools were reopened, and China's new revolutionaries for an old cause went back to their newly decontaminated and somewhat sterile classrooms.[6]

Indonesia's Student Revolution

Indonesian students also played a tremendous role in national politics in the sixties. The student wing of the Indonesian Communist Party, known as PKI, alone had tens of thousands of members, but a 1965 Communist coup attempt nationally discredited both the PKI in general and its student membership in particular. Following the attempted revolution, Indonesia's army massacred thousands of suspected dissidents. Student groups opposed to Communist student organizations used the opportunity to launch an aggressive attack on the PKI, destroying the PKI headquarters and the offices of a number of affiliated student groups.[7] Anti-Communist students identified Communists for execution, and armed by the military, many students participated in the actual killings.[8]

In 1965 anti-Communist student representatives formed a new national organization; the purpose of the Action Command of Indonesian Students, or KAMI, was the absolute destruction of the PKI, as well as the reformation of Indonesia's government and economy. The Action Command's membership soared, and the organization grew powerful. Student demonstrations succeeded in reducing public transportation rates, and early in January 1966 President Sukarno was meeting with KAMI leaders in an effort to come to terms with this new force on the Indonesian political scene (Sukarno's control over the government and Indonesia's military was already tenuous). When

Sukarno openly attacked the organization, KAMI students responded with street demonstrations, marches, and urban warfare. In February thousands of KAMI members and thousands of workers surrounded the presidential palace in a massive and violent demonstration. Sukarno immediately outlawed KAMI, declaring all further student protests illegal. The threat to Sukarno's government, however, had only begun.

The president sponsored and presided over his own student demonstration several days later, a demonstration that turned into an armed student assault against the University of Indonesia. KAMI members raced to the Jakarta military base and successfully pleaded with troops to secure the university and shield the student organization; the Jakarta troops formed a defensive ring around the university and blocked the attack by Sukarno's supporters. The president subsequently shut down the university. KAMI nevertheless met en masse and organized a long-term strategy for revolution. The organization continued its barrage against the government in flyers, posters, newspapers, and illegal radio broadcasts, and the multimedia onslaught worked: KAMI gained the support of an Indonesian public tired of the nation's corrupt bureaucracy and troubled economy. Thousands of KAMI students led large public demonstrations throughout Jakarta for Sukarno's ouster. When workers and even renegade troops joined the student protests, Sukarno decided a change in locale was in order, and he evacuated to an outlying stronghold.

At that moment military general Suharto stepped into the limelight, convincing Sukarno to allow him to take control of the situation, to quell the riots, and to assert his control over the military. Acting as the leader of Indonesia, Suharto arrested Sukarno's cabinet members and filled the government with his own men; in March 1967 Suharto officially replaced Sukarno as the president of Indonesia, and Sukarno's regime was over. KAMI thus brought public support behind the demise of Sukarno's government, as Suharto deftly choreographed a military coup. Following the fall of Sukarno's government, Indonesia's military purged the country of Communists and executed tens of thousands of opponents and suspected dissidents. KAMI continued to play a role in politics for a while, but with the loss of its unifying opponent, the organization fell prey to factionalism.[9]

Revolution and Reforms in India

After the National Union of Students fell apart, student protests in India remained localized and relatively small. A few organizations endeavored unsuccessfully to unite, represent, and control India's studentry in the early 1960s, but some demonstrations nevertheless were surprisingly effective; in 1964, for example, students in Orissa protesting against Orissa's minister of the state were able not only to remove the official from office but to topple the local government itself. And the following year in southern India, students protested the mandate to nationalize Hindi as the primary language; the students' demonstrations erupted into full-scale riots that left dozens of people dead in the regions where Hindu was not the dominant language. The destructiveness of the demonstrations and the violence they fostered forced the government of India to reconsider its plan for nationalizing Hindi.[10]

In 1966, hundreds of students went on strike and occupied administration buildings in India to champion university rights in the face of government suppression. To show defiance to the state, students destroyed university and city property, and even kidnapped university officials. Demonstrations became a public threat, and areas around universities were evacuated. While many students were running wild in the streets, battling police, or vandalizing university property, however, others were organizing a representative group and drafting a petition, which included calling for new laws guaranteeing rights for universities. The students' demonstrations, in concert with strikes, forced the government of India to seek a diplomatic resolution; in a series of meetings with officials in the winter of 1966, the student representatives and the government began the slow process of reforming India's universities.[11]

The State of Student Resistance in France

The Union Nationale des Etudiants de France continued to lead the French student movement, though by 1960 factionalism was taking a heavy toll on the union. Having internally debated the question of Algerian independence since the mid-1950s, the Union Nationale finally took a stand in 1960 favoring independence; it began staging protests for Algerian liberation and sheltering students from military induction. The union's pro-Algerian stance alienated many students, and a number of member organizations sought to distance themselves from the parent group.[12] In 1961 the Fédération Nationale des Etudiants de France organized, linking politically moderate and right-wing students; either supporting the French government's position on Algeria or seeing the Union Nationale as generally counterproductive to their careers, members of the Fédération Nationale opposed the union and seriously challenged the progressives in university reform issues, especially after the French government withdrew its economic support of the union. The French government readily, and continually, funded the professionally oriented federation. The union increasingly agitated against French authorities and national policies, and in 1962 the government universally outlawed university student demonstrations.

Although severely weakened, the union was not yet dead; in 1963 it staged a series of national student strikes demanding a wide range of educational reforms. Although many of the demonstrations remained peaceful, others erupted in violence, particularly those in the Latin Quarter. When thousands of students demonstrating for better educational facilities and a lower cost of living for students gathered at the Sorbonne, thousands of police troops arrived, armed with sticks, and smashed the student demonstration, arresting as many of the students as they could catch. Although the demonstrations received sympathetic attention from both the press and the public and hundreds of thousands of students across France went on strike to protest the government's action, the French government continued to suppress individual demonstrations and ignored the demonstrators' demands. Students and faculty (many of whom supported the student actions) remained frustrated by their government; the union, however, continued to organize demonstrations in the following months, and student resentment continued to grow.

In February 1964 the union had its final major clash with the French government. The group helped to organize another demonstration for educational reform at the Sorbonne, which happened to coincide with a visit to the university by the president of Italy. All parties involved anticipated that the announced protest would immediately get out of hand, and Latin Quarter police outlawed the demonstration. Nevertheless thousands of police troops amassed in the area in preparation for the protest, and the Sorbonne was emptied and occupied by police. The government warned that if the demonstration occurred in any form, the union would be terminated. In an attempt to alleviate the crisis, union leaders tried to keep the demonstrators on the Right Bank to prevent violence, but several thousand students scuffled with police troops there, and that led to the jailing of student protesters. In response, students occupied the Sorbonne to protest the police actions, and students across France staged sympathetic marches. Although the French government ignored the protests, it did not ignore the Union Nationale, cutting all financial support to the organization and refusing to recognize its existence. The Union Nationale continued to agitate and promote its causes and democratic ideology through the remainder of the 1960s and '70s, outside official channels, where its lack of resources and access to the government greatly reduced its political leverage and efficacy.

German Students Go Radical in the 1960s

Students in the Soviet-controlled German Democratic Republic found themselves within a zone of increasing intolerance of political agitation following the division of Germany after World War II, which continued through the 1960s. Dissidents met covertly, and what student resistance occurred manifested itself in meetings and small forbidden demonstrations. Such actions were immediately and ruthlessly suppressed. The Federal Republic of Germany, however, witnessed a revival in German student activism and acts of student resistance. The Sozialistischer Deutscher Studentenbund, or SDS, which had been the leading student organization in Western Germany since World War II, split between conservative and liberal factions in 1960. Taking cues from its European and United States counterparts, the SDS reformed itself as a New Left organization, downplaying the revolutionary power of the working class, privileging the role of intellectuals in transforming societies. The new student ideology sought to engage intellectually with highly political issues, such as remilitarization and U.S. involvement in Vietnam, and did not shy away from taboo subjects, even addressing the relationship between the current state and Nazi Germany in an exhibit it sponsored at the Free University called *Ungesühnte Nazijustiz* ("Unexpiated Nazi Justice").[13] The SDS viewed the current government of West Germany as in many ways related to that of Nazi Germany; the perceived association became stronger as the decade wore on, and leftist student activists grew increasingly radical in their leanings and in their protest actions.

Small, local student protests sporadically appeared in West Germany and Berlin, but it was the October 1962 arrest of the editors and publisher of *Der Spiegel* magazine for treason that provoked hundreds of students to protest against the government's clamping down on the freedom of the press and the freedom of expression. Members of the SDS grew more alarmed when the two dominant national parties, the Christian Democrats and the Social Democrats, began working together. The SDS contended that the Federal Republic lacked any substantial political opposition, a dangerous situation that seemed all too familiar, while the government and many university officials countered the student attack with the recollection of the role that a national student organization played in the development of Nazi Germany. Both sides accused the other of trying to take the country toward an extremely dangerous political situation. In 1965 the SDS and other student organizations met in Bonn to organize a campaign against the coalition, resulting in a series of campus and street demonstrations.

The first major acts of German student resistance in the 1960s occurred at the Free University in 1965. Students wanted Erich Kuby, a journalist and outspoken critic, to address a commemorative ceremony of the Allied victory over Germany. Outraged by their selection, the university rejected the students' choice. Upset, the students of the Free University turned out for a massive protest against the administration's actions. The administration upset the students yet again when it dismissed an instructor who had attacked the university in a local newspaper. Following the action, thousands of students took to the streets, holding demonstrations and marches and staging strikes for months, and thousands more signed petitions against the administration calling for reform. Although the student protests pressured limited reforms out of the administration, students also were punished for their actions, forbidden by the university to hold political meetings on campus.[14] Incensed at yet another infringement on their freedom of expression, students held large demonstrations that eventually forced the revocation of the new policy. Other assaults on the rights of university students at the Free University met with similar protests.[15]

German students had concerns apart from their own rights and liberties, and the anti-oppression demonstrations blended with anti-imperialist protests. As the government continued to support domestic and international policies that students perceived as oppressive, their resistance increased. Protests against the Vietnam War generated violent clashes with German police, and students perceived the government's turn to physical force as justification for their own; in 1968 and 1969 student groups would increasingly resort to violence to resist their government and the war.

One massive demonstration in June 1967 united those agitating for student rights, those fighting the state's international policies, and those protesting against Iranian persecution of political dissidents, but it also ended up galvanizing student opposition throughout Germany. The shah was touring Berlin, and massive numbers of students converged on the Berlin Opera House, where he was to see a performance. A police line guarded the entrance and secured the shah's safe arrival, and while students were focused on the shah's motorcade, police flanked the demonstrators. With the shah safely inside, authorities ordered the police troops to attack the demonstrators, and they did so— at once and from all sides. The students were overwhelmed, yet the police continued to hit the demonstrators even after it was clear the officers controlled the area. Students, bystanders, even medical personnel trying to rescue the injured were clubbed.

Police kicked one student unconscious, and while they dragged the comatose Benno Ohnesorg to a police wagon, another officer put a gun to the student's head and shot him. The brutal murder provided a cause and a martyr for the student movement. Tens of thousands of students gathered for Ohnesorg's memorial service and a massive

protest for university and political reform. They drafted a general statement on the dire need for radical reform to both higher education and
the state government.

Rudi Dutschke (popularly known as "Red Rudi") led the students in
their resolution and the movement it engendered. In addition to blam-
ing the government and the undemocratic university system for pro-
grammatically suppressing students' rights, Dutschke identified an
enemy for the cause, again directing the students' anger toward a chain
of newspapers owned by Axel Springer that distorted the public's view of
students. In a move reminiscent of medieval universities, radical students also created the floating Negative University, which had neither
buildings nor set curriculum; it offered ad hoc courses centered around
strategic resistance. In the spring of 1968 Dutschke was shot and sidelined; students blamed the newspapers for inciting the would-be assassin and began attacking distributors of Springer papers and vandalizing
their offices. From 1968 on, radical students increasingly resorted to violence to prevent the distribution of Springer papers, raiding stores and
firebombing company offices.[16]

As the 1960s progressed, both German students and police used violence, resulting in paranoia on the part of both sides, with rough arrests
leading to violent protests and more arrests. The situation escalated rapidly. In April 1967, for example, police arrested and roughed up eleven
student members of the Commune for planning to assassinate U.S. vice
president Hubert Humphrey on his trip to Berlin; acting on a tip, police
hit the group in a preemptive strike and discovered a large cache of
homemade "weapons" made of pudding, yogurt, and smoke bombs.[17]
But even if some student resistance actions were prankish, the violent
tenor of the student movement was no laughing matter. In December
1967, for example, students protested in a ritzy shopping area of West
Berlin just before Christmas, showering holiday shoppers with images
of Vietnamese dead and shouting slogans critiquing thoughtless consumption at a time when thousands were being killed due to German
indifference to the war in Vietnam. Berlin police reacted swiftly, with
enough force and brutality to disperse the marchers almost instantaneously—confirming the students' claims of state oppression as they
freed the streets for the holiday. The brutality of police suppression and

the government's forceful response to the growing German student movement of the mid-1960s set the stage for the 1968 turmoil to come in Germany by radicalizing student activists and fostering a situation in which student extremists saw violence as the only viable course of action. In 1968 and 1969 student groups launched a terrorist campaign that captured government and media attention, but also discredited the student movement for most of the German public.

A Different Face of Radicalism: Student Actions in the Netherlands

Throughout the 1960s, a group of Beat-influenced students and intellectuals calling themselves Provos sporadically appeared in the streets of Amsterdam to call attention to the faults of modern civilization: air pollution, materialism, mass conformity, and a profound lack of humor. Their journal, *Provo*, was promptly banned by the government for obscenity. The group was at best a loosely connected coterie of students and avant-garde activists centered around a sorcerer/window cleaner. The group of provocateurs staged street actions and wore white during their demonstrations to emphasize the need to clean their dirty, industrial society. Their intentionally provocative and often nonsensical banners, slogans, and actions did not discourage Amsterdam police from brutally suppressing them, but the combination of demonstrations and police actions made for terrific headlines and great news copy; thus the group and their issues received a tremendous amount of press coverage, and the state came under media fire and earned public scorn for its often brutal suppression of the peaceful and entertaining protesters. When the popularity of the Provos grew to the point that they threatened to become a political party, their horrified founding members ceremoniously buried the tainted organization with a wake and a funeral.

Czech Studentry and the Prague Spring

In 1967 hundreds of students spontaneously gathered during a blackout and marched through the streets of Prague holding candles and shouting for power, sparking a vicious suppression by police. When the press blamed the students for causing a riot, saying that the police were only restoring order, the students retaliated by plastering posters throughout the city documenting the police force's excessive violence through both photographs and eyewitness accounts. The students' efforts to set the record straight quickly evolved into an antiauthoritarian fight for civil liberties, which won some victories in the form of political and social reforms. But the "Prague Spring" passed quickly—the Soviet military had crushed the progressive movement by the fall of 1968.[18] In the following years students attempted sporadically to protest against the Soviet presence and their own lack of freedom of expression, but they were immediately and brutally suppressed. The desperation of the Czech student movement was evident in the tactics students employed to bring attention to their causes, tactics that ranged from terrorism to public suicide. Althrough they sometimes garnered tremendous international attention, the students could not generate enough power to combat suppression. Czech students would have to wait some time for the opportunity to protest effectively.

Turkish Students Catalyze a Coup

In April 1960 Prime Minister Adnan Menderes of Turkey capped a ten-year repressive regime by launching an attack against all political opponents of the ruling party; the goal was the eradication of all opposition to his government. When over a thousand students held a demonstration at Istanbul University to protest Menderes's latest act, Istanbul police swarmed the campus to suppress the students; and once the police opened fire on the demonstrators, the campus erupted into a massive riot, and in the ensuing chaos, hundreds of students were injured. With the protest growing into the thousands and more students joining all the time, the police went on the offensive, launching gas grenades and charging the protesters with a cavalry division. The police on the ground continued shooting, killing a number of students and injuring scores of others. Under fire, the students fled, but they regrouped and tried to demonstrate through Istanbul, only to be hit once more by heavily armed riot troops. A similar student uprising, complete with violent police suppression, occurred at Ankara. Effectively prevented from large demonstrations because of military intervention, students held small riots throughout both cities; their suppression only fueled their anger and they too resorted to violence. The turmoil was a harbinger of a coup.

Menderes shut down Turkey's universities and declared a state of emergency, but in May Turkey's military seized power. Following the takeover, the new government decided a purge of the universities of dissidents was in order. The students' claim of some responsibility for Menderes's fall had the effect of emboldening Turkey's studentry, however; over the next few years they successfully demonstrated for a number of university reforms. On the off campus post-coup political scene, though, which was one of tension and competing political factions, the students made little impression, even as they continued to organize and demonstrate.[19]

The Fires of Student Resistance Burn in Africa

The National Union of South African Students continued to fight apartheid in South Africa during the 1960s, but in 1961 radical members, frustrated with the limited achievements of the organization and eager to take stronger measures against the government, formed the African Resistance Movement.[20] ARM, a secret group dedicated to the eradication of apartheid and to government reform through terrorism, had ties with the banned African National Congress. Its campaign of resistance—consisting of dynamiting railroads, electrical facilities, communication lines, and train stations—resulted in several deaths. By mid-decade the South African government effectively suppressed the organization through a series of police arrests.[21]

Students played a significant role in the newly independent Republic of Congo in 1960, but more at the behest of Joseph Mobutu than through their own collective resistance; in 1960 Mobutu actively recruited university students (many of them were attending foreign universities at the time) as cabinet members in the government body controlling the republic, but the inept student government, unable to rule, fell to infighting and was terminated early in 1961. That same year, however, students increased their participation in other activities, including the Union Générale des Etudiants Congolais, which heavily criticized the failures of the cabinet. But, the union itself soon fractured and succumbed to internal conflicts. Student strikes in Congo, which occurred from time to time, achieved negligible long-term effects; although some were well attended, the Congo military or local police effectively suppressed them.[22]

After the 1962 Algerian independence and a government shakedown of Algeria's universities and student political organizations, students scrambled for control of the remaining organizations. Student power struggles largely mirrored those occurring on the national political scene. Some groups supported President Ahmed Ben Bella; others opposed him. When Houari Boumedienne wrested the government of Algiers away from President Bella, thousands of students took to the streets to demonstrate against him, but they were immediately suppressed. Student groups sponsored other protests, but although they were sometimes of significant size, they could do nothing against the forces unleashed against them; student opposition leaders were eventually replaced by those more supportive of the new government.

In contrast to those in Algeria, students achieved great success in Sudan, where students at the University of Khartoum went on strike in 1964 after the government announced a decision to put the university under state direction. Originally aimed at securing university autonomy, the strike sparked a national general strike against the military government; riots erupted all over Sudan. The demonstrations escalated in size and vehemence, with workers joining in, and Ibrahim Abboud eventually stepped down. The Sudan student uprising was unique in that a government attack on a university's freedom led directly to that government's demise; the students of Sudan were able to generate far more power than Abboud or his military government realized.

The Student Fight for Freedom in the United States

In February 1960, four African-American students quietly walked into a segregated department store in Greensboro, North Carolina, and sat at a "whites only" lunch counter; the waitress did not serve them lunch, but their presence did not go unnoticed. In the days following, the counter had dozens of African-American student demonstrators quietly sitting at it, waiting to be served.[23] Similar actions had been tried before, even in Greensboro, but this one gained tremendous media attention and sparked a rash of sit-ins at segregated dime stores and restaurants throughout the South.[24] The students' quiet protests dramatized social injustice and infuriated police and Jim Crow supporters; protesters were often met with violence and jailings and, once released, faced expulsions from their schools because they brought public anger and financial pressure from white philanthropists on their institutions. Six weeks after the Greensboro action, hundreds of students targeted lunch counters in bus depots and state and federal buildings in Atlanta for sit-ins.[25] Many of the students were arrested; some were beaten and jailed for their actions, but they allowed the authorities to take them without resorting to violence themselves.[26]

Inspired by the nonviolent student demonstrations occurring throughout the South, students attending a civil rights conference in April 1960 decided to create a national committee to link the various student groups agitating for civil rights. In October the organization was officially named the Student Nonviolent Coordinating Committee (SNCC), with Marion Barry sworn in as its first leader. From its beginning the organization's purpose was the strategic deployment of forces in what it perceived as a war for social justice.[27]

Over the next few years SNCC organized voter drives, protests and demonstrations, sit-ins at restaurants and other segregated places, Freedom Rides, and boycotts, mobilizing 100,000 students, both African-American and white, in the nonviolent fight for civil rights.[28] SNCC's actions had limited immediate local effect, but were extremely effective at focusing national media attention on segregation and thus generated great pressure on their opponents.[29] When the first two buses with Freedom Riders from CORE (Congress of Racial Equality) were viciously attacked in 1961 by mobs in Alabama and their passengers brutally beaten, SNCC rallied to urge the federal government to desegregate bus and train stations, helping organize more Freedom Rider trips and supplying volunteers for them.[30] Within the year, the national fallout from the violent attacks on the Freedom Riders forced the

Interstate Commerce Commission to desegregate both travel and travel stations in the South. Subsequently, activists attacked specific instances of such injustice through litigation.

Desegregation battles were not only waged off campus, though. Throughout the South, students fought on both sides of the war over integration of the region's colleges and universities.[31] The University of Georgia was finally integrated in 1961 after a vicious struggle, and James Meredith successfully integrated the University of Mississippi in 1962—yet these successes were in many ways just harbingers of a larger struggle that would last for years to come.[32]

In 1964 SNCC organized the Mississippi "Freedom Summer," and began teaching hundreds of students how to act nonviolently when arrested by Mississippi police. SNCC then bused the predominantly white students to the state, where they helped local civil rights volunteers in voter drives and with education and health programs for African Americans.[33] The students were met with virulent racism, tremendous hostility, and violence from local law enforcement and white supremacists; three were killed by Klansmen in June.[34] For the price paid in blood, bruises, lives, and burned property, the Freedom Summer registered thousands of black voters, extended health and educational services into areas where they were virtually nonexistent, encouraged the adoption of the 1965 Voting Rights Act, and focused massive, negative media attention on the state.[35]

When Stokely Carmichael, who had been a Freedom Rider in Mississippi and a member of the Congress of Racial Equality (CORE), took over the leadership of SNCC in 1966, the group became much more radical, ejecting all whites from its ranks and promoting black nationalism. The organization's political power, however, suffered for it, and SNCC membership dwindled.[36]

The nonviolent methods of protest that had been so effective in the civil rights campaign in the 1950s and early '60s were immediately adapted by students across the United States for other ends as well. In May 1960 a subcommittee of the House Un-American Activities Committee began hearings at San Francisco's City Hall to explore the degree to which Communism had permeated and corrupted California. Hundreds of students quietly attended the first day of the hearings. On day two, however, several hundred vocal students and other boisterous protesters converged on City Hall to oppose the hearings more audibly; San Francisco police drove the demonstrators from the building and brutally beat them. The next day the hearings were again disturbed, but this time by thousands of protesters who had heard about the treatment of the students the day before. Large numbers of police guarded the building, which was engulfed by chanting protesters. The brutal reaction to the students' nonviolent protests resulted in demonizing both the state and the federal hearings; police treatment of unarmed and peaceful, if vocal, dissenters was broadcast in every state, and the national media evoked tremendous public sympathy for the students and their cause. The attention drawn to the presence of the House Un-American Activities Committee in California also served to alarm a significant portion of California's studentry.

The House Un-American Activities Committee had its student supporters as well, though, most notably the Young Americans for Freedom. This group of students was vehemently anti-Communist and pro-business. Like most political student organizations, the Young Americans for Freedom perceived themselves as oppressed, and their main source of power lay in resistance—in this instance, resistance to leftist student groups that attacked their ideology. By the mid-1960s, the Young Americans for Freedom boasted thousands of members and endeavored to block leftist student actions in campus politics. Its existence alone helped conservative politicians cast leftists as nonrepresentative radicals.

In terms of power, the leader of leftist student organizations in the United States during the 1960s was Students for a Democratic Society. Originally the Student League for Industrial Democracy, a student affiliate of its parent group, the students broke away in 1962 at a conference held in Port Huron, Michigan, took a new name, reset their goals, and elected their first president, Tom Hayden.[37] From its inception, SDS was to be an organization for direct action and political conflict. Hayden had traveled with SNCC in the South, as had many of those involved in the new organization, and thus it is not surprising that, although it had a broader political agenda, SDS had similar motives and relied on tactics similar to those used by SNCC. Hayden's first act as executive officer was to oversee the writing of the Port Huron Statement, a declaration of the agenda and interests of SDS general enough to encompass most leftist activist students in the United States.[38]

One conceit of the Port Huron Statement was that students would lead a social movement that, in contrast to the old left's class-based attack on capitalism through the mobilization of workers, would endeavor to attack poverty, racism, and imperialism through nonviolent protest, education, and the uniting of various student activist organizations and outside communities. The statement claimed that the role of the intellectual activist was central to social change. Heavily influenced by the writings of C. Wright Mills and Howard Zinn, the statement had an existential, if utopian, commitment to direct action, and was literally handed across the nation as thousands of university students at hundreds of universities distributed it to their colleagues.[39] It was nothing short of a strategic call to arms. For the next few years SDS members at campuses across the United States organized sit-ins and local demonstrations, as well as large protests for a wide variety of causes, including the 1965 March on Washington to End the War in Vietnam, in which twenty thousand protesters rallied at the nation's capital. Although the Port Huron Statement was drafted in 1962, it was not until 1964 that the SDS attracted its thousands of members, following an unaffiliated and spontaneous demonstration at a University of California campus.[40]

The Berkeley uprising began after a campus official declared a section of land that ran along the campus's main entrance off limits for student political activities. For years, students and off-campus political organizations had used the Bancroft sidewalk strip as a place to set up card tables on which they displayed political literature to inform the university community about issues and to gain support for causes. On September 16, 1964, the university startled activists volunteering at the tables by claiming that the sidewalk was university land, and that the students must fold up their tables at once and desist using the area for any and all political activities. Activists refused to obey the orders, and when five of the illegal table sitters were called to appear before the dean of men on September 30, a petition was passed and signed by hundreds of students (including both Goldwater supporters and CORE members) claiming an equal responsibility with the five charged with breaking the ban; if they spread the blame, they hoped, no one would suffer. The chancellor ignored the petition, and subsequently hundreds of students gathered within Sproul Hall and refused to leave, using the time to organize the Free Speech Movement, a coalition of political students with the express goals of changing the university's regulations regarding free speech and political activities and battling what they perceived as the evolution of the university into a factory intended to produce cookie-cutter students to serve industry.[41]

On the first day of October 1964, in an open act of resistance, students once again set up their card tables and passed out political literature on the Bancroft strip; the police arrived and arrested a student manning a CORE table, hustling him into a squad car amid a throng of students who immediately converged on the car.[42] Though the students were unable to prevent the arrest, they could keep the police vehicle from moving; spontaneously, they sat down before and behind it, hemming the car in. Protesters used the automobile, which was stuck in the crowd of students for the next thirty hours, as a platform from which to address what was quickly becoming a free speech rally. Another contingent of students occupied Sproul Hall. The following day university officials and the protesters negotiated a deal in which the students would disperse, the activist would be released, and the university would establish a committee to address political activism on campus. Both sides claimed victory.

Nevertheless, the university decided to press charges against the students who had led the protest, a decision that united the student body once again, and it demanded the university drop the charges. When university officials ignored the students, they again occupied Sproul Hall, where many, including one of the accused, Mario Savio, gave impromptu speeches; Joan Baez appeared and sang songs, and others held political workshops or slept. Governor Pat Brown Sr., however, soon ordered hundreds of police officers to invade Sproul Hall; they arrested all of the students, who allowed themselves to be taken without physical resistance. Although no one was seriously injured, rumors of police brutality spread throughout the university, and the sight of armed police and national guardsmen occupying the campus the next day convinced thousands of Berkeley students to support the Free Speech Movement.

The students met at another rally on Berkeley's main plaza on December 4; thousands turned out to hear the speakers, who, wearing black shirts with large white V's on them, railed against university and state government officials and the state police and called for a general strike, which immediately went into effect. A few days later the president of the university addressed a summoned crowd of sixteen thousand students and teachers, condemning the actions of the students; his speech was spontaneously followed by one by Mario Savio, the ringleader of the movement. The university faculty held a meeting to discuss freedom of speech and politics on campus; siding with the students, they voted to lift speech restrictions on campus. Encouraged, the students held another massive rally and continued the strike, and university life ground to a halt. Professors resigned over the university's handling of the issue, and on January 2, 1965, the university's regents forced Berkeley's president out of office.[43]

The Berkeley revolt inspired student resistance and activism across the United States and throughout Europe as well. Its tactics were adopted by protesting students across the nation, and the press picked up the events, drawing national attention to hitherto largely ignored student issues.[44] At other universities students followed the example of the Berkeley students in an attempt to reform and to humanize their own schools. The Berkeley uprising made political protest exciting to a lot of previously uninvolved students; it identified the university as the site par excellence for fashionable dissent, and popularized student organizations as had no other incident in U.S. history. SDS was quick to capitalize on its success.[45]

While political protest was becoming chic on campuses, nevertheless at the heart of the student movement were individuals seriously engaged with, idealistic about, and committed to their causes—willing to take them beyond hanging posters on dormitory walls, and coffee shop or classroom discussions. SDS launched a series of community outreach programs, sending students into impoverished inner-city areas to educate and to agitate for the establishment of public social services, and SNCC continued its work in the South; their efforts gained broad media attention, but these were only the most visible of student activism efforts. Many others were occurring as well. A group of Puerto Rican students calling themselves the Young Lords, for example, took to the streets of Spanish Harlem in New York in 1965 in an attempt to capture media attention to help the area's residents. The first Young Lords campaign was the literal cleaning up of Spanish Harlem: students literally picked up tons of garbage and piled the trash into heaps along the curbs. When New York City sanitation workers went to work and discovered the hills of garbage waiting for them, they promptly ignored the stacks of trash; the city simply left it in piles along the streets. The students responded with protest marches. The target of their resistance, and one of the most difficult to overcome, was blind indifference. Previously uninterested city officials responded to their subsequent agitation, dispersing the students with police troops, an action that only succeeded in bringing in the press, and the publicly embarrassed city officials soon made an effort to get the garbage removed.[46]

For the majority of students—and student activists—in the United States, the Vietnam War overshadowed any domestic political struggle.[47] In 1967 tens of thousands of students gathered in antiwar demonstrations at hundreds of campuses, culminating in October in "End the Draft Week," seven days of intense nationwide protests and student demonstrations against the Selective Service, in which many draft cards were publicly burned or gathered, marked "Return to Sender," and en masse dropped into mailboxes. In Oakland the demonstration resulted in a massive attack on the municipal Induction Center; Oakland police battled with fifteen thousand demonstrators for several days before finally capturing the neighborhood surrounding the center. Students at the University of Wisconsin picketed against Dow Chemical, which had representatives on campus, staging a sit-in when university officials refused to eject the representatives of the company that produced napalm for the military.[48] When police attempted to forcibly remove the peaceful students, they found themselves surrounded by a few thousand angry students. The confrontation turned serious when the ring of students surrounding the police began throwing objects at them; trapped, the police panicked and radioed a call for help. Hundreds of troops rushed to the scene, violently overwhelming the students. One day later the demonstrating students called a general strike, but lacking leadership and without a clearly defined agenda and attainable goals, the strike withered.[49]

The national End the Draft Week itself culminated in a march on the Pentagon, an anti-Vietnam demonstration attracting approximately thirty thousand protesters, many of them students. The marchers stopped en route to listen to speeches at the Department of Justice and at the Lincoln Memorial before crossing the Arlington Bridge and converging on the Pentagon, where they were met by local police, national guardsmen, and military police. The peaceful protest erupted in violence at the Pentagon, when a faction of the demonstrators suddenly surged to the front of the protest and charged the police and military troops defending the front of the building. Police repelled the protesters and subsequently launched a counteroffensive, beating and arresting hundreds of protesters; the battle waged back and forth until a regiment of troops arrived and pushed the demonstrators back. Many of those gathered at the Pentagon, who were there demonstrating for peace, were seriously injured in the fighting.

The battles fought at Berkeley, at Madison, in Washington, D.C., and throughout the country in the early and mid-1960s served to draw lines between "the establishment" and "the radicals"; by the end of 1967, a greater war was beginning to heat up in earnest. One early casualty of the domestic war was the National Student Association, originally founded at Wisconsin in 1947. The organization of student governments, which had taken an anti–Vietnam War stance and supported many of the peaceful student antiwar demonstrations, was nevertheless rumored in 1967 to have been supported by the Central Intelligence Agency since the early 1950s.[50] The group lost most of its support among leftist university students, but it continued to exist. During this period, many student groups became paranoid about government infiltration. In 1968, however, a more open warfare in the United States would be unleashed against the radical students.

Latin American Students and the Turn to Extremism in the 1960s

The student actions taking place in Latin America in the 1960s varied in duration, degree, and goals; many activists tried to respark the energy characteristic of earlier educational reform movements, while others widened the wars to include government or social reform. Generally, however, government force ruled the day. As the decade progressed, protesters increasingly turned to acts of desperation and to guerrilla organizations, anticipating the violent, student-led upheavals of 1968.

Anti-Communist student groups at the University of Havana began to agitate for democracy at the start of the 1960s, publicizing their views in pamphlets and on posters and even in public demonstrations. Terrorist groups also formed that targeted government facilities for sabotage. In 1961 one took out Havana's main power plant with a bomb. The democracy movement did not, however, last long, and by the end of the year those terrorists who had not fled the country had been hunted down and arrested; many were executed.

The Dominican Republic, which witnessed strikes and demonstrations in the late 1950s by students against the repressive regime of General Rafael Trujillo, saw the dictator mercilessly retaliate, arresting, imprisoning, and executing hundreds of students in his effort to control the nation. After his assassination in 1961, students at the University of Santo Domingo formed a national union and demonstrated for university autonomy; Dominican police smashed the protest, and violent riots subsequently broke out in the streets, resulting in numerous student deaths. One year later, students again protested en masse—but peacefully—when a military coup toppled the civilian government of Juan Bosch; but even so the marchers were again attacked and overwhelmed by police.[51]

Since the early 1960s, the Central University of Venezuela had been a site of political unrest; in 1966 police attempted definitively to secure the university. Students responded with riots and strikes that the police violently suppressed. As a result of the unrest, Venezuelan president Raúl Leoni ordered the Central University shut down indefinitely in 1967. Students in Ecuador agitated for government and social reform in the early 1960s, and were likewise brutally suppressed for their efforts. As the years passed, the students' antigovernment protests intensified, and in 1966 the government retaliated by sending troops against students agitating at state universities. The actions resulted in the killing of several student protesters and the military occupation of schools. But in the face of violent suppression that often left activists wounded or dead, students continued to fight the government of Ecuador.

Students waged a variety of protests in Colombia in the 1960s, many for university reforms and against police violence. Holding strikes for as long as four months at a time, rioting in Bogotá and other major cities, the students often verged on anarchy. Police were often called by university officials to quell student uprisings. In 1965, students called a general strike in which tens of thousands of students nationwide participated to protest university administrators' use of police to suppress on-campus demonstrations. To stifle the growing student rebellion, Colombia's government replaced the unpopular university officials.

Latin American student movements in the 1960s looked back to history for inspiration and examples, but the political climate of the region and the universities had drastically changed. The student movements were now more politically oriented, and the activists more willing to resort to violence—in large part because of the widespread use of police suppression by the individual rulers of Latin American nations. Inspired by the tactics in Che Guevara's *Guerrilla Warfare*, and encouraged by the success of Fidel Castro's student-supported revolution, students throughout Latin America envisioned their own revolutions based on political issues, deriving their force not from the working class or peasants but from the ideology of students.[52] Throughout the 1960s, students in Colombia, Ecuador, Guatemala, Haiti, Honduras, Nicaragua, Peru, and Venezuela met and formed guerrilla organizations modeled on Guevara's and Castro's examples. As the end of the decade drew near, the numbers of such student groups increased, and their resistance actions, which ranged from organizing street protests to sparking riots, sabotage, kidnappings, and even assassinations, intensified. The embers of revolt were glowing once again.[53]

1968 and 1969
Student Power, Part I

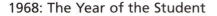

8

1968: The Year of the Student

No year has been written about more in relation to student activism, no year is more mythologized or brings more sighs of melancholic yearning to aging activists, than what has come to be known as the Year of the Student, 1968. From Paris to Tokyo, Mexico City to Dakar, in one single year students staged an unprecedented number of major resistance actions, actions that dramatically changed the course of their respective nations and the world; students all over the globe pushed their individual movements to crisis points as the international media watched, reported, and capitalized on their stories, applauding or condemning the movements' issues, strategies, and heroes. Many of the actions begun in 1968 continued in 1969 (and indeed, some of the most important effects of 1968 student actions weren't felt until the 1970s), but as for a historical moment that crystallized the global power of the student—1968 is it.

The Year of the Student and the Students of France

In January a group of students at the University of Paris, Nanterre, calling themselves Les Enragés, or the maniacs, after an extremist group in the French Revolution and borrowing the tactics of the Situationists—an anarchist, antibourgeois, anticapitalist group of antiaesthetic agitators—began creating disturbances on campus, disrupting university lectures, classes, and events. Situationist-inspired slogans—"The more you consume the less you live!" or "I take my desires for reality because I believe in the reality of my desires!"—began appearing on Nanterre university walls.[1] Les Enragés, composed of highly motivated student radicals and scores of willing followers, extended their disruptions throughout the campus, at first hurling only insults at those whom they perceived as fascist bourgeois professors and speakers, but soon hurling stones as well; they called for immediate educational reforms (co-ed dormitories topped their list of demands), but they also demanded the destruction of imperialism, the military, the bourgeoisie, and the university itself. Situationist propaganda had primed the students of France for action; *On the Poverty of Student Life*, a radical call for insurrection, was first published in 1966 by members of the Situationist International and a group of Strasbourg students, and by 1968 it had circulated throughout France's universities, with over 300,000 copies printed.[2] Although the students took themselves seriously, the Situationists were using them to sow anarchy and using their student union funds to print Situationist pamphlets. Independent Situationist-inspired organizations already existed in schools across the nation by the time Les Enragés students were scaling the entrance to the Nanterre campus at night to hang banners reading, "Never Work!"[3]

From the start, the 1968 student upheavals were an international potlatch of strategies and concerns. In March 1968 Les Enragés seized an administration building at the Nanterre campus to protest the arrest of students suspected in a series of anti–Vietnam War bombings. Led by Daniel ("Danny the Red") Cohn-Bendit, the radical students at Nanterre modeled themselves on Fidel Castro's July Twenty-Sixth Movement, calling their own revolutionary action the March Twenty-Second Movement. They also endeavored to start an urban revolution as they protested against the Vietnam War, Western imperialism, and militarism. The surprising success of the Tet offensive in Vietnam, the embarrassing defeat of overconfident American forces in an impoverished third-world country, and the growing and highly visible unrest of American students fueled the revolutionary fires of the French radicals, who claimed they would start their own war in France. Hostilities on the campus between the demonstrators and the administration threatened to erupt, and the president of the school temporarily closed the university. Shortly after the school opened again, demonstrations and disruptions again occurred on campus, and the administration reclosed the school, announcing that disciplinary hearings would be held for the Enragés core members on May 6 at the Sorbonne. The radicals had only a few days to prepare for their defense. Instead, they went on the offensive.

Les Enragés met other radical students from the University of Paris at the Sorbonne to address a large crowd of Sorbonne and Nanterre students.[4] When police began arresting those students gathered, Sorbonne students raised an alarm and attacked the police. Provoked, the police charged into the unruly students with clubs, and the entire area erupted in a riot in which hundreds of students and bystanders were injured. The largely unorganized student uprising continued the next day, spreading through Paris and then through the nation as student organizations and unions went on strike and joined the demonstrations against police oppression. By May 5, most of the major student organizations, including the Union Nationale des Etudiants de France, supported an immediate national strike.

On the supposed day of the hearings, May 6, students numbering in the thousands demonstrated on the Boulevard Saint-Michele to protest the violence of May 4 and the police occupation of the Sorbonne. In spite of massive Parisian public support (the numbers swelled as the march continued), the police brutally attacked the demonstrators as they approached the Sorbonne. This time the students refused to run, and when the police fired tear gas grenades, the protesters covered their faces with wet rags; they organized themselves into long columns, passing bricks and paving stones torn up from streets blocks away up to front lines of students facing off with police. The students continued the assault for over seven hours, until police troop reinforcements finally overwhelmed them in a concerted push. The entire quarter became the scene of rioters and police run amok; students, onlookers, residents, emergency health workers—police attacked them all. Groups of students and police officers fought each other throughout the night. Relying on urban guerrilla tactics—many of them Blanquist—the students had, in a fashion, started their own war on the Left Bank after all.

On May 7, the Union Nationale des Etudiants de France held a massive demonstration on the Champs Elysées; forty thousand students attended—the Arc de Triomphe floated in a sea of waving banners. Over the next few days students in each of France's major cities held huge

demonstrations, demanding the release of arrested students and protesters, the recall of police presence from universities, and a gamut of
educational and social reforms. Even though the protesting groups
often professed disparate beliefs, and the relations between them were
sometimes strained, Communists and hard-line Trotskyists marched
together with anarchists and Situationists, united in opposing the
Gaullist government and the brutality of French riot police. For several
days students and police waged battles in the streets of the Left Bank.

By May 10 tens of thousands of students had taken over the Left
Bank, where they fashioned barricades in the streets out of furniture,
cars, bricks, bicycles, and anything and everything that they could carry
and stack. The demonstration was by and large leaderless; and although
the lack of centralized control diluted the protest's power, it also made
suppression of the students difficult. Supporters continued to mass, and
by nightfall the streets swarmed with thousands of demonstrators armed
with stones, bottles, bricks, Molotov cocktails, and whatever they could
use as missiles, bombs, or clubs, standing on or behind massive barricades. The upcoming fight in many ways was unavoidable. De Gaulle's
government was damned if they attacked the barricades and damned if
they didn't; to attack would cast the police once again as the brutal
oppressors, while to delay would be to appear weak. De Gaulle was not
one to back down, and early in the morning of May 11 thousands of
police troops charged the barricades. The clash of sticks, the thuds
of truncheons, the clattering of thrown stones, the explosions of gas
tanks, the firing and hiss of tear gas canisters, and yells and moans filled
the streets of Paris. After intense fighting, the students were thrown off
their fortifications, and many discovered too late that they had neglected
to provide themselves with escape routes. Police beat protesters, even
storming apartments suspected of harboring them. Many terrified
and pleading protesters found sanctuary and protection in the homes
of sympathetic residents, but a great many did not. For the remainder of
the night, students skirmished with police troops throughout the
Latin Quarter.

The French government tried to defuse the situation by withdrawing
troops from university campuses, but the revolt by then had too much
momentum to be diverted; workers' unions announced their own gen-

eral strikes for May 13, the tenth anniversary of de Gaulle's ascension to power, and the workers brought their own demands to the protest.[5] Workers at major industrial plants occupied their factories or joined in public demonstrations; suddenly millions of French factory workers were striking. Public service, shipyard, and other workers joined the strike—all with their own demands for government or labor reform. France's workers had grown increasingly upset at rising work demands, the lowest wages in industrialized Europe, and a growing national unemployment rate. The government's economic policies had slowly pushed blue-collar workers to a flash point: the Paris student riots simply ignited the flame. In an effort to consolidate power, many student groups marched to factories to establish relations between striking laborers and students. As Paris erupted in riots, and industrial France ground to a halt, de Gaulle found his grip on the country in serious jeopardy. The French workers offered the more dangerous threat to the government, but the students kept Paris on the edge of revolution.

Les Enragés and the Situationists officially joined forces, and the two groups continued to try to radicalize the exploding student movement. The core group of students at the Sorbonne, however, were no longer in control of the student uprising, nor would the studentry adopt the increasingly militant stances of the radicals, who now sought de Gaulle's overthrow. Frustrated with the general student masses, who no longer listened to them, Les Enragés and the Situationists abandoned the Sorbonne to the students.

The division between the radical learners, the more moderate masses, and those students simply rioting for the sake of it spoke to other fractures in the tenuous coalition of resistance. The protesting students could not agree among themselves on their goals, while the workers wanted concrete economic reforms and wage increases. Trouble soon plagued this partnership as well, as the laborers perceived the students as irresponsible, too radical, and unpredictable.

Nevertheless, by May 27, de Gaulle's government's demise seemed imminent. Students kept protesting, and labor unions held out for wage increases and other reforms. The seventy-seven-year-old president abruptly left Paris at the end of May. His departure stunned the populace of Paris, and students claimed victory; but the aged war veteran was determining if he still enjoyed the support of the military, and he did. One day later he returned to Paris to give a public radio speech in which he called for national elections. After de Gaulle's speech, a spontaneous rally of hundreds of thousands of his supporters marched down the Champs Elysées waving French flags and intoning the "Marseillaise." By this time the general public had grown frustrated with the students' abuse of property, their general disorganization, and their radicalness; urban residents also began to feel the strain of the interruption of daily life and of social services (public transportation had long since been discontinued, and the cities had run nearly, if not completely, out of gasoline). De Gaulle's first decisive move of his new campaign came on June 1, when he had all the gasoline stations restocked with fuel for the long Whitsun weekend; traffic once again flowed in Paris, and the tide of fortune turned against the students and workers as the general public began to appreciate a society that worked. Strikers at factories tried to hold out against the reenergized regime but eventually succumbed to police troops, and the police overran the Sorbonne early in June. On June 23 the Gaullist government swept the elections, and immediately instituted educational reforms and a wage increase, which satisfied students and workers enough to return the majority of them to their former employments.[6] By the end of the month de Gaulle was once again securely in power, and students were once again sitting at their desks.[7]

Thus although the students and the workers of France pushed the Gaullist regime to the brink of disaster, they lacked the leadership and the political power to topple it. When both movements stalled, de Gaulle was able to rally his political and police forces against them. Satisfied the military backed him, de Gaulle used his political power to call elections, relying on nonurban popular support and frustrated city residents who had grown impatient with the protests and the interruptions to daily life and of public service. The students and workers generated enough power to threaten de Gaulle's regime, but they were unable to focus it effectively and decisively.

The People's Democracy in Ireland

In the fall of 1968 the Northern Ireland Civil Rights Association began a series of marches to protest Protestant domination of Northern Ireland;

in October two thousand (mainly Catholic) protesters marching peacefully in Derry were suddenly attacked by police. Images of police clubbing marchers were televised all over Ireland; at Queen's University in Belfast thousands of students angered at the beatings marched on City Hall. Protestant police troops turned them back, but the protests did not end in violence; the students returned to the university to form a resistance group, the People's Democracy, and agreed to march on City Hall again to raise issues regarding Catholic unemployment and the scarcity of public housing for Catholics. To hold such a demonstration legally, students needed a permit and someone willing to file for it; for this decidedly risky honor, Bernadette Devlin, a twenty-one-year-old student, volunteered her name, claiming before the committee that as she was an orphan, she had little to lose. This demonstration too occurred without violence, and encouraged the People's Democracy to stage a sit-in at Northern Ireland's Parliament building one week later.

The Northern Ireland Civil Rights Association struck a more conciliatory pose with the prime minister, but the students pressed their demands for social reform, which included new electoral boundaries, housing based on need, the awarding of jobs based on qualifications, freedom of speech, and the abandonment of the Special Powers Act that gave the police force extraordinary powers over Northern Ireland's citizenry.[8] Approximately seventy-five People's Democracy marchers gathered on the morning of the New Year, 1969, and began a trek from Belfast to Derry directly modeled on Dr. Martin Luther King Jr.'s march from Selma; the march was a lightning rod for media attention and thus also one for the Irish Republican Army, who took it upon themselves to escort and to guard the marchers when they camped at night. Police also warily trailed the marchers. As the demonstration progressed it grew in size, attracting supportive Catholics and a number of sympathetic Protestants. The march almost made it to Derry.

On the fourth day, however, the protesters were ambushed by a mob of right-wing Protestants, who attacked them with homemade weapons, clubs, and chains as they approached Burntollet Bridge. The police did not interfere or offer assistance to the unarmed marchers, whose only options were to run or be beaten, but there were few avenues of retreat not blocked by unsympathetic police or locals. Nearly one hundred of the marchers were injured in the ambush, and many were hospitalized. Those who survived uninjured, however, regrouped and began marching again, only to be assailed again as they drew near Derry; this time their assailants attacked with rocks and Molotov cocktails before rushing the marchers with clubs. When the rumor of the violence spread, a riot broke out in the Catholic ghetto of Derry, which police quelled by sweeping through the area and attacking anyone found in the streets. Catholic residents responded by erecting barricades in the streets and fighting back; the battles raged for over a week.

Meanwhile Bernadette Devlin entered the February general elections for Parliament to use her candidacy as a platform for the People's Democracy. Devlin's political star rose; to the surprise of many, she was elected, and the People's Democracy quickly gained support from Catholics throughout Northern Ireland. Derry, however, continued to witness violence; what had begun as a student action grew to major social unrest, its new participants quickly outnumbering the original student members. Over the next several months Derry and Belfast repeatedly erupted in riots and police battles. Devlin herself participated in the defense of a barricade following her election and was afterward convicted of inciting a riot.[9] But by August 1968 the students were peripheral to the struggle, which failed to make the transformation to viable political force, exhausting its strength in an ongoing series of violent riots and an increasing number of individual acts of terrorism. Militancy and internal power struggles alienated the moderate participants in the social movement, leaving the future of the struggle in the hands of those who promoted change through violence. The People's Democracy, too, divided over the turn to violence and rapidly declined in strength.

English Students Act

In the wake of the 1968 French student movement, previously apolitical students throughout the Western world began to rebel, joining their politically minded colleagues or acting on their own, and acts of resistance became de rigueur at previously untroubled campuses. Apart from the troubles in Northern Ireland, however, the English government and English university officials had relatively few problems in 1968 and '69.

The most significant student resistance efforts in England were generated from the larger anti-Vietnam campaign; in 1968 at the University of Essex, a small group of students were expelled after they attempted to interrupt a lecture given by a scientist working in biological weaponry. They had originally planned a peaceful response to the lecture, a series of questions as a form of rebuttal, but when the speaker would not engage them and police arrived on the scene with dogs, a frustrated student rushed the stage, dumped a bag of mustard on the scientist, and decried the horror of mustard gas.[10] The expulsion of some of the students after the event sparked a large demonstration and the student occupation of the campus. The administration unceremoniously reinstated the offending students, thus effectively defusing the situation, which had drawn public attention to Great Britain's involvement in biological and chemical weapon production.[11]

The Vietnam War was the only issue that British students rallied around with any substantial force during the late 1960s; in October 1968 many students participated in a massive anti–Vietnam War march in London. The 100,000-person march was viciously attacked in newspapers and journals, but the British government refrained from forcibly opposing the march. Students staged other acts of resistance aimed at the Vietnam War at universities in England in 1968 and '69, but the marches drew students off campuses as well, diluting the strength of campus-centered protests.

Protests aimed at local university reforms also occurred on campuses. At a number of universities, students occupied buildings, trying to establish free universities and to reinvent their institutions; at Hornsey College in May 1968, for example, rebelling students evicted the institution's workers and administration and occupied and ran the university, from its administrative offices to its kitchens, for six weeks. Inspired by the Hornsey occupation, students at dozens of other colleges occupied their schools as well. Unlike their counterparts in the United States or in France, however, the English and local educational governments did not immediately react with force—they waited in most cases until students grew tired and the strength of the occupations weakened before retaking the buildings, and then afterward punishing the dissidents.[12]

Following an anti-Vietnam protest at the London School of Economics campus, for example, the administration decided to install gates around the campus to prevent future demonstrations. The students responded by taking sledgehammers to the gates, whereupon school officials shut down the university for a month. A few students retaliated by breaking into the swimming pool of the University of London and skinny-dipping, but activists were unable to generate enough energy to challenge the administration. Again, officials waited until the university was reopened before taking action against those involved in the original protests and the subsequent defacement of school property.

Inspired by the resistance they saw occurring in the countries around them, students throughout Britain often challenged their institutions and governments in 1968 and '69, but they were unable to generate any sustained or even relatively cohesive movement. The British government and university officials, too, had witnessed the threats posed by students in France and other countries and learned from the mistakes made by de Gaulle and his education officials in dealing with those threats; they refused to be provoked and remained flexible in their dealings with dissident students, either effectively defusing situations before they exploded or consciously indulging students' political outbursts. What force police exerted they did for the most part later, and quietly.

German Student Radicalism: Assassination or Suicide?

The massive Socialistischer Deutscher Studentenbund, or SDS, continued to grow in membership after the murder of student Benno Ohnesorg in 1967. Encouraged by an international climate fostering student resistance, the SDS began a powerful campaign of agitating at all major universities throughout West Germany.[13] The most visible leader of the German student movement, Rudi Dutschke, was an extremely vocal socialist who loudly criticized the government and the "apoliticality" of the general public. "Red Rudi" spearheaded student demonstrations against the capitalist authoritarian state in April 1968 that spontaneously gave way to general student rioting in several major cities. Violent police suppression of the students only incited more students to join the ranks, and for close to a week hundreds of students battled against police in a number of cities. Three students died in the conflicts. "Red Rudi" was another victim of the violence, though he did not die; during the uprisings a mentally imbalanced painter stalked and shot the student leader. Wounded but not dead, Dutschke was nevertheless sidelined, and the SDS lost its leader.

The SDS blamed the government and the media for the assassination attempt, vocally attacking them both. The campaign of destruction waged against Springer offices and property increased. And student support for the SDS also rose following the attack on Dutschke, but the students made the mistake of isolating themselves from the general public and alienating government officials through their untempered vitriol. Like their counterparts in Paris, the German students sought an alliance with labor and attempted to transform their wild social power to political power. The West German trade unions, however, refused to answer the call.

Blocked in the attempt to publicly widen the political war and unable to confront police on the streets effectively, the students found themselves confined to their campuses; radical students turned their anger on their own institutions, disrupting lectures, defacing property, and occupying buildings. Frustrated students occupied Frankfurt University and renamed it the Karl Marx University; the new institution existed for almost three days before police overran it. The students continued to agitate, but the SDS was quickly becoming marginal. No bond was forged with labor, the general public was tired of the student disturbances, and the government maintained a zero-tolerance policy in handling student uprisings. With no place to go, SDS members began turning on themselves, and factional infighting tore the organization apart from within. The return of de Gaulle to power in June, followed shortly after by Soviet tanks ending the Prague Spring in August, added to the general feelings of defeat among West German student agitators. By the end of summer the end of the German student resistance movement was in sight.

The radical elements of the studentry did not, however, retire. During the rapid decline of the German student movement in 1968 and 1969, and for years afterward, small militant terrorist groups—which included students among their members—desperately turned to violence to effect change. The Baader-Meinhof Gang, hoping that their acts of terrorism would incite the general public to revolt against the government, began a seven-year arson campaign. When the burning of buildings failed to start a revolution, they began exploding bombs—most notoriously at a U.S. military base in which U.S. soldiers were killed. Such instances of violence only further alienated Germany's student activists from the public, dooming a priori their future revolutions. In 1969 the German student movement of the 1960s, had for all practical purposes, expired.[14]

The Power of Learning and Labor in Italy

In the late 1960s, student resistance in Italy blossomed into a massive movement that, uniting with a labor movement, spread beyond university walls. Eventually the wider cultural revolution would leave students behind. The student struggle at the Trento Institute of Social Sciences from 1965 to 1968, however, attained allegorical proportions. Holding demonstrations and teach-ins, the students at Trento initially fought for the recognition of the importance of sociology as a discipline. By the 1967–68 school term the struggle with the university's administration was expanded to include major university reforms. It was a complete success, as the university gave in to the angry students and began instituting reforms.

That same term at Turin University students were launching similar battles. In 1967–68 students occupied key university buildings, and their campaign continued most of the school year. The students of Turin were protesting the lack of official student representation at the university and, more generally, against the feudalistic structures of Italy's educational systems. By spring 1968, however, the length of the occupation was wearing down the protesters, and the movement was rapidly losing steam.

Meanwhile a nearby Fiat assembly plant had recently expanded massively, drawing close to 100,000 migrant workers to Turin by 1968, but neither the city nor the plant could provide accommodations for the vast number of impoverished, unskilled laborers and their families who had flocked to the factory. The young workers found themselves exploited, living in terrible conditions, unappreciated by city residents, and without representation in their factories. Students tried unsuccessfully in the spring of 1968 to join forces with the workers, but by the fall, the frustrated laborers were ready for an alliance. Having recently organized a student force, fought an authoritarian system, and theorized their own disenfranchisement, the students of Turin University were in a position to articulate the plight of the auto workers and provide the means for their revolt against their exploitation. Frustrated with their own revolutionary actions, the students jumped at the chance of translating their rhetoric into direct action and resuscitating their movement.

Students printed and distributed flyers, joined the workers striking at the factory gates, organized demonstrations, and sent representatives to other factories throughout Italy to spark similar protests, demanding wage increases, shorter hours, representation in the workplace, and the reformation of factory hierarchies. In the spring of 1969 workers held massive strikes at the Turin Fiat complex, and these quickly spread to other factories. When police brutally attacked a student demonstration in March in Rome, media coverage generated widespread public support for the students. Students and workers throughout Italy found their concerns making national headlines again in July when police charged thousands of workers and students blocking the gates of the Turin Fiat plant. Following the example set by the university students, high school students throughout Italy began striking against and occupying their own institutions, demanding educational reforms, and swelling the numbers demonstrating at factories. In a rare display of their own political position and social status, the high-schoolers successfully articulated a concern for their future beyond secondary education and protested what they saw as their probable future exploitation.

In the fall of 1969, at the height of the student-worker movement's power, trade unions began making serious bids to regain control of labor as the unions saw the opportunity to negotiate contracts for millions of workers in discussions with beleaguered factory owners. When unions successfully bartered for contracts that included wage increases, a forty-hour work week, and limited representation at local factories, they siphoned off a substantial portion of the student-worker movement's forces. The student movement suffered another blow when a fatal bank bombing in Milan erroneously blamed by the government on radical leftists discredited militant students in the public's eyes. And as more workers joined the movement, bringing with them social concerns and an emphasis on attainable concrete results for workers, rather than more extreme and abstract revolutionary goals, radical students found themselves sidelined. Able to field political strength far in excess of what the students could, the Communist Party, the Republican movement, the powerful trade unions, and the Italian government all vied for political control of the worker uprising. Replaced by worker leaders and trade union representatives and defeated by powerful political parties, the activist students were left with two options: return to their universities or abandon their institutions for traditional or radical political organizations.[15]

Those continuing their fight beyond the walls of the university either accepted that the resistance movement was now a different animal, largely beyond their individual control, or turned extremist and sought change through more violent means. The student-worker movement had within one year become a viable political force in Italy, and it was precisely at the moment of its transformation from social to political force that the students lost their power to more sophisticated, battle-tried political organizations, which successfully focused the concerns of the workers on attainable social issues rather than radical political positions.

Student Resistance Flares and Fizzles in Eastern Europe

A few acts of student resistance occurred in Eastern Europe as well, although none so prominent as those in the west. Students from Warsaw University held a large protest against the expulsion of dissident students in March 1968 but were met with a ferocious police attack that overwhelmed the demonstrators and shocked the public. After a student was beaten to death by police, the conflict escalated into a three-day riot. Over the next two weeks, students scuffled with police, which only resulted in more students being hurt. Sympathetic demonstrations were held throughout Poland, but by the next month all of the universities were systematically purged of dissident students. Police oppression effectively killed the uprisings in Poland.

In Belgrade students caught the fever for student revolution and answered the international call for student strikes during 1968. The strikes were, however, short-lived and thus could not cultivate labor

support. Fearing Soviet aggression, Yugoslavia gave in to student demands for reform rather than risk riots. In terms of relative power, it was
an opportune moment for students to agitate.[16]

Uprisings in Africa and the Middle East

The characteristics of the sporadic student uprisings in Africa and the
Middle East during 1968 and 1969 were as varied as their host countries;
causes of student resistance ranged from miniskirts to apartheid, and
their subsequent effects ranged from radical changes in national governments to the reinforcing and strengthening of the very powers challenged.

In 1968 a group of students from Haile Selassie University in Addis
Ababa reacted against a provocative fashion show by attacking run-
way models and spectators. Outraged by the students' behavior, the
Ethiopian government shut down the school, which incited student
demonstrations and riots and retaliatory police action for several days.
In response, the students decided to strike against the university. Over
the next year and a half, university students organized themselves, formulated a list of university and government educational reforms, and
staged a series of marches. The government indulged none of the
demonstrations, dispersing them with untempered police violence and
arresting and imprisoning agitators. The police killing of student protesters in 1969 sparked large student uprisings that were followed by
more police attacks and prison sentences for demonstrators. By the end
of 1969 police were openly targeting students. What had begun with
local protests, such as resistance to aristocratic decadence, had evolved
into a fight against an oppressive state. However, through sheer physical
force, mass expulsions, and the threat of imprisonment, the Ethiopian
government brought the nation's radical students under control.[17]

In protest for educational reforms, students at the University of Dakar
in Senegal called for a general strike and the occupation of the university
in May 1968, and for days students held the buildings before police violently attacked the demonstrators, killing students in the process.
Students subsequently rioted throughout Dakar for several days, fighting police and destroying government property. Prescient labor movement leaders saw this as an opportune time to press their own concerns,

and further their own movement; they voiced solidarity with the student demonstrators and began their own series of strikes. The government was forced into action; officials immediately began negotiating with the labor unions and successfully ended their strikes within a matter of days, but it largely ignored the students' demands for reform. Student representatives eventually negotiated with government officials for moderate reforms, greater student representation, and increased autonomy from the state. However, when the students held a strike in support of students purged from Senegalese schools, the government abandoned diplomacy and seized the University of Dakar. By the end of 1969 the government of Senegal, acting with French approval, agreed to reform the university to better reflect its African constituency and agreed to structural and political reforms as well.[18]

Elsewhere in Africa, students were less successful in generating enough resistance to influence university reforms or national politics. In May 1969 African and European students held massive demonstrations against the Rhodesian government's attempt to change its constitution to legally sanction apartheid. The protests were ineffective, however, failing to elicit enough white, nonstudent support to raise a serious challenge. In 1970 the government proclaimed Rhodesia a republic under apartheid.

In October 1968 students at Lovanium University in the Congo protested against the encroachment of party politics on the university administration and for university reform. The students held futile demonstrations over the following months, but in June 1969 the frustrated students of Lovanium University took their protest to President Joseph Mobutu directly; a massive group of protesters marching on Mobutu's headquarters were blocked by police and army units, and when they did not disperse, the army began firing on them. Several students died, many were arrested, and the government shut the university down. A number of the students were convicted and imprisoned, though Mobutu later suspended their sentences. The student demonstrations netted a number of deaths and a decrease in university student power—after the protests, student organizations not officially sanctioned by the government were illegal, and university campuses witnessed an increase in government presence.[19]

Student Power in Pakistan

By contrast, in Pakistan a massive student uprising led to the eventual demise of the country's reigning political powers. In 1968 Pakistani police managed to kill a student in their zeal to put down a small demonstration. The death sparked a student riot that was too large for municipal police to control, although government troops eventually subdued the demonstrators. Angered, students continued to protest, but they also began to organize and challenge the government.

An assassination attempt and recent political challenges to his presidency convinced Ayub Khan to initiate a national crackdown on opposition. The arrests of prominent resistance leaders began a cycle of demonstrations and police suppression—protesting students were beaten and sometimes killed, and this, in turn, incited other protests, beatings, and killings. By 1969 students were demonstrating and clashing with police and army units throughout Pakistan. Labor unions joined the fray and threw their support behind the students. In March 1969 the president simply abandoned his office. Thus a national government fell victim to the increasing momentum of popular revolt initially generated by a series of student resistance actions. Although students lost control of the movement as it grew, in less than six months, what began as Pakistani student resistance efforts had grown large enough and generated enough social power to overwhelm a presidency.[20]

1968 and 1969
Student Power, Part II

Student Resistance in Japan: The Anti-Imperialist Push

Infighting characterized the student political landscape of Japanese universities throughout the early 1960s; in 1968 radical groups formed federations to unite their efforts against university administrations, oppressive ideologies of the establishment, and government political actions.[1] The willingness of warring student groups to join forces signaled both widespread perception of a common enemy and the realization among student groups that they would need to generate a lot more power than they could individually to fight their administrations or government. Anti–Vietnam War and anti-U.S. imperialist sentiments ran high among Japan's studentry, uniting student groups in a shared cause; recent battles with police defending a "collaborative" government provided forces with which they could physically battle. In January 1968 the docking of the U.S. aircraft carrier *Enterprise* at the Sasebo Naval Base before it headed to South Vietnam brought hundreds of students to the base, where they were overwhelmed by overzealous Japanese police troops. The students made several futile attempts to enter the base, and paid heavily for their efforts. Japan's studentry nevertheless grew bolder. For example, when U.S. marines, wounded in Vietnam, began arriving in Tokyo, demonstrating students battled police guarding the hospital, setting vehicles on fire and accidentally killing a local resident. Not all student uprisings were as organized as those against the U.S. military presence in Japan, though many were as violent, and as police forces continued to suppress the demonstrations, the focus of student resistance shifted: students began to attack the police, whom they viewed as their oppressors, more openly. Students turned up at demonstrations wearing hard hats and gas masks, and armed with sticks and sometimes Molotov cocktails. In October 1968 demonstrating students and workers rioted in several districts of Tokyo, destroying train stations and torching police vehicles. Riot police brutally dispersed the demonstrators, though it took some doing, as students came prepared for a fight; similar incidents occurred at a number of stations and universities throughout the year, with similar results. In 1968 and 1969, students were ready and willing to riot in their struggle against oppression and for political change.

Other acts of student resistance were aimed at practical university and governmental reform; students rocked Tokyo University with protests and demonstrations for much of 1968 and '69. For example, one 1968 protest begun by students fighting proposed curricular reforms led to massive occupations and the eventual destruction of many university facilities. In January, students began a protracted strike and held numerous demonstrations. Administrative threats brought thousands of Tokyo University students to the protesters' support, and in June the main body of students declared a strike at the university. Over the next month, the students and the administration negotiated; after officials offered to step down the students ended their strike. The administration, however, subsequently adopted a hard-line stance and refused to negotiate further with the protesters; in response students throughout the university joined in a general strike, occupying and barricading themselves in university facilities. Unable to deal with the students, who had armed themselves and turned the university buildings into fortified strongholds, the university's president stepped down. Meanwhile, the different student groups, with individual—and often disparate—concerns, demands, and strategies, claimed various university buildings. Some groups peacefully and respectfully occupied a building, while others ransacked offices and held university staff hostage; other factions fought one another over choice buildings. The new president resumed a strategy of diplomacy with the students, but violence was breaking out between the individual groups. Thousands of students faced off with each other on the campus, and even began raiding one another; large-scale war was clearly brewing. Frustrated, the president of Tokyo University gave the police the go-ahead to remove the occupiers, and in January 1969—one year after the initial strike had been declared—an army of police, supported by armored trucks, began their assault. The various buildings fell to the police one by one, but the battles were intense, and many people were hurt. The assaults on the buildings and the arrest of thousands of students were aired around the world.[2]

The fight over Tokyo University was not an isolated event. Following student-administration disagreements, thousands of leftist students demonstrated at Nihon University in June of 1968 in a peaceful strike, forcing university officials to meet with the students to negotiate. During the meeting, the leftist students found themselves under assault by a massive faction of radical right students; police troops arrived and joined in the attack. The leftists responded by locking themselves within a number of university buildings and holding them for months; police could not dislodge students from university buildings until early September.

Although the police eventually succeeded in dislodging the students, the action escalated the conflict; thousands of students swarmed to support those arrested. After students poured onto the campus and occupied buildings in all of the departments, officials agreed to meet with the radical leaders; but when students emerged to discuss terms, they found themselves arrested instead. The remaining students continued to occupy their buildings, but by the beginning of 1969, the occupational forces fell to police forces building by building.

The Nihon University and Tokyo University occupations sparked imitations at schools across Japan; radical students at dozens of institutions formed organizations, demanded university reforms, and when they were ignored, barricaded themselves in campus buildings. The violence with which they were inevitably removed from their fortifications radicalized more students, who increasingly resorted to more violent tactics. This eventual turn to violence, however, catalyzed the opposition of the majority of students—who could support activism and resistance to oppression, but could not condone terrorism—to the radical groups, adding to their isolation. Seeing their future on campuses endangered, radical students began to abandon campus politics for larger political struggles.

In 1969 the Japanese government aggressively planned reforms to the Japanese university system, passing a law that gave university presidents greater power in settling university-based conflicts, as well as giving the department of education the ability to remove dissidents from universities that showed chronic signs of student unrest. The government clearly signaled to students that police force would in the future be used on campuses to suppress uprisings. The effectiveness of Japanese student movements subsequently suffered because as the radical factions argued for more and more violent means to effect change, the government guaranteed it would respond to demonstrations with force. Slowly, inexorably, the situation continued to heat up as the radicals increasingly turned to violence. In 1969 student protesters demonstrated against a meeting between Prime Minister Sato and U.S. President Nixon in Washington, D.C., and again attempted to lay siege to Haneda airport, as they had done in 1967. Radical students wearing helmets and armed with sticks clashed with police and opposition student groups, but could not overcome them; in desperation they set fire to train stations. Lacking numbers and strength, the thousands of demonstrators were overwhelmed by police, just as they were in 1967.

The majority of students, even those demonstrating for reforms, were generally opposed to an escalation of violence, and so the Japanese student movement itself began to grind to a halt. Some radicals refused to give up, however, and moved beyond the university, forming small militant student groups that went underground and embraced terrorism. Members of the terrorist Japanese Red Army, for example, in the 1970s began a lengthy campaign of airplane hijackings, embassy bombings, kidnappings, and assassinations. As in other countries rocked by student protests in the latter half of the 1960s, in Japan the general public, including the majority of students, withdrew their support of student causes when frustrated radical students turned to terrorism.[3]

Massacre in Mexico

During the summer of 1968, Mexico City police suppressed a number of university and high school demonstrations with extreme force. Protesting the beatings, students subsequently broke into and occupied high schools in the capital for several days. In July police troops attacked the students holding the schools; when the barricades fell, a number of the defenders were killed by overzealous troops, galvanizing student opposition throughout Mexico City. Students demonstrated in massive numbers against the government's zero-tolerance policy and the brutality of the Mexico City police.

Seeing that the student protests were increasing in strength, and fearing that they might have an adverse effect on the world's perception of Mexico City during the upcoming October Olympic events, the government closed Mexico's vast Autonomous University and sent its students home. Police and military troops were assigned to protect the campuses from expected protesters; realizing that the government's actions would be scrutinized by the international community, students from the Autonomous University judged it was an opportune time for a strike and issued demands to Mexico's government that centered around eliminating the problem riot police and awarding restitution to the families of students they had recently killed. The government and the newspapers blasted the resistance actions, but the residents of Mexico City supported the students, who held marches and passed out protest flyers to anyone willing to take them. The government, however, ignored the students' demands, and as the Olympics approached, the students increased their efforts, demonstrating in massive numbers daily, strangling Mexico City's traffic.[4]

Thousands of students and supporters peacefully protesting at the Plaza of the Three Cultures on October 2 found themselves surrounded by fully armed military troops, some carrying machine guns. The protesters began shouting at the soldiers, and tensions increased between the gun-toting troops and the angry students. When a few shots rang out, the demonstrators tried to run from the area, but they were blocked on all sides by troops. The thousands of angry and frightened demonstrators rushed at equally frightened police troops anyway, and a number of the soldiers surrounding the plaza began firing; the plaza erupted in chaos as more and more troops opened fire, even with the machine guns. Trapped on the plaza, the protesters ran into gunfire wherever they turned. Soldiers killed and wounded hundreds of people—demonstrators and bystanders both—and arrested thousands more. The government blamed the students and refused to release the numbers of people killed in the attack (estimates range from 50 to 500).[5] Both students and the government claimed the other fired the first shots (and recent studies contend that snipers from the president's own elite guard might have fired on both students and soldiers from the rooftops of buildings surrounding the plaza);[6] in any case, in 1969 President Diáz Ordaz accepted full responsibility for the event, without however explaining his involvement. Following the October massacre, a pall fell over the student movement. The Olympics witnessed no major student interruptions; only a handful of radicals received prison terms for their involvement in ongoing protests, and although the government made some minor social reforms, allowing for more freedom of speech and press, its actions were largely superficial. While students continued to demonstrate and to garner much public sympathy, they were unable to field the numbers of protesters and supporters that they had before October 2.[7]

Students all over Latin America demonstrated for university reforms or against U.S. involvement in Vietnam in 1968 and '69, but no action comparable to Mexico's October massacre occurred. In Venezuela, for instance, students protested against President Rafael Caldera's attempts to control university government. Demonstrations turned into riots in 1969, and clashes with police repeatedly rocked campuses over the next few years; similar struggles over educational reforms and police suppression broke out at numerous universities and high schools in 1968 and 1969. By the early 1970s Venezuelan student resistance against government oppression was intense, with demonstrations often ending in brutal police suppression. Despite the zeal with which they pressed their causes, the students were ultimately unsuccessful in combating police or their government's control over the nation's universities.

The United States Scene

Politically motivated students in the United States generally fell into camps with specific concerns and goals, and although the various groups at times formed alliances, on the whole they remained distinct from one another. Civil rights, the Vietnam War, student representation, and social revolution were some of the general issues fought for; although specific instances of resistance were at times highly effective in provoking public outrage or sympathy, the various campus forces could not be welded into a greater unified movement. Acts of resistance and protests inspired many students, but what united studentry in the United States more than anything else was the defining of the opposition. In 1968 students on campus all over the country answered a popular call to arms based more on resistance to "the establishment" than on specific, attainable goals. This is not to say that organized student groups did not lead actions or demonstrations, only that the numbers that swelled those actions were not as focused or as committed as the core groups protesting; thus when large demonstrations were met with overwhelming force, the majority of students tended to abandon the struggles. And like many groups in other nations, radical U.S. student groups faced decisions about whether to accept the limitations imposed by governmental forces and adopt different goals and strategies, to abandon campus causes and join larger social struggles occurring beyond the walls of academe, or to go underground and become extremist.

In 1968 African-American students from the South Carolina State College protested against segregated businesses and public spaces in Orangeburg. After the demonstrations resulted in a series of minor scuffles with police troops in February, the governor of South Carolina declared a local state of emergency, called out the National Guard, and had troops stationed around the town and on campus. In response the students redoubled their efforts, increasing the size of their protest to include both more local students and outside volunteer organizers from the Student Nonviolent Coordinating Committee. Several days into the protest the demonstration turned ugly as students on campus began assaulting police troops and guardsmen; afraid, police panicked and began shooting at the students, killing three and wounding twenty-seven more. This overreaction caused a tremendous outcry from the African-American community of Orangeburg, which subsequently declared a boycott of local white businesses and called for justice and a federal investigation. Residents also joined the students in their demonstrations and held marches of their own. Angry citizens squared off with national guardsmen. The state withdrew the troops, and the federal government began an inquiry—although one year later, it found that the troops were not at fault.[8]

The student deaths in Orangeburg lit fires of resistance at other campuses across the United States—at Bowie State, at Fisk, but most notably at Howard University, where for years students had agitated unsuccessfully for university reforms, many of which centered around race-oriented curricular changes, student representation, and greater political freedoms. Following the violence in Orangeburg, however, students at Howard stepped up their agitation efforts against authority, calling for the removal of Howard's senior administration officials. Militant protesters called for a university-wide uprising against the school's government, and in March thousands of students protested and seized control of an administration building. In response, the university canceled all classes and tried to send students home, but thousands of students showed up on campus every morning in order to support the peaceful occupation. Negotiating with university officials, the students succeeded in procuring increased student representation and their own freedom from formal charges regarding the occupation of the building, but they did not substantially reform the university, its administration, or its curriculum. The occupation, and the impression of a successful protest, did, however, encourage a series of similar occupations at other universities and colleges.[9]

The occupations and strikes by students at traditionally African-American schools generally centered around increased recognition of African Americans and race issues in mandatory courses.[10] For the most part, the few concessions that the occupations gained through negotiations—when they gained any at all—tended to be superficial, the concessions vague enough to allow the students a face-saving way out of a situation that could only end in violence, and yet also vague enough to allow administrations not to institute substantial changes. In the 1960s, university reforms were instituted on many U.S. campuses, in large part due to a public pressure on colleges to change with the times, but university administrations generally made reforms on their terms, not on those of unruly students. Direct challenges to authority were most often met with suppression. The bad publicity surrounding the police brutality in Orangeburg forced state officials to pause before using force—but only to pause. And yet provoking violence was the only way many groups could call attention to their causes. At Bowie State College, for example, students who seized the campus and demanded educational reforms were ignored until they took their demonstration in April to the State House, where they were forcefully arrested.

Students at Columbia University upped the ante on campus resistance in the United States after two political groups formed a coalition late in April. African-American students protesting the construction of a new gymnasium on city park property, which lay between Columbia and a Harlem neighborhood, led one of the factions; they argued that the proposed gymnasium displayed the university's imperialism into the area, and that Columbia's grabbing of public park property for a project was blatantly racist because it would exclude primarily black Harlem residents from most of the facilities. The other faction spearheading the revolt was the Students for a Democratic Society; Columbia's SDS had been protesting against the university's relationship to the Institute of Defense Analysis, which did war-related research (a successful demonstration against a university's affiliation with the IDA had been led by SDS at Princeton in October 1967).[11] The two groups demonstrated together at Columbia's Low Library, where they decided that some kind of action needed to be taken. A bullhorn-holding Mark Rudd, a proponent of participatory democracy, tried to elicit suggestions for their next move, but he could not control the restless students, who spontaneously made for the grounds of the proposed gymnasium; once there, the hundreds of students were again flummoxed regarding what to do next. Rudd again tried to organize a democratic decision-making event, proposing a future student strike, when someone shouted that the demonstrators should regroup at the Columbia sundial. Frustrated, the students moved again, but at the sundial, Rudd decisively stepped forward and suggested they take a hostage and occupy Hamilton Hall, the main classroom building of Columbia.

While Dean Henry Coleman patiently served as the students' hostage, the students did their best to redeem the haphazardness of their actions by rapidly organizing themselves within the hall; Rudd appointed a steering committee, and students immediately began drafting demands, organizing a standoff with authorities, and decorating the building with Che Guevara posters and fashionable political slogans. On April 24 factionalism broke out; the African-American students ejected their white colleagues from the building and began fortifying against police attack.[12] Thrown out, Rudd and the SDSers stormed the Low Library, where they took over the office of President Grayson Kirk. Student support for the occupation grew rapidly, and students seized and occupied other university buildings. Tom Hayden, one of the original founders of the national SDS, led one such occupation.[13] Students flocked to their support. Striking students formed supply blockades around the occupied buildings and prepared for a lengthy protest; when nonstudent protesters began marching on the city campus, President Kirk suspended classes and called in police to secure the university. In a move to pacify the students, the university announced that Columbia would stop construction of the gymnasium, but student-administration negotiations over the next four days resulted in a deadlock, with students insisting on amnesty for the demonstrators and the administration fearing that to accede to that particular concession would legitimize such actions in the future. Meanwhile, leaders of the Student Nonviolent Coordinating Committee arrived to speak with the Hamilton Hall occupiers and, once there, endorsed their political stand.[14]

With major facilities of the campus held by student radicals, a growing national interest in the students' revolt, and the threat that residents of Harlem might decide to intervene, President Kirk gave the police permission to remove the students on April 30, eight days into the occupation. Approximately fifteen hundred New York City police troops entered the campus. In the face of a no-win situation, the students in Hamilton Hall gave up, but the activists in the other buildings refused to submit to the police, who had to drag the students out one by one. Many students and faculty members tried to place themselves between the buildings and the police troops in an effort to prevent violence, but those that did so found themselves under attack. During the police raids, officers injured hundreds of students and faculty members and arrested hundreds more in what became popularly known as the Battle of Morningside Heights.[15]

A tremendous number of students subsequently went on strike to support the students officially disciplined for the uprising and to protest the university's handling of the affair. In May, students and police again fought on Columbia's campus, and police again forced students from occupied buildings. In protest against the administration's handling of the students, students and faculty dramatically marched out of Columbia's official commencement ceremonies in June and held a counter-commencement exercise, officiated by former Sarah Lawrence College president Harold Taylor.[16]

The widely unpopular President Kirk resigned in August, and eventually many of the students' demands were met by a university eager to move beyond the incident and avoid others in the future. Authorities suspended Mark Rudd, however, along with many students involved in the destruction of school property. Nevertheless, through international media coverage, the event was an inspiration to politically active students around the globe, and it also served as an example of how not to handle student revolts. Kirk's strategy—his early reluctance to call in police, his ineffective negotiations, which allowed the media time to set up cameras and generate public interest, and his subsequent permission for a brutal police sweep—formed a case study in how not to resolve such a crisis.[17] To the students, the Battle of Morningside Heights set the stage for future protests, specifically identifying the campus as that stage. The incident immediately ignited a number of student power demonstrations on campuses throughout the United States, fueled more by antiestablishment sentiments than by specific attainable goals.

The Columbia University revolt showed students that the protected ground of the university was the perfect site for protests; U.S. campuses were liberal enough to allow some dissension, but were also quasi-neutral zones where limited police action and media coverage also existed. The university thus became a fashionable site where idealism and freedom of expression were—at least theoretically—on equal footing with political realism and could engage in power politics. Even if this was not always practically so, the disjuncture was a provocative issue that could get attention.[18] In other words, in its very balance between ideals and practicality, the American university was the perfect environment for fostering relatively low-risk political resistance.[19]

On the eve of this realization, nevertheless, the general student movement in the United States was set on a course of destruction—much of it self-destruction. Several factors contributed: an uncompromising, if belated, use of police suppression of demonstrations, the deaths of protesters and key political and social leaders, including Dr. Martin Luther

King Jr. and Bobby Kennedy, and the subsequent extreme radicalization of the left. These elements combined to give most students a distaste for student revolution; the apathy of the masses highlighted the divisions among radicals who could not define or work together toward common goals. Factionalism continued to tear the movement apart. Although provocative, general notions such as "revolution" or Black Power or Student Power were not necessarily conducive to long-term strategies of resistance; they tended to alarm the public, and they provided few attainable goals. As state and government forces reacted more quickly and with greater force to protests, the number of demonstrators dwindled through expulsions, arrests, and fear.[20]

After Bobby Kennedy's assassination in California, the anti–Vietnam War movement lost any real hope of success in the upcoming election; Eugene McCarthy promoted peace, but he was far behind Vice President Hubert Humphrey, an assumed advocate of the war, in the race for the Democratic Party's nomination. Thus although many SDSers worked on McCarthy's campaign, the SDS itself turned to radicalism, electing new and militant leaders and refusing to demonstrate during the 1968 Democratic Convention in Chicago. Many SDSers went to the convention and protested anyway, but they were unorganized and fell in with other groups demonstrating against the war or for McCarthy.

Other organizations, however, went to Chicago in force to make their cases public. One of the groups, the Youth International Party, or Yippies, led by Jerry Rubin and Abbie Hoffman, planned to hold their own Chicago convention for the countercultural youth contingent, during which they would play rock 'n' roll music, read poetry, have a "grope-in for peace," sponsor mass meditations, and eventually nominate a pig for president.[21] The Yippies were an antiwar group who promoted aesthetic, artistic, and cultural revolt; the "Yippie revolution" was to occur not through violence but through pleasure, excitement, humor, and fun. Students drawn to the Yippies tended to be revolutionaries of everyday life whose major concern was social rather than political reform.

Another large group demonstrating during the Chicago convention was the National Mobilization Committee to End the War in Vietnam (MOBE); this federation of student and other smaller protest groups planned a more conventional and focused demonstration than the

Yippies. Many of the participants in MOBE and the other large groups involved in the massive demonstrations and riots that were about to consume Chicago were SDSers and student supporters of McCarthy. The month before the convention, the various groups involved, especially the Yippies, began advertising their upcoming demonstration in journals and on radio shows, generating intense interest among students, revolutionaries, and anarchists, and tremendous concern among Chicago city officials and residents. Chicago mayor Richard Daley reacted by erecting a large fence around the convention center and mobilizing every available police officer for the event, as well as stationing national guardsmen within the city.

Those protesting and their supporters—who numbered in the thousands—took over Chicago's parks during the week of the convention, exchanging ideas, supplies, and support and holding continuous rallies and sporadic marches. On the last day of the convention, which was in the process of voting Hubert Humphrey the Democratic Party's candidate, police charged demonstrators, who had assembled for a final protest in Grant Park. The suppression was extremely violent as troops in full riot gear, "holding the line" before demonstrators, began beating anyone not wearing a police badge—student protesters, spectators, Yippies, hippies, and journalists. Tear gas canisters exploded into clouds over the park, through which club-wielding, gas-masked police troops attacked. Police barricades closed all the exits to the area, and when the gassed protesters attempted to flee by pressing against the barricades, the police violently pushed them back. Trapped, hundreds of people, including members of the press, were clubbed by police troops; television networks, some with injured or missing reporters, broadcast the police violence live to millions of viewers across the nation. Particularly disturbing were reports given by wounded, even bleeding journalists who had been beaten.

Besides shocking people across the nation, the violence hurt the Democratic Party, severely weakening Humphrey's presidential bid in a race he subsequently lost to Richard M. Nixon.[22] It also radicalized protest movements, which after Chicago were forced to accept that liberal reforms through elections were not a viable option; frustrated, those committed to working for social or political change suddenly had to make strategic choices—either accepting defeat on the larger political stage and scaling back their aims or turning to militant extremism, a model of which was readily available in the Black Panther Party. In Chicago the student demonstrators, those against whom they demonstrated, and the city government all learned tough lessons in understanding the power relations in such a massive, well-publicized demonstration. The ordeal was far from over for the principals involved, or for the nation, however. Both members of the Chicago police and a number of students were subsequently tried for their roles in the riots.[23]

Administrators at many universities analyzed student resistance actions to develop strategies of overcoming them. The Columbia occupation, for example, had shown that waiting too long before using force to suppress a student uprising was a mistake—radical students would dig in, generate collateral student or public support, and alert the media; the "Siege of Chicago" demonstrated to authorities that when force was used, it should be controlled and used away from the media. Administrators and governors recognized the effectiveness of a zero-tolerance policy. In January Governor Reagan ordered state police troops to suppress student demonstrators at the Berkeley campus of the University of California; Reagan's strong-arm tactics would make him extremely popular among the general population of California, though a demon to the leftists. That same month, on the opposite coast, MOBE members, SDSers, and many activists upset over Nixon's win held a demonstration and march during Nixon's inauguration as president of the United States. The demonstration erupted in violence when a faction attempted to intercept Nixon's motorcade and was suppressed by secret service and police forces. Nixon's successful bid for the presidency was a tremendous blow to students agitating against the war in Vietnam, and although they would make a few more concerted public efforts at demonstrating against the war, their struggle at home over the war abroad suffered from the results of the national election.

Students agitating for racial equality and representation in universities, however, were still gaining in power and momentum in early 1969. One of the most notorious events occurred at Cornell University—

where African Americans then were less than 2 percent of the school's total enrollment—after a cross was burned outside a residence building where African-American women resided; the terrified students called campus security, and security members removed the cross. No further actions were taken, however, and this caused students to be upset. The next morning a group of students—outraged at Cornell's blasé attitude toward an overt act of aggressive racism—occupied the university's student union in protest, ejecting the guests staying there and barricading the doors. Before security or police arrived, a fraternity angry over the activists' actions attempted to breach the barricades, and a battle ensued between the students; SDSers interceded and formed a line between the students within and without the union, demonstrating and protecting the African Americans within, some of whom had, meanwhile, armed themselves with shotguns. Police officers and reporters were soon on the scene as administrators attempted to negotiate with the armed and angry students, negotiations that successfully achieved clemency for the demonstrators and eventually aided the institution of an African-American studies program. To ensure that the administration complied with the settlement, thousands of students supporting the African-American radicals occupied another building on campus until they did—a victory for the students, but one that ultimately had little immediate effect on the structure of Cornell.[24]

University students increasingly turned to violence in the late 1960s; their actions generally met with extreme police force.[25] In May 1969 students at a North Carolina technical school violently demonstrated after police suppressed a high school demonstration in Greensboro; African-American students from the university attacked whites who happened to be walking by the school. When people reported shots being fired, Greensboro police arrived in force and found the demonstrators already besieged by a mob of angry whites. Tensions between the students and the police and the town increased after a student was murdered. When a student in a dormitory began shooting at a group of police on the campus, the governor of North Carolina ordered the National Guard to take over the campus; the dormitory was hit with tear gas and then charged, and hundreds of students were arrested.[26]

In April 1969 students at Berkeley were again resisting their administration; this time they took over a university field slated to be the location of a future residence hall. Hundreds of students and local residents decided to turn the vacant lot into a children's playground, planting grass and flowers, and naming the space People's Park. The administration responded by hiring a local construction company to raise a chain-link fence and post "No Trespassing" signs around the area. Seeing the tremendous student support for People's Park, and fearing the worst, the administrators called local police in to guard the area. On May 15 thousands of students attempted to possess the park physically; police troops at the park and close to two thousand national guardsmen assigned to control the site and the campus by Governor Reagan repelled the students by shooting tear gas at the demonstrators and then opening fire on them with shotguns loaded with birdseed.[27] Although the birdseed was intended to sting the legs of students and make them run away, the troops discharged their weapons at too close a range and aimed too high, hitting a number of protesters in their faces, blinding one and killing another. The situation was soon beyond control; students and troops rushed to the campus to reinforce those already there and joined the mêlée. When students and faculty held a wake for the dead protester, riot police attacked the procession; and whenever students gathered they fell under attack by police and guardsmen. At one point National Guard units that were attempting to disperse protesters at the park and other demonstrators on the Berkeley campus sprayed them with irritants currently being used by U.S. marines in Vietnam. This last gesture was too much, and the federal government intervened. Berkeley students held a meeting and a majority favored keeping the park, and the press excoriated the excessive use of violence against the students. In the face of public and federal opposition, Reagan reluctantly recalled the soldiers. The park remained a park.[28]

But even as student resistance actions continued to garner tremendous national media attention, the student movement itself was beginning to fly apart. At its 1969 convention, the national SDS split over which direction to take the organization. A radical group of members calling themselves the Weathermen (inspired by the Bob Dylan lyric: "You don't need a weatherman to know which way the wind blows") pressed for a revolutionary agenda, militarism, and open confrontation with the establishment to combat the government and to rectify social injustice. Another faction of SDSers protested the domination of the organization by men, claiming that women's issues had been ignored for too long a time (many women subsequently abandoned the organization). Indeed, women involved in student and civil rights organizations of the 1960s, such as SNCC and SDS, realized that their energies and skills could be used for women's liberation and joined local efforts, such as the Boston-based Nine to Five or national organizations, such as the National Organization for Women (NOW).[29]

After the 1969 SDS convention, many student group coalitions officially dissolved their connections, and although some continued to work together, the radical groups generally scared off the moderate ones. The tumultuous 1969 convention revealed the extent of the factionalism destroying the SDS. Because of infighting, the increasingly violent suppression of student demonstrations by local governments, and a corresponding increase in the popularity of militarism among student agitators, the Weathermen asserted a tremendous influence over what was left of SDS; the radical group dominated the national organization and set its own agenda.

During the remainder of 1969 the Weathermen pursued provocative and confrontational tactics; the group's exploits included marching in public shouting Communist slogans, occupations of and demonstrations at high schools and university buildings, and invasions of public events where media would be gathered. Their provocative tactics frequently ended in violence and did little to endear student causes to the U.S. public or to convince mainstream students to become activists. Following an October 1969 demonstration promoted as a revolution, in which a few hundred protesters ran amok in Chicago, shouting antigovernment slogans and smashing store windows before thousands of police troops avidly suppressed them, the Weathermen splintered into tiny cell groups, went into hiding, and became the Weather Underground. Over the next few years they began a war of terrorism through bombings and arson.[30]

The winds of change were indeed blowing for student activism in the United States, as indeed they were for all activists in the country. The increasing militancy of groups such as the Black Panthers, the drug culture of the Woodstock Music Festival, and even the murders by the Charles Manson gang—all served to exacerbate public disaffection with any "revolutionaries," whether students or not. As students were faced with either resorting to violence or retooling their resistance machines for slower, less confrontational tactics, many students chose simply to drop out of the political scene and to "do their own thing." Those who were left found themselves opposed by an increasingly hostile government and intolerant general public.[31]

Although coming apart at the seams, the U.S. student movement had enough life in it to stage a few more large-scale efforts. In October 1969, students launched a massive national protest against the Vietnam War; thousands of students and nonstudent supporters held demonstrations in major cities and on campuses across the nation, setting the stage for a national antiwar demonstration held in Washington, D.C., one month later. With students and other protesters numbering over a quarter million, it was by far the biggest protest against a war in the history of the United States. A simultaneous demonstration in San Francisco attracted over 100,000 participants. For the most part, peace reigned at the two-day demonstration in Washington in November, although occasional violence broke out.[32]

In 1969, when desperate revolutionary students were turning to more extremist tactics, arrests, defections, and deaths had seriously weakened student groups, and the SDS was splintering under factionalism, a few student groups remained focused on central issues. One group that generated a massive student following began at the University of the Pacific in Stockton, California, in 1969. Let Us Vote (LUV) fought for voting rights for all citizens over eighteen years of age; it immediately spread across the country—fueled in large part by growing anti–Vietnam War sentiment among U.S. youth, who saw a problem in the fact that they could be drafted and die for their country but were too young to choose government representation, but also by a need for a positive outlet for dissension, one that was not explicitly antigovernment, radical, or racially charged. This relatively "safe" voting issue would move to the foreground in U.S. student politics in the early 1970s.[33]

The 1970s

Campus Killings and Student Fury

Terrorism and the German Greens

The power of 1960s student activist movements continued to be felt well into the 1970s in Europe, although much of the momentum was by then lost. Isolated incidents of student resistance occurred—in England, in France, in Italy—but widespread police suppression, arrests, the deaths of radicals, and a more general public disapproval forced students in Europe to make the same choices facing those in the United States: return to campuses, look for alternative ways to protest (such as litigation), or turn to terrorism and go underground.

The Sozialistischer Deutscher Studentbund self-destructed in 1970, and West Germany's activists pursued their campaigns in smaller organizations. Antiwar activists, feminists, environmentalists, and many other issue-oriented students pursued their interests in specialized organizations. Willie Brandt, the Social Democratic chancellor, gave amnesty to thousands of protesters who broke antidemonstration laws in 1970, but the government also made it clear it would not tolerate further threats to social order; the federal criminal investigation agency received a massive increase in funding in 1970, and domestic terrorism headed its task list. Many West German students, however, did not accept their new political limitations or growing public apathy so passively. As in the United States, fringe groups in Germany that condoned violence resorted to acts of terrorism and had a negative influence on the general public's opinion of radical organizations of any sort, student or otherwise. The environment for radical movements was becoming increasingly inhospitable in West Germany after the 1960s.[1]

Nevertheless, the Baader-Meinhof gang stepped up its terrorist program in the 1970s in the hope of sparking a general revolution; the small group escalated their campaign of arson to include bombing U.S. military buildings, assassination attempts, and numerous attacks on property and personnel of the Springer publishing firm, whose newspapers remained critical of student protests, generally, and the Baader-Meinhof gang in particular. These actions outraged the general public, and government officials came under tremendous public pressure to arrest the members of the group. In June 1972 police separately captured Baader and Meinhof and thereafter systematically hunted down, arrested, or killed the other members of the gang. The remnants of the gang made a final stand in 1975, taking a number of hostages and demanding the release of their incarcerated partners. Police troops overwhelmed the gang members, killing two of them in a raid to free the hostages.[2] Independent terrorist groups continued to set off bombs and start fires throughout the 1970s, however, and by the 1980s, such groups had perpetrated well over one hundred bombing and arson attempts, claiming over fifty lives.[3]

After the fall of the SDS and the dispersal of terrorist factions, small self-interest groups dominated the German student political scene; most were concerned with university reforms or social issues, including feminism, the environment, and the peace movement. Students involved in extra-university issues were often absorbed by social organizations that drew them away from campuses, such as the massive antinuclear demonstrations occurring between 1975 and 1977. But the tenor of the German activist confrontations had definitely changed, with the police showing restraint and taking care not to create any martyrs. In the face of a politically moderate student body and police who refused to be provoked, the German student movement disappeared. Desperate terrorist groups continued their campaigns to spark general revolt against the "oppressive state"; in 1977 radical groups, for example, still set off bombs in public spaces, killed innocent bystanders, took hostages, attempted airline hijackings, and assassinated attorney general Siegfried Buback and bank chief Jürgen Pont. Conservatives in the government called for hard-line responses to civil disobedience and a tightening of control on civil liberties, while leftists found themselves arguing that although wrong, the radicals were fighting against what they perceived as a trend toward fascism in the government. Thus one of the long-term effects of the disintegration and radicalization of the

German student movements of the 1960s was the political polarization of the country. Chancellor Helmut Schmidt, however, successfully moderated between the polarizing forces and negotiated for tolerance and liberalization, but within federally sponsored institutions; he was able to keep the left committed to the republic, even if they battled the government over atomic energy plants, and to keep the conservatives in power from further dividing the nation.

In 1977 the Green Party was founded, and its existence and energy helped temper the 1970s political scene. But whether moderate or radical, the majority of causes had moved off campus, and although resistance actions continued to flare from time to time, the political and social environment was hostile to their thriving; the resurgence of the Cold War in the late 1970s captured the political focus of the nation. Meanwhile the Green Party offered a progressive alternative for voicing social opposition, and by the end of the decade, student resistance on West Germany campuses was by and large neither radical nor powerful.[4]

Universities remained relatively quiet in the 1970s in France and Italy—political campus energies seemed to have been spent in the 1968 and '69 actions. Although the general studentry displayed a serious lack of élan, many of the more vocal or committed agitators continued to fight for their causes, but they did so off campus, in larger, public organizations or radical underground groups. In 1977 the University of Rome witnessed a surge in demonstrations linked to labor concerns, but these began off campus and were supported more by labor union members than by students. Throughout Europe, students seemed to have abandoned the general call to activism sounded in the prior decade; instead they focused on academic issues and their own individual concerns.

Students Continue to Rock Campuses in the United States

Students on campuses all over the United States celebrated the passage of the Voting Rights Act in 1970. Let Us Vote (LUV), the National Students' Association, and many other groups had much to celebrate, but after the victory many students found themselves activists without a cause. Shortly thereafter, the Students for a Democratic Society gasped its last breath as well.[5] And yet despite the fact that some major struggles ended and some large organizations died in the beginning of the decade, a number of groups—and a number of issues—refused to go away.

Students at the University of California at Santa Barbara demonstrated against the 1969 dismissal of a faculty member in a series of protests in 1970; once the protests turned violent—with thousands of students participating in riots, vandalism, and arson—Governor Reagan appeared on the scene with the National Guard and suppressed the violence.[6] When it resumed three weeks later, police troops opened fire on students with birdseed and wooden plugs, injuring several protesters and killing one.[7]

At the end of April 1970, President Nixon declared that the United States would begin bombing Cambodia, setting off a wave of student protests across the United States. In May over fifty thousand demonstrators gathered in Washington, D.C., in a massive but peaceful protest against the escalation of the war. Splinter groups tried to provoke police and cause riots, but they were immediately suppressed. At campuses across the United States, students took stronger than symbolic measures of protest, and university and state administrations responded with force: a small group of students from George Washington University bombed the U.S. National Guard's main office.[8] Demonstrating Ohio State University students met with a tear gas and birdseed assault launched by the National Guard and local police. The administration evacuated the university, and six thousand National Guard troops patrolled the campus. Sizable demonstrations occurred at dozens of universities, with more than a few meeting with armed suppression.

Students at Kent State University began protesting against the war and for greater African-American presence on campus at the beginning of May. Although the original conflict began as a typical town-and-gown riot, with students wreaking havoc outside bars in Kent, police suppression brought antiwar and university reform activists out in droves, and these burned the campus's Reserve Officer Training Corps building.[9] Radical students then attacked those attempting to put out the fire, and police retaliated against everyone in the area with tear gas and clubs. Governor James Rhodes directed the National Guard to secure the campus and outlawed all further protests; students sporadically harassed guard units, but they were unable to launch any significant challenge to the troops. On May 4, however, over a thousand students gathered, and the guard moved in with tear gas to disperse them; they were met with a barrage of stones and bottles thrown by students. The guard fell back, regrouped, and began firing on protesters and bystanders, killing four outright and wounding others.[10] Most students ran for cover, but many remained on the field, facing off with the troops and shielding the wounded students.[11]

May was a month for violence on U.S. campuses; two weeks after the Kent State massacre, local police killed two students at the historically African-American Jackson State College in Mississippi. The police shot demonstrating students on the campus after a number of whites driving by the campus reported that their cars had been hit by rocks. The U.S. government immediately instigated a federal investigation of the shooting, and assigned FBI officers to the campus. In June, President Nixon ordered a federal inquiry into the Jackson State College and Kent State University shootings and other instances of campus violence.[12]

Students protesting the Vietnam War and agitating for increased African-American presence on campuses were not simply fighting local or state police and National Guards, however; the physical forces fielded by the establishment were a symbol of the greater social forces the activists faced. Anti-antiwar, anti-civil-rights, anticounterculture, and antistudent sentiments ran high in mainstream America; in May 1970, for example, anti–Vietnam War protesters on Wall Street found themselves overrun by angry construction workers.[13] Adding to the tensions on and off campuses, radicals bombed the University of Wisconsin Physics Building in 1970, and the Weather Underground continued its campaign of terror, bombing New York police buildings in June of that same year and the U.S. Capitol building in Washington, D.C., in May 1971.[14] Other factors exacerbated student-establishment tensions, such as extensive media coverage of student and ex-student involvement in radical groups including the Symbionese Liberation Army, which murdered Oakland's school superintendent in 1973, kidnapped Patty Hearst in 1974, and perpetrated numerous robberies and acts of terrorism.[15] Thus while the Kent State and the Jackson State massacres brought public sympathy and support to students as victims of overzealous police and state troops, the radical students taking increasingly violent measures to effect change were turning that same public against student activists.[16]

When the Vietnam War ended, so too did much of the student movement in the United States. By the mid-1970s the student activist movement had splintered and collapsed. Even though students continued to agitate for university and social issues, including greater minority enrollment and representation on campus, for civil rights, for gender equity, and for environmental issues, the ability to call for widescale revolution, to physically threaten establishment forces, and to provoke sizable governmental actions or reforms was a thing of the past by mid-decade. But as the political and social climate of the United States turned more and more conservative, universities became sanctuaries for liberals; students and faculty began turning their attentions to reforming and fortifying those sanctuaries, developing liberal politics as much as possible within them. The reactions of university and state administrators to prior student activism generally forged a stronger bond between students and faculty, and together in the 1970s they set about reforming the institutions housing them. Pioneering black studies programs gave other oppressed groups incentive to create intellectual, academic programs and disciplines.[17]

Women's studies programs blossomed on campuses as the women's liberation movement gained steam; female students, who realized they had often been treated as "grunts" in male-controlled political groups, organized themselves, held consciousness-raising sessions, and agitated for their own rights. Since the late 1960s women radicals on campuses had begun challenging male dominance in various campus-affiliated political organizations, from SDS and the New MOBE to the Black Panthers.[18] Valerie Solanis, for example, had published the SCUM Manifesto in the *Berkeley Barb* in June 1968. SCUM (the Society for Cutting Up Men) contended that no genuine social revolution could be perpetrated by men, as men were inherently inhumane and always attempting to establish hierarchies of power—a characteristic that inevitably led to enslavement and death.[19] By the 1970s, women's organizations on campuses had gained substantially in numbers; they published important journals and newspapers, including *off our backs* or *The Furies*, formed specifically around the need to articulate the social, intellectual, and political situation of women. Such journals and larger women's organizations, including the National Organization for Women, fanned the fires of campus activists, and women at colleges and universities across the United States began forming organizations and agitating for respect, women's studies programs, and curricular changes.[20]

Institutions often responded to such activist efforts on campus in the 1970s by taking the initiative away from students and faculty and creating university-approved specialized studies programs that both accommodated and tempered the various groups agitating for their creation.[21] Under the official stamp and control of academia, specialized programs forced student radicals to join them or further isolate themselves, especially since the more politically moderate would be placated by the university's "progressive" innovations.[22] Encouraged by the effectiveness of ethnic and gender studies programs, gay and lesbian organizations and student unions formed and began agitating for university recognition in a series of legal challenges; sexually stigmatized minority student unions attacked campus ROTC programs by launching antidiscriminatory suits against the state-sponsored programs. They generally met with little success in their reform efforts, although they increased awareness, provided information and local support groups, and set up national organizations and networks.[23]

By far most of the actions happening on a national level, though, concerned antiwar efforts, and the majority of the rest aimed at university reforms. This is not to say that the effects of student actions did not continue to reverberate through larger political movements in the United States; numerous student actions set the stage for or significantly contributed to social or political movement. On November 20, 1969, for example during a symbolic reclamation of Alcatraz Island by Native Americans, a student of San Francisco State College named Richard Oakes deviated from the agreed-upon plan of tribal elders to sail around the abandoned island in authentic costume, beating on drums, and singing: he stripped off his shirt, dove from the deck of the rented sailboat into the bay, and swam for "the rock." The immediate effect on his fellow activists was electrifying: others followed him into the freezing waters of the San Francisco Bay, and that night dozens of

Native Americans, many of them college students, officially occupied the island. Citing an 1868 treaty between the Sioux Nation and the U.S. government that allowed Native Americans to claim abandoned federal lands, the activists fortified themselves within the cold and crumbling prison. Richard Oakes became a national Native American hero overnight and garnered tremendous media attention for the Native American movement; San Francisco residents supporting the occupation ran a Coast Guard blockade to deliver supplies to the activists; and for nineteen months an armed group of Native Americans—men, women, and children—held the island, setting up a community with a school and a clinic.[24] Throughout 1970 and into 1971 the occupants of Alcatraz grew to include student activists, local business owners, families, and members of various tribes from all over the United States who had heard about the occupation and wanted to participate.[25] The occupiers issued a proclamation that began,

> We, the Native Americans, reclaim the land known as Alcatraz Island in the name of all American Indians by right of discovery.
>
> We wish to be fair and honorable in our dealings with the Caucasian inhabitants of this land, and hereby offer the following treaty:
>
> We will purchase said Alcatraz Island for twenty-four dollars (24) in glass beads and red cloth, a precedent set by the white man's purchase of a similar island about 300 years ago.
>
> We will give to the inhabitants of this island a portion of the land for their own to be held in trust by the American Indian Government and by the Bureau of Caucasian Affairs to hold in perpetuity—for as long as the sun shall rise and the rivers go down to the sea. We will further guide the inhabitants in the proper way of living. We will offer them our religion, our education, our life-ways, in order to help them achieve our level of civilization and thus raise them and all their white brothers up from their savage and unhappy state.[26]

The Alcatraz Proclamation also noted that the island was perfectly suited for reservation territory, as it lacked all modern conveniences, had no fresh running water, was without education, sanitation, or health care facilities, and came without industry, or mineral and oil rights; despite all the hardships, the Native Americans claimed they would make use of the island's rocky, unproductive soil, as they were used to such conditions and familiar with being prisoners on their own lands. The national media had a field day, and the plight and issues of Native Americans were broadcast nightly across the United States. But as the months wore on and the leaders of the Alcatraz community spent more and more time off the island lecturing, organizing, or holding press conferences, the numbers of activists on the often freezing island slowly dwindled as food supplies, media attention, and enthusiasm among the agitators were depleted. Support for the occupiers by Bay Area residents died when those living on the island lost political focus, and the occupation devolved into general anarchy. When some of the newer buildings were set on fire in 1971, the U.S. government sensed the time was right for action and quietly retook the island.[27]

Although Oakes fell from the limelight relatively early in the occupation, and the occupation fell apart, the momentum set in motion by the student leader's action continued. The student-led action garnered a tremendous amount of media attention and helped raise Native American activism in the United States to a new level, with profound results.[28] Inspired by student resistance actions of the 1960s, Native American activists subsequently occupied government buildings, reservation lands, and museums, protesting the United States's treatment of Native Americans, corruption in the Bureau of Indian Affairs and in reservation management, and the poverty on reservations—all leading up to the March 1973 armed stand by members of AIM, the American Indian Movement, at Wounded Knee.

As the decade progressed, U.S. student political radicalism decreased in popularity. Given a bad rap by the violence of extremists, faced with rampant apathy and careerism on campuses, and without the unifying cause of the Vietnam War, the U.S. student movement splintered and disintegrated.[29] Political students were unable in 1977, for instance, to generate enough interest at Kent State to block the university from building a gymnasium on part of the area where the National Guard had confronted and killed four students.[30]

Clashes Continue in Mexico

In Mexico, students continued to agitate against the Mexican government for social and political reforms; many of those involved in the 1968 protests had never ceased their efforts, and student demonstrations consistently interrupted Mexico City traffic or blocked entrances to state-sponsored events in the 1970s. After the 1968 massacre, public outcry against the use of police or military force on students was at a fever pitch, and for several years students tried to capitalize on the situation, staging massive demonstrations and directly challenging the government. Unable to use police suppression for fear of a general uprising, Mexico City officials resorted to other counterresistance measures, including training radical right-wing organizations to do the police troops' dirty work for them. In June 1971 one such group, the Halcones, ruthlessly beat students protesting at a demonstration in an incident that resulted in hundreds of wounded students and bystanders and eleven deaths.[31] The ill-conceived strategy cost the mayor and the police chief their jobs, and subsequent Mexico City officials chose to ignore student demonstrations or to disperse them with less violence. But if the students suffered violence or indifference during their demonstrations, they also sometimes achieved results; organizing and staging sit-ins and other peaceful demonstrations, student activists effectively bartered for university and social reforms throughout the 1970s, in part due to government officials' unwillingness to risk their positions over bloodshed and public outrage.

Japan and the New Student Samurai of the Seventies

As government suppression became more effective in the early 1970s, and factionalism began to take its toll on Japan's activist organizations, the student movement fell apart. The turn to terrorism among radical students in the Western nations in the mid- to late 1970s characterized student fringe groups in Japan as well. The most notorious of student groups suppressed in Japan's universities, the Red Army, began recruiting nonstudent radicals, taking global liberation as their cause; they targeted Japan's government, among others, for destruction. In the 1970s, they began a series of airplane hijacks, bombings of embassies and Shinto shrines, kidnappings, and assassinations. One widely covered Red Army exploit, known in the international press as the Samurai Skyjacking, began in March 1970. The group took command of a full commercial jet departing from Tokyo and insisted the plane be flown to North Korea. The jetliner flew to Seoul, South Korea, instead, where the hijackers swapped hostages and negotiated safe passage to North Korea, where they let the plane's hostages go. While the event brought international attention to the Red Army, the group did not elicit much international sympathy, and in fact exploits such as skyjackings, which were increasingly perpetrated by radical ex- and nonstudents, did much harm to dedicated but less militant student political groups peacefully struggling for respectable social and educational reforms, as the general public often mistakenly associated them with radical terrorists.[32]

Unrest in Thailand and Indonesia

After a 1971 military coup in an economically depressed Thailand put unpopular officials in power, student activists began agitating for economic and political reform and met with severe government suppression. By 1973, however, the general public had had enough economic hardships (daily rice lines had formed in Bangkok). When protesting students and professors were arrested in Bangkok in October, and thousands of students demonstrated for their release, the residents joined them in a massive surge that brought hundreds of thousands of antigovernment demonstrators into the streets. On October 14, they began to riot. In the face of such forces, and hamstrung by internal government factionalism, the ranking officials could do little else but abandon the state. Thus in October 1973 a massive student-led revolt (with the timely intervention of King Bhumibol, who weighed in on the side of change and ordered the government officials to step down) overthrew the military rule in Thailand and restored the country's parliamentary system. Euphoria ran high as students filled the streets of Bangkok, but high spirits soon gave way to the sobering recognition that the country was still under severe economic duress. The new system of government was strong enough neither to address the country's economic troubles nor to control its power-hungry military leaders. Three years later, another military coup swept the parliament aside, and the new regime simply did not tolerate student resistance. The new military regime brutally suppressed the Thai student movement.[33]

In January 1974 Indonesian students began demonstrating in the streets of Jakarta to protest Japanese imperialism during a tour by Japanese officials, but the students were also shouting antigovernment slogans, demanding economic and political reforms. The demonstrations continued in Jakarta and other major cities for several days, and the Jakarta student protesters were joined by workers whose added enthusiasm sparked massive riots in which vandals targeted Japanese businesses. Police and government troops swept through Jakarta, opening fire on rioters, killing and wounding many. With the rioting suppressed, Suharto purged his government and the Indonesian military command of political opponents. Not well planned, and certainly uncontrolled, the student-instigated Jakarta riots of 1974 served as an excuse for Indonesia's leader to flex his own government muscle, which neither the students nor challengers within the government could resist; thus the student uprising only solidified Suharto's control of Indonesia in the long run, strengthening and stabilizing his government.[34]

Trouble on Tiananmen Square: Student Resistance in China

China's universities reopened in the 1970s, after being thoroughly purged during the Cultural Revolution, but political dissension on or off campuses remained out of the question for many years. In April 1976, however, students gathered on Tiananmen Square during a memorial for the recently deceased premier, Chou En-lai, and began to voice publicly some of the problems they were having with Maoism. The impromptu gathering swelled into the thousands and evolved into a full-scale protest, with students and disgruntled citizens loudly airing grievances and demanding reforms until police troops arrived and attacked them. Mao's government made Deng Xiaoping the scapegoat for the anti-Maoist sentiment in Beijing, but he escaped before he could be accused and indicted. After Mao Zedong's death in September 1976 and Deng's rise to power in 1978, Deng co-opted the students' spontaneous "counterrevolutionary action" as a precipitate anti-Maoist "revolutionary action." The appropriation of the Tiananmen Square incident facilitated Deng's undermining of the power of those in government who had publicly condemned him and the students' actions. Deng adopted a policy of supporting democratic student activists who attacked Maoism or any of Deng's current political opponents, but his tolerance for democratic movements extended only as far and as long as they were of political use to him.

In the late 1970s, however, most Chinese university students showed little interest in ideological battles, turning their attention back to academic affairs; the democracy movement was primarily left in the hands of others. In 1977 the government instituted national entrance exams as the single determinate for the selection of university-qualified students. Millions applied, and a small percentage were accepted; those few generally chose not to risk their spots in the universities by challenging the powers that be. It would not be until 1985 that China would again see a significant rise in the number of student resistance actions.[35]

The Quelling of Student Unrest in South Korea and in Southeast Asia

Students in South Korea took to the streets in protests after President Park Chung Hee was reelected in 1978. Early in his career, Park had exhibited leftist leanings, but he was also a rigid authoritarian, and by the late 1970s South Korea's growing middle class yearned for more freedom. Park responded to the student demonstrations with brutal physical suppression and extensive infiltration of the universities to identify and remove dissidents. Nevertheless, students protested for political and government reforms throughout the remainder of the year and well into 1979, although their demands were ignored and their demonstrations quickly suppressed. They did not, however, cease their activities, and by mid-1979 the sporadic, beleaguered demonstrations had evolved into a full-fledged, large-scale student movement. With the memory of the massive student uprisings of 1960 still fresh, the government attempted diplomacy, but the small efforts at negotiating failed as students saw this as an acknowledgment of their power. In 1979 chaotic student demonstrations in Pusan, Kwangju, and other major cities evolved into battles with troops that left numerous students dead. The anxiety sparked by the protesting students exacerbated the factionalism and political strife within the national government. When another South Korean government official had President Park assassinated in October 1979, the students lost their momentum, and their power dissipated as quickly as it had been generated.[36]

Southeast Asian countries generally saw little student resistance activities during the 1970s. Following the Vietnam War, for example, the Khmer Rouge not only purged all of Cambodia's universities, it annihilated them. In the last half of the decade, the Khmer Rouge strove to turn Cambodia into a primitive society, outlawing commerce, culture, and religion, and destroying all products of foreign or bourgeois origin, including literature. The Khmer Rouge burned libraries, historical collections, and art throughout the country, and hunted down, imprisoned, or executed students and professors. Those attempting to resist the Khmer Rouge were simply murdered (the death toll of Cambodians killed under the Khmer Rouge approached 2 million). It was not until the 1980s, during the Vietnamese occupation of Cambodia, that universities began to reappear in the country.

Student Resistance in Rhodesia

Students held strikes and demonstrated for political and social reforms on campuses throughout Africa in the 1970s, but they were especially active in Rhodesia, South Africa, and Zambia. The governments of all three countries violently suppressed student actions. In Rhodesia, however, students were particularly effective in their actions, although it took most of the decade to get results, with the colonial government brutally suppressing demonstrations as quickly as they occurred. At the University of Rhodesia, for example, students demonstrating for political reforms in 1973 were dispersed by police, but they regrouped and nevertheless continued their efforts, despite violent police suppression. The focus of the protests, however, quickly evolved into antiwhite and antigovernment demonstrations. Rhodesia's colonial government had faced growing African student agitation for some time, and the white minority resorted to increasingly harsh measures to keep control over the African majority. On August 7 government troops mercilessly attacked the African demonstrators with extreme violence, the brutality of which signaled both the intolerance of the government and the desperation felt by the country's leaders in the last decade of colonial rule.[37] Over the next few years the resistance efforts by students merged with those of the general populace and turned into a full-fledged independence movement, which finally met with success in April 1980, when Rhodesia became the Republic of Zimbabwe. Unlike the students in Rhodesia, however, those protesting for reforms in Zambia and South Africa were unsuccessful; these respective movements were crushed by their governments. Zambia was particularly harsh in its treatment of student dissidents.[38]

Riot and Revolution in Iran

Throughout the 1960s, student resistance efforts against the shah's regime had been violently suppressed, but in 1970 Iranian students began to challenge the almost two-decade-old ban on public demonstrations. Students in Tehran, for example, led a massive demonstration of tens of thousands to protest local economic reforms; the focus of the demonstration immediately shifted, however, to direct criticisms of the shah's regime. Police met the demonstrators with untempered violence, killing many and wounding hundreds. The shah's police cracked down on the universities and suppressed dissension.

Militant groups that often included students stepped up their own campaigns of violence in the 1970s. As terrorism increased, so too did the counterterrorist efforts of SAVAK, the brutal Iranian secret police. University students organized and helped foment rebellion by distributing pamphlets and agitating on and around campuses. They made a serious effort to spark a revolt, but they could not control the masses who turned out to protest in Iran's major cities in September 1978, following the end of Ramadan; millions of citizens—all suffering under extreme economic hardship—and supporters of the Ayatollah Khomeini, a popular reformist Shi'ite Muslim cleric, poured into the streets, calling not only for political reforms but for the end of the regime as well. In the face of a popular uprising, the government proclaimed martial law and sent troops and tanks into city streets to suppress the demonstrations; soldiers opened fire upon the crowds, killing thousands of people. Demonstrators continued to clash with troops throughout the following months, and in December 1978 the government began to crumble. Within the first two months of 1979, the shah sought asylum in the United States and the government fell to its fundamentalist opposition. As the United States had supported the shah and was in 1979 harboring him, the nation was not particularly well liked by the revolutionaries in Iran.[39]

In 1979, radical student leaders guided students from various Tehran universities to the U.S. embassy in Tehran, where they plotted how to capture and to hold the twenty-seven-acre compound. For weeks, students stationed at buildings surrounding the compound monitored the activities of the embassy, charting attack routes and waiting for the right opportunity to act.

The students had aligned themselves with militant cultural conservatives who sought not the establishment of a counterculture but a return to tradition and the rejection of Western imperialism. On November 4, 1979, hundreds of students took the U.S. embassy efficiently and dramatically. While the students were victoriously shouting "Death to America" on the compound after capturing fifty-two hostages, the country's fundamentalist leaders were busy figuring out how to use this sudden media windfall.[40] The students planned to hold the hostages for a few days as a protest against U.S. presence in and influence over Iran, but once they grabbed the embassy, they found themselves the center of tremendous national and international attention, active players—and pawns—in power games for which they were unprepared. The secular provisional government, which had been in place since the shah fled, was in the midst of a battle with religious clerics; when the ayatollah and the clergy endorsed the students' actions, members of the provisional government stepped down in protest, essentially handing over the government to the opposition. They were immediately replaced by members of the clergy who began drafting a new theocratic constitution and a government that had to answer to the Ayatollah Khomeini. Meanwhile, the students ended up holding the captured Americans in the compound for over a year.[41] On April 25, 1980, the United States attempted a disastrous rescue mission that severely strained U.S.-Iranian relations, blackened Jimmy Carter's presidency, and helped

Ronald Reagan win the November 1980 U.S. presidential election. Although the Iranian students in the U.S. embassy and many U.S. citizens perceived the hostage crisis as a testing of U.S. strength and a display of general anti-imperialist or anti-U.S. sentiment in Iran, the students' actions also played a significant role in a power struggle over the control of Iran between fundamentalists and pro-Western moderates. An end to the embassy crisis was eventually negotiated between the United States and Iran through efforts of quiet diplomacy and the release of substantial sums of U.S.-controlled Iranian assets.[42]

During the political turmoil in Iran from 1979 to 1981, the Iranian leftist students' interests—once highly visible on campuses—were left behind in the struggle over Iran's government. Although they did much to seed resistance to the shah—printing flyers, organizing rallies, and demonstrating in the streets—leftist students were simply overwhelmed by the conservative forces dominating the revolution, which viewed outside influences, including Marxism, as a threat to Iran's future. Indeed, supported by Muslim clerics, an organization called the Hezbollah, often armed with clubs, began viciously physically suppressing leftist student rallies and demonstrations. The leftist students—who were taking advantage of the freedoms available with the departure of the shah by printing up thousands of Communist-oriented pamphlets and other leftist materials and distributing them on the streets—discovered postrevolution that they were the new enemy of the republic. In 1980, the Islamic Revolution not only purged the government of pro-Western moderates but also purged the universities of leftist students and faculty members, obliterating real and potential opposition to the ongoing cultural revolution. Following the cultural revolution, acts of student resistance in the eighties against the new regime were virtually nonexistent.

Revolution in a Postmodern World, 1980–1989

Student Protesters in Chile: The Dangers of Direct Assault

After General Augusto Pinochet Ugarte overthrew the socialist government of Chile in 1973, he brutally suppressed political dissidents, including students, banning student political organizations and demonstrations. The universities were no sanctuary for radicals—Pinochet put military personnel in charge of their administrations. Many students protested against the new restrictions placed on them, and some went so far as to criticize the government, but public protests came with severe consequences; consequently, the majority of Chilean university students decided they were not politically motivated in the late 1970s, and those who were did not align themselves with political parties in the way that student agitators had in the 1960s. Those committed to opposing Pinochet generally abandoned the universities and joined movements that relied on guerrilla terrorist campaigns, or they focused on firmly but peacefully and carefully maneuvering for university reforms.[1] Most students recognized the latter option was in their own best interest, as universities were the breeding ground for future business and government leaders of Chile; given Chile's economy and political climate, most of those who made it into the universities felt privileged to have done so. In the 1980s, however, student activism began to resurface; in the first few years of the decade students began organizing and even demonstrating. In 1984 and 1985 students demonstrated in support of striking workers, and when they were suppressed, students demonstrated against the suppression. Student organizations were resurrected, and for several years students were able to elicit enough public sympathy when suppressed to force Pinochet to make some concessions in reforming Chile's universities. In 1987, for instance, students successfully campaigned for the removal of the rector of the

Universidad de Chile, José Luis Federici.[2] But students typically fought, however, for university reforms and a greater voice in individual schools primarily to improve their own educational opportunities and future careers; they were careful not to challenge Pinochet directly. Paradoxically, such a focus, in the long run, led to greater influence in an extremely repressive political sphere.[3]

UNAM Students Strike against Reforms

To say that Mexico's public universities—losing money, physically falling apart, and overflowing with students who had been guaranteed admission on graduating from high school—were suffering in the 1980s is putting it mildly. Students could attend an Autonomous University of Mexico (UNAM) school for practically nothing in fees; they could attend sporadically, retake failed tests an unlimited number of times, and faced no time-to-degree limits. In 1986 the Mexican government, which contributed 90 percent of the school system's budget, supported a plan to revamp the bankrupt public higher education system radically. With UNAM's enrollment five times what it was in 1960, the university's rector, Jorge Carpizo, decided to institute dramatic reforms, including substantially raising the cost of tuition, well beyond the reach of the poorer university students. Part of the reform agenda was aimed at ridding the UNAM campuses of a significant number of academically inactive students, who devoted tremendous amounts of time to extrauniversity activities—including political activism—while keeping their student status and privileges. In 1986 a typical UNAM undergraduate took an average of eight years to graduate.[4]

The rector proclaimed his proposed reforms—entrance exams, a fee increase, attendance policies for students and professors, and time-to-degree limits—and students called a national strike. Mexico's 1917 constitution, which guarantees free and available public education to all, was at the heart of the students' protest. Pouring into the streets of Mexico City and strangling the city's already horrible traffic, students beat on cars and taunted police. With the 1968 student massacre still a vivid memory (and evoked provocatively in the demonstrators' banners), Mexico City officials restrained police and let the demonstrations happen, and pressed the federal government and UNAM officials to resolve the crisis. Fearing to resort to force in the midst of an election period, the government supported a timely decision by UNAM administrators to drop plans for reforming Mexico's public universities. UNAM promised to keep tuition at its token level, and scrapped plans for time-to-degree limitations. One decade later, the government of Mexico and UNAM would again attempt reforms, and again students would strike to keep the universities free, resurrecting the specter of the October '68 massacre to good effect. Mexico's studentry realized the power they held and used it to keep themselves students—defined in terms they had grown accustomed to.

The United States: New Tactics for Old Fights—Economic Warfare against Apartheid and the Sound of Silence at Gallaudet

Following a series of particularly brutal acts of suppression in South Africa, a large protest movement—situated primarily in civil rights and African-American church organizations—swept the United States, taking many politicians and corporations by surprise and forcing tremendous changes in foreign policy and business practices. The movement protesting apartheid in South Africa thus already had momentum in the United States when college students took up the cause across the nation in 1985.[5] While members of the anti-apartheid movement were staging demonstrations outside the South African embassy in Washington, D.C., students at a number of universities began holding sit-ins, claiming they would not cease until their universities divested their investments in corporations operating in South Africa or transacting business with South African companies.[6] Nonviolent and nonconfrontational, the 1985 student divestment demonstrations sought to bring economic sanctions on South Africa about by drawing media coverage to U.S. campuses and framing the protests against specific universities in moral terms. Students endeavored to distribute information and to institute political discussion—the stances they took were those of educators, not of combatants.[7] At first, university administrators refused to even consider divestment; police arrested the demonstrators, and universities prosecuted them. But school officials underestimated their opponents, who were extremely effective at pointing out to both colleagues and the media that the central issue was a moral one—that defending monetary gain at the expense of human rights was, well, indefensible. The movement was extremely popular on campus and off. The anti-apartheid movement on campus developed along nonpartisan lines, enjoying support from national leaders, labor, and the general public. Students passed out petitions asking for university divestment on hundreds of campuses, and hundreds of thousands of students signed them. Lobby groups subsequently used the petitions to pressure congressmen to impose sanctions on South Africa. Back on campuses, students also erected shantytowns to draw attention to the effect of apartheid on South Africa's poor.[8] Using the opposition they initially met from university administrations, demonstrators launched rallies and demonstrations on a scale not seen in the United States since 1969.

The pressure on universities to divest was tremendous, and within two years, well over one hundred universities had divested their holdings in the country, with significant financial repercussions; the University of California, for example, withdrew over $3 billion from companies with business ties to South Africa.[9] Of course, the negative publicity seriously hurt the corporate and public funding the universities themselves received, and thus made the choice to divest easier. The divestment movement on campus helped the greater anti-apartheid movement in the United States and proved popular enough among the general public to force many politicians previously opposed to revise their positions; the popularity of the movement forced President Reagan to support imposing limited economic sanctions on South Africa. With administrations backing down to local protesters at scores of prominent colleges, including Yale and the University of California system, U.S. colleges across the nation, many of which faced their own anti-apartheid demonstrations, began divestment efforts. The issue itself entered the national political arena in the late 1980s, and by the end of the decade the United States joined other nations in bringing crippling economic sanctions against South Africa.[10] Once the success of the U.S. anti-apartheid movement was assured, activists discovered the issue-oriented student movement was itself at another end; student political activism vanished in the nation as quickly as it had appeared.[11]

Students demonstrated for other issues as well in the 1980s. Over one hundred and twenty years earlier, Gallaudet University had been founded in Washington, D.C., to educate deaf students, but by 1988 Gallaudet had yet to have a deaf university president. A series of retirements and appointments in the mid-1980s left the university administration reeling, and at the beginning of March 1988 students peacefully protested for the selection of a deaf person to the vacant office. The university board considered several persons, two of whom were deaf, for the position, but offered the job to a nondeaf candidate. Hundreds of Gallaudet students protested on the campus before taking the march to the streets, where they again peacefully demonstrated. Deaf organizations across the nation threw their support behind the striking students at Gallaudet, and throughout the United States deaf students also went on strike to show solidarity with the demonstrators. The Gallaudet students demanded a deaf president, changes to the university's board, and amnesty for the students demonstrating. Although the officially approved candidate was willing to negotiate, the students would not back off their demands or suspend the strike; the university, they claimed, simply was not listening.[12]

The protesters occupied the campus. At a meeting, the Gallaudet faculty overwhelmingly voted to support the students. The newly elected president and the chairman of Gallaudet's board resigned, and the trustees met and appointed one of the deaf candidates as president. The students returned to their classes, led, for the first time in over a century, by a deaf president.[13]

Of course, students protested at many institutions for a vast number of different reasons during the 1980s, and by far the greatest number of actions were aimed at university reforms, such as the institution of ethnic, women's, or gay and lesbian studies programs.[14] But if U.S. students were getting more sophisticated in their protest strategies (a plethora of student activism studies appeared following the student movements of the 1960s and '70s that aided student rebellion), so too were administrators (who read the studies as well): most university officials in the 1980s sought to defuse situations before they grew out of hand. Still, a number of demonstrations escalated into major situations. At Howard University, for example, angry students took over the administration building when Republican National Committee chairman Lee Atwater was made a member of Howard's board of trustees. After troops in full riot gear squared off with the students, and it appeared that an invasion was imminent, the Reverend Jesse Jackson and Washington mayor Marion Barry convinced university officials to negotiate and avoid a potential disaster. But on the whole, in the 1980s, U.S. universities opted for negotiations over combat, restraint over force.

Pakistani Student Warfare

At the University of Karachi, student resistance actions took aim primarily at students throughout the 1980s, as rival political parties battled one another through their student affiliate groups. Beatings, kidnappings, and assassinations occurred on the campus, and dozens of students died violently during the decade. The effects of this open warfare were not confined to student activists, however; innocent students were often injured, and members of various organizations often intimidated professors into assigning unearned credits and grades. In July 1989 student members of the Muttahida quami Movement wielding AK-47s forced their way into a mass of students registering for exams, grabbed three student members of the Pakistan People's Party, marched them to a nearby wall, and executed them. The situation could no longer be ignored by the government.

The university responded by banning all political and extracurricular activities and stationed fully armed military personnel on the campus who screened all individuals entering the campus and patrolled the grounds around the clock. Students covertly participated in the political groups, but the military presence forced them to wage their wars off university grounds. Using the event, Pakistani officials subsequently blamed political students for many of the hundreds of terrorist actions occurring in Karachi during the 1980s and '90s. The military eventually controlled most of the violence on university campuses, but battles continued to break out sporadically over the next decade. (One fought with bottles, clubs, and chains erupted in April 1999, leaving dozens of students injured and at least one dead before army personnel crushed it.) On-campus security and off-campus violence intensified over time, especially following the civil war in neighboring Afghanistan, partially because fully automatic rifles and other weapons became readily available and easily acquired through Pakistan's black market.[15]

The Intifada and Student Resistance in Palestine

As members of the Palestinian resistance movement, students had been holding demonstrations protesting Israel's domination of Gaza and the West Bank ever since the 1967 Six Day War; Israeli occupational forces routinely closed the universities and schools when protests became threatening or violent. In the early 1980s, the demonstrations gained in strength as Israeli forces sought to establish non-PLO-affiliated Palestinian administrations of their choosing in occupied territories. In 1981 Palestinian students from Bethlehem, Hebron, and other universities led massive demonstrations that ended in skirmishes with Israeli troops; following such incidents, Israeli forces occupied and routinely closed universities. Throughout the early and mid-1980s, activists in the occupied territories often staged violent demonstrations against the occupational forces, which retaliated with brutal force and university closings.[16]

In late 1987 the greater Palestine resistance movement, of which university students were a part, exploded into full-scale urban war; known as the Intifada, the war was carried out mostly by boys and young men, who attacked Israeli soldiers with rocks, set fire to Israeli equipment, and tried to make the area uncontrollable by Israel. University students organized and led resistance efforts, but most of the agitators were between ten and eighteen years of age. Older teenagers seriously wounded Israeli soldiers, and thus were the first to be imprisoned when Israel responded to the massive uprising through a program of violent suppression directed against the general populace. Israel's military closed universities, sometimes for a year at time, identified and jailed politically active students, invaded houses, and indiscriminately arrested Palestinian boys. As time passed, the desperate battle for Palestinian liberation was increasingly fought by children, and Israeli forces found themselves over and over again hunting Palestine's young. The Intifada and the brutal tactics employed to suppress it continued through the remainder of the decade and into the next, decimating student activists. As the war went on, and Israeli troops killed hundreds of people and wounded and imprisoned tens of thousands, groups inside Israel and many of the Israeli soldiers in Palestine became disenchanted with the official suppression strategies.[17] Due to the growing unpopularity of fighting an unwinnable war waged primarily against children and the acute awareness that Israel could not indefinitely suppress over 3 million Palestinians in the midst of hostile Arab states, Israel turned to diplomacy in the 1990s to resolve the uprising. In the mid-1980s, university students had provided leadership in the Intifada, but because the military targeted them early in the uprising, students were among the first casualties of the conflict.

The Velvet Revolution in Czechoslovakia

In Czechoslovakia students led a different sort of revolution. In November 1989 university students staged a nonviolent demonstration on Wenceslas Square to commemorate the student martyrs of the 1968 Prague Spring. Police riot troops arrived and surrounded the students, who remained peaceful but staunchly refused to end the demonstration; infuriated by the students' unwillingness to disperse, the police brutally beat the protesters. The reports of the beatings spread quickly, and almost immediately, larger demonstrations against police violence erupted at campuses all over Czechoslovakia, with widespread public support. Controlled by a repressive Communist government and under tremendous economic strain, Czechoslovakia was ripe for a popular uprising. The protesting students called for drastic government reform and for democracy; students proclaimed a national strike and—joined by Czechoslovakia's counterculture and intellectuals—took their protests to the streets, demanding radical change. Carrying flowers and trying to incite dialogue, the proponents of the Velvet Revolution marched in the nation's major cities. The demonstrations were the largest the country had witnessed in decades; in Prague alone those marching numbered over 200,000. After initially trying to suppress the uprising with force, the country's leading government officials responded to the massive, peaceful popular revolt by resigning, and by the end of December a new and non-Communist-dominated government headed Czechoslovakia, with the '68 Prague Spring veteran Alexander Dubcek as chairman of the National Assembly and Václav Havel as president. International media marveled at the gentleness of the revolt, how the will of the masses prevailed without violence, but foreign governments remained skeptical of Czechoslovakia's future or stability, especially after images of brightly painted military vehicles, including pink tanks, rolled across the airwaves. Nevertheless, the new government immediately went to work with reform measures, and Czechoslovakia somewhat successfully, if a bit awkwardly, leapt out of a Communist state into a free market economy.[18]

As far as student resistance strategies go, the Velvet Revolution was an example par excellence of a successful student-led revolution; a group of students provoked police into violence, subsequently sparking widespread sympathy and a national uprising that because of its sheer size led to a peaceful revolution. Following such examples, students demonstrating throughout the world often would endeavor to provoke police suppression with the realization that violence draws media attention, and that nothing brings large numbers of people behind a cause as quickly as the perception that the nation's youth is being oppressed by the state. Of course, governments learned this lesson as well, and, responding to the same examples, many governments adopted policies of restraint in dealing with student demonstrations. In Mexico City in the 1980s and '90s, for instance, police troops escorted student demonstrations, especially those occurring on the anniversaries of the '68 massacre, but, following orders, refused to be provoked by the demonstrators, suffering verbal taunts and even minor acts of physical aggression to keep student protest situations from escalating.

Revolution in Romania

Not all nations adopted policies of restraint. When Romanian university students, joined by the general public, called for a massive uprising in 1989, police, local militia, and units of the Romanian military ruthlessly attacked the demonstrators. Although poorly equipped for waging a war, the rebels raised enough people and force to overcome armed soldiers and police to liberate the city of Timişoara. Aided by massive defections from Romania's military and swelled by a general public tired of the dictator Nicolae Ceauşescu, the revolution of Timişoara inspired uprisings in other cities. The entire nation erupted in a revolt that within days became unstoppable. Government officials, including Ceauşescu, abandoned their positions and attempted to flee the country, only to be caught and executed. Nevertheless, members of the old guard soon gained control of the new government.[19]

A Flash of Revolt in Burma

General Ne Win had ruled the country ever since a military coup toppled Burma's democratic regime in March 1962. By the late 1980s, Burma was financially broke, and the extent of poverty in the country was incredible, but the Burmese people still feared complaining publicly (Ne Win had retired but still held tremendous influence over the government). In 1987 massive numbers of students began demonstrating against the ruling regime's economic policies. In dire economic straits and suffering under a repressive government that had recently experienced a power vacuum, the country was ripe for a popular uprising. Students sprang into action, leading a reform drive that swept the country, bolstered by the presence of Aung San Suu Kyi, the daughter of Burma's national hero Aung San. By the middle of the summer of 1988, Burma's demonstrations had become a prodemocracy movement; hundreds of thousands of students and other demonstrators protested against the government's economic and social policies, demanding radical political reforms. Such actions did not come without a price, however; in the fall of 1988 the Burmese military brutally suppressed the demonstrations, in one incident killing hundreds by indiscriminately firing on a mass rally in Burma's capital. Throughout the remainder of 1988, the military continued to suppress protests violently, destroying the movement.[20]

The Fires of Protest in South Korea

After an aide of Park Chung Hee assassinated South Korea's president of eighteen years in 1979, the masses yearning for a more democratic and open Korea were suddenly infused with hope for the future of the country.[21] General Chun Doo Hwan, however, moved into the vacuum created by Park's fall. Stunned by Park's death, the student movement stumbled, but Chun's power grab reinforced its urgency, and student activism levels again surged. Protests broke out all over Korea. The country had already been straining for more democracy against the strictures of Park's autocratic rule, and when the nation fell under a new military rule, it was simply too much for many to bear; radicals and moderates, including many businessmen and politicians, began actively pushing for more civil and political freedoms in spite of Chun's threat of reprisals. Within months demonstrations by student and other activists grew to gigantic proportions.

The students demanded increased democracy, free elections, freedom of speech and of the press, and educational autonomy.[22] Students all over Korea protested against martial law and were attacked by police, but in Kwangju, police violence sparked a massive uprising in which students and citizens rose together to take control of the city. Declaring the city liberated and democratic, the revolutionaries apprehensively waited for the state's response. At the time, Korea's military command was bound by a pact to clear all Korean troop movements with the U.S. military command in Korea; thus students were counting on interference from the U.S. military to keep Chun's army away from Kwangju long enough for a larger democratic rebellion to take hold. But the gamble did not pay off—within one day the students and citizens holding Kwangju saw armored Korean army units taking up positions around the city.

Much anti-U.S. sentiment already existed among students, who viewed the Western nation as an imperial power and a source of state government corruption; thus when those holding Kwangju saw the approaching army, they not only knew there would be no outside succor, they assumed the United States supported what would certainly be a massacre. And yet as Korean troops and armored vehicles beyond the city prepared for an all-out assault, the students refused to surrender. After amassing a sizable force outside the city, the Korean army moved: a division of soldiers armed with assault rifles and bayonets began a relentless push against the students and citizens massed in Kwangju's barricaded streets. Although relatively poorly armed—the majority of defenders could only throw things at the advancing soldiers or set fires before the armored trucks—the students refused to give way; showing little mercy, often firing indiscriminately before them, the professional soldiers overran the city. Surviving students and subsequent research claimed that as many as two thousand were killed in the assault alone, with thousands more wounded and arrested. Many subsequently disappeared into Korea's prison system.[23]

The massacre resulted in exacerbating anti-U.S. sentiment and radicalizing the student movement, which increasingly turned to violence; terrorist student groups actively began calling for an end to Chun and his military regime. In 1981 Chun was elected president, but many students and radicals openly opposed what they perceived as a thoroughly corrupt government. Demonstrations continued to shake Korea's principal cities; student revolutionaries firebombed buildings, and radical elements participating in larger demonstrations hurled Molotov cocktails, bottles, and bricks at police troops, who began attacking even moderate student protests.

Radicals set fire to government buildings and U.S. centers to draw attention to their issues, and they also used fire on themselves to achieve similar results. Self-immolation by scholars as an act of remonstrance against an unjust ruler had long been a method for inciting reform in Korea, and students increasingly turned to the practice during the 1980s as a way of drawing media attention to their commitment to anti-imperialist causes. In 1986—a year that witnessed dozens of self-immolation events in Korea—a flaming student leaped from a third-story window in Seoul, for instance, shouting, "Out with American imperialists!"[24] The students also began agitating at factories and in rural areas, trying to spark a nationwide people's movement, while the government responded with arrests and the placement of secret police in factories.

The students, however, found a receptive audience in the Korean public, who were upset with Chun's repression; organized and committed in their resistance to Chun's policies, the students were able to reach, inspire, and mobilize large numbers of people from all walks of life. As the world's attention turned to Seoul in preparation for the 1988 Olympics, students increased their anti-Chun and anti-U.S. agitation efforts. Their reform movement eventually coerced Chun in 1987 not to run for a second term, and the government fell into the hands of moderates in the 1988 general election. As Korea subsequently became more politically progressive and more democratic, the student movement lost its momentum and focus; activists had difficulty identifying an opponent to resist. Anti-U.S. sentiment still pervaded the student movement, but because Korea's studentry had lost its most immediate and most tangible enemy—Chun—the movement disintegrated.

China's Student Democracy Movement and the 1989 Tiananmen Square Uprising

In the early and mid-1980s, acts of student resistance in China occurred over a myriad of different issues, ranging from local government policies to Japanese imperialism. Students held hunger strikes in Changsha City in 1980, and massive outdoor demonstrations in major cities throughout China in 1985, but on the whole, the first half of the decade saw a relatively low level of student agitation. In December 1986 however, two student protests—demanding more democracy at the University of Science and Technology in Anhui Province—spearheaded the first struggles of a major new student movement. The level of student activism in China was about to change dramatically. That same month students from Tongji, Jiaotong, and other Shanghai universities began a poster campaign in Shanghai, taking to the streets in small groups of a few hundred, marching and shouting, and carrying signs reading "Minzhu wansui!" ("Long Live Democracy!").[25] On the nineteenth, a group of several thousand protesters marched on Shanghai's People's Square, demanding greater democracy and calling on the government to accelerate its economic and social reform programs. The march was relatively uneventful, but late that night a student run-in with local police brought charges of police brutality from the students. The circulating rumors sparked a flurry of student agitation in the city: posters decrying police oppression or demanding more civil rights, the freedom of expression, and greater democracy appeared all over the city's universities and throughout the city itself. Thousands of students marched in the streets of Shanghai in protest, and within days the number of students in Shanghai swelled into the tens of thousands.

Although small student demonstrations were by this time relatively common in China, what occurred in Shanghai was unusual; nonetheless, the students participating in the demonstrations did not think of them, at least at first, as particularly risky enterprises, for there was at the time a strong push within China's government to institute progressive changes, and the government was currently, albeit cautiously, experimenting with social reforms and granting more political freedoms. Protesting students did not directly criticize the Chinese Communist Party (CCP) or the government, but called only for an acceleration of the government's own reform efforts.[26] Government radio and television broadcasts, however, hinted that further student actions would be perceived as challenges to the government and, as such, elicit reprisals. The joint fear of hurting China's fledgling reform movement and of possible repression effectively defused the Shanghai student movement within the month.

Similar student democracy movements flared up in Nanjing and Beijing at the same time, but like the incident in Shanghai, those too died following successful government propaganda campaigns. After the demonstrations ended, however, hard-liners in the CCP used the incidents to clean house and purge top offices of the party of liberals; the most notable target of the purging was progressive Hu Yaobang, a reformist whom the students had singled out as a leader they particularly favored. The party blamed General Secretary Hu for failing to control the student demonstrations effectively and expelled him in 1987. The movements that swept through Shanghai, Nanjing, and Beijing for several weeks thus precipitated a purging of the CCP and a backlash against powerful political advocates of China's reform movement, thereby hurting the prodemocracy movement; but they also demonstrated to the students of China that massive student power could still be mustered in the 1980s. For students already agitating, the incidents and their repercussions confirmed that soon such forces would have to be raised, for the window to liberalization so recently opened in China appeared to be closing quickly. Another round of democratic reform demonstrations flared up again in 1988, but it was not until the Tiananmen Square demonstrations in 1989 that China witnessed a massive student movement.[27]

In the spring of 1989 China's government announced it would suspend its experiments regarding a level self-determination for professions among university graduates, an action that alarmed most of China's students.[28] Then, on April 15, Hu Yaobang, the student-friendly CCP official purged from the government in 1987, died of heart failure; the progressive leader immediately became a martyr for the student prodemocracy cause. Students began to gather on Tiananmen Square, the world's largest public square, in increasing numbers over the days following to praise Hu publicly and to speak of the need for a prodemocracy movement; leaders of prodemocracy student groups, such as Wang Dan, saw an opportunity to bring their interests before the public eye and to force the state to recognize the legitimacy of student demands for reform. Three days after Hu's death, thousands of students from Beijing University and the People's University held a funeral–protest march for Hu that wound through the streets of Beijing before arriving at Tiananmen Square, where approximately five thousand students held a prodemocracy rally. The students unsuccessfully attempted to present a petition to the government, asking for an official revision of the life of Hu and social reforms.

Thousands of demonstrating students massed in Beijing turned their attention directly on the CCP complex also just down the road from Tiananmen Square. Again the state ignored their demonstrations. On April 20, students started a scuffle with CCP security guards at the gate of the complex. Although minor, the incident sparked greater agitation among Beijing's studentry as rumors of police brutality spread. Students demonstrated in Nanjing, Shanghai, and other major cities as well, and the leaders of the various prodemocracy groups began working together to maximize the effects of their resistance efforts. At a CCP-sanctioned commemorative service for Hu held on Tiananmen Square on April 22, hundreds of thousands of spectators gathered; students used the opportunity to speak to the many residents and workers on the square, who, frustrated by China's economic difficulties and government corruption, heard a voice for change in the growing student movement. Following the ceremony, three student representatives climbed the steps of the People's Hall and, humbly bowing, knelt to symbolically deliver their demands to the premier. Again they were ignored. In response, students called a general strike.

Meanwhile the CCP-controlled media excoriated the students for threatening China's stability. But the propaganda worked against the CCP, alienating students from the party, and increasing public support for the protesters. The students, however, posed no real threat to the state at this point, and Deng was already occupied with upcoming state-sponsored public celebrations of the seventieth anniversary of the May

Fourth Movement, an unanticipated power grab by a political rival, and a state visit by Mikhail Gorbachev, during which Deng wanted to showcase both his own political strength and China's advances in social and political reform.

The prodemocracy students did not cooperate with Deng's plans, however; on April 27, over 100,000 protesters illegally marched through the streets of Beijing and around Tiananmen Square. Enormous crowds of people supporting the students gathered to watch the marchers and mitigated police violence by physically placing themselves between police units rushing to the scene and the students. With an overwhelming feeling of victory, surrounded by supportive and enthusiastic Beijing residents, the students took over Tiananmen Square, gave speeches, discussed democracy, and organized future events.

Embarrassed by the student march, China's government escalated its propaganda war. On May 4, students retaliated by holding their own anniversary celebrations of the May Fourth Movement on Tiananmen Square, where the original demonstrators had gathered in 1919. Again, the students' actions were met with reprimands and threats by the government, but not with reprisals, for a group of reformers in the government used the diversion created by the students and Gorbachev's impending visit to try to wrest control of the government from CCP conservatives. During the week following the May 4 rally, students continued to meet and to demonstrate, but without further government antagonism against which to renew their resistance, the People's Movement began to weaken.[29]

At this crucial moment in the life of the movement, approximately twelve hundred undergraduates gathered on Tiananmen Square and announced a hunger strike. The strike galvanized China's studentry, and tens of thousands of students from all over China traveled to Beijing to support the hunger strikers and the cause. The students were not alone; the sight of a couple of thousand students willing to die for democracy, fainting from hunger and heat exhaustion, brought Beijing citizens and workers onto Tiananmen Square in droves; they brought the demonstrating students water, supplies, and encouragement. In the middle of this unrest, Gorbachev arrived, and to Deng's embarrassment, the students continued to march in the streets, waving banners of protest and verbally attacking the CCP; they also sent letters to Gorbachev explaining the terrible problems in China due to the backwardness of the country's leadership.[30] The CCP canceled most of the public events scheduled to impress the Russian leader and had to dodge around the multitudes in the streets in their efforts to keep Gorbachev from seeing signs of massive unrest. The unrest grew, and within days, over 1 million people protested in Tiananmen Square. The progressives in the CCP were defeated by the hard-liners, and fearing that Beijing's masses might unite with the students after all and rise against the state (the demonstration had already lasted three days), the now unified government declared a state of emergency. Violence was now unavoidable, and radicals took over the leadership of the student demonstration, ended the hunger strike, and began preparing for the onslaught.

Knowing that a massacre was coming, many students—mostly those from Beijing schools—began slipping away from the square, until fewer than 50,000 students remained. Soldiers tried to enter the city, but residents, who had remained in the streets in massive numbers, physically blocked them. A die-hard core of students remained camped on the square in a nonstop prodemocracy rally for several days as over 100,000 students from universities all over China continued to pour into the capital. A "Goddess of Democracy" was raised on the square directly opposite the poster of Chairman Mao; a massive student-built sculpture over thirty feet high, the goddess combined features of both the Statue of Liberty in New York's harbor and popular Chinese deities. For the next three days, students nervously watched the avenues leading to the square and shouted for democracy.[31]

Tiananmen Square itself had become a massive and extremely complex camp, with tents, "roads," various zones corresponding to different levels of student security clearance, clinics, workshops, student security guards, and moped couriers. Everywhere banners flew, proudly identifying schools, academic disciplines, and various student groups, and displaying prodemocracy slogans and icons. Workers, too, joined the protests and had their own zones, organizations, and agendas. The worker presence on the square was a crucial factor in the government's decision to employ military force to clear it, for if agitating students were a nuisance, an uprising of workers constituted a real threat to the state.[32]

The appearance of autonomous worker unions in Beijing, and other cities, inherently challenged the CCP's claim to represent the working people of China; from the perspective of China's leaders, the rebellious workers, the revolting *laobaixing*, had to be crushed, and crushed immediately. Troops had already been denied access to Beijing, primarily by masses of workers, and in other cities, such as Shanghai, workers aided students in creating barricades. The seeds for a massive popular rebellion had thus been sown, and the state knew it must act quickly if it wanted to prevent those seeds from sprouting.

On the evening of June 3, the government imposed a media blackout on Beijing, and tanks and armored personnel carriers began moving into the city, supported by battalions of troops armed with both clubs and automatic weapons. The troops operated under the command of leaders imported from outlying provinces, who, unlike those they replaced, would not hesitate to use force on the city's residents. Masses of rioting workers attacked them, throwing anything they could at the oncoming soldiers—bricks, bottles, trash cans, Molotov cocktails—and retreating workers set barricades on fire to stop the troops' advance.[33] As the conflict escalated, groups of soldiers indiscriminately opened fire with automatic weapons on the rioters before them; the masses retaliated, throwing objects at bayonet-wielding troops or rushing on isolated or stalled vehicles, pulling soldiers from their vehicles and beating them to death. Reports on the details of the Beijing massacre vary widely, but they generally agree that hundreds, perhaps thousands, of workers and residents were killed by soldiers in the military's push toward the square; they also agree that many soldiers were violently and often gruesomely beaten to death by rioting crowds.[34] But the massacre principally took place in the streets leading up to Tiananmen Square, not on the square itself; and the main targets of suppression were not the demonstrating students, most of whom were back on the square, but the rioting workers and residents of Beijing. In many cases, students on the square came to the aid of isolated and beleaguered groups of soldiers and police, helping escort them safely away from the enraged mobs of workers assaulting them.[35] Responding to the vehemence with which they were opposed, the soldiers increased their own use of force, and the sound of automatic weapons filled the streets of Beijing.

By the time the army reached Tiananmen Square in force, most of the students had long fled, and the majority of the few thousand remaining gathered closely around the Monument to the People's Heroes and the Goddess of Democracy; ignoring the students, the soldiers continued to subdue workers and citizens around the square. Military reinforcements arrived by the thousands. Wearing steel helmets and armed with assault rifles and bayonets, troops took up positions around the entire square. Hundreds mounted the steps of the buildings bordering the area, ostensibly so they could rush down into or shoot into the square, and a line of tanks rolled into formation at one end of the giant plaza. Through sheer intimidation—which included firing volleys at the monuments above the students' heads—they encouraged those left on the square to leave. The numbers actually killed in the massacre are still unknown, but clearly those who suffered the most were not the demonstrating students. Soldiers beat and killed students during the drive to the square and upon their first arrival on the square, but the workers rioting in the streets of Beijing were the primary targets and victims.[36] The government eventually claimed officially that soldiers killed several hundred people in the incident (saying students numbered a few dozen), but students and many foreign journalists put the number of victims much higher. Fueled primarily by assumptions and imagination, and aided by the fact that troops allowed very few journalists to remain on the square after the soldiers arrived, Western news media erroneously claimed for months afterward that soldiers had brutally massacred a great number of students on the square itself.[37] Rumors of a government conspiracy to hide the number of casualties ran rampant both in China and across the world, but the CCP purposely, and for good reason, tried to avoid the martyring of several thousand students on Beijing's most prominent revolutionary landmark.

Police arrested tens of thousands of students and other demonstrators during the weeks following the incident, and many received lengthy prison sentences. In official statements Deng claimed victory in defeating an illegal rebellion in Beijing. Although none of the arrested students ended up serving more than a few years in prison for their roles in the prodemocracy movement, the warning had been given to students contemplating future demonstrations.[38] The message to workers of the city contemplating a popular uprising had been made clear in the streets of Beijing: they had no chance of successfully challenging the CCP, and to attempt to do so was to risk the harshest of penalties. After the massacre in Beijing, demonstrators protesting in other major cities in China at the time briefly continued their protests, but changed their tactics to avoid a repetition of the Beijing massacre.

In Shanghai, prodemocracy activists immediately adopted new strategies, departing from the standard massive marches and rallies on squares to institute a strategic attack on Shanghai's economy by strangling the city's transportation and traffic systems. Aided by radical labor union members who defied the government's warnings, students used buses to block intersections and major streets in June, erecting barricades throughout the city; they also gathered at railway stations to stop Shanghai's trains. One massive traffic jam paralyzed the city for several days. The advantage to this strategy was the pressure it put on businesses, and thus the government, to negotiate, while effectively preventing large contingents of troops from entering the city. Violence erupted throughout the city, however, when the CCP authorized ad hoc militia groups of loyal workers to break apart the student barricades. At least one train ran over protesters blocking its path. But as more and more militia groups attacked students—while "officially" Shanghai police forces showed restraint—it became clear to the students that they could not continue their blockade of the city; the increase in violence and the rumors from Beijing heightened the Shanghai students' fear of the inevitable reprisals, and they released their hold on the city. The Chinese Communist Party reexerted control over China, and the prodemocracy movement was forced to go underground. For those continuing to oppose the CCP, the misinformation originally broadcast by journalists about a Tiananmen Square student massacre eventually served the Communist Party because the state subsequently used the "false claims" to undercut claims by individuals and human rights groups about massacres that occurred elsewhere, such as in Muxidi and Nanchizi.[39] Nevertheless, the suppression of the uprising severely strained many of China's international political and economic relations for over a decade and made international heroes of its students.[40]

Student Unrest on the Eve of a New Millennium

12

Latin American Student Agitation: On the Rise Again

In 1992 Brazil witnessed a massive wave of student demonstrations, the like of which it had not seen since the 1964 protests against the military. Except for sporadic minor attacks aimed at tuition hikes or the military regime, Brazil's student political scene had been relatively uneventful after the overwhelmingly brutal police suppression of students in the late 1960s, which included mass arrests, imprisonments, and torture. Following the fall of Brazil's dictatorship in 1985, radical students tried to revive the once intense interest in political activism on the country's campuses, but the students of the 1980s were not receptive; individual concerns and careerism held the day. All that changed in the summer of 1992, however, as Brazil's newspapers revealed the extent and depth of government corruption tainting President Fernando Collor de Mello and his colleagues.

Outraged by the revelations, students demonstrated in the tens of thousands, chanting for the president's impeachment and carrying banners accusing him of corruption. The student protests were joined by labor unions, which held massive demonstrations of their own, and the number of demonstrators in the streets of Brazil grew to hundreds of thousands. Notably, neither the demonstrators nor city police turned to violence (indeed, many of the police supported what the students were doing), and members of Brazil's congress, a significant number of whom had been student leaders in the 1960s, were moved by the student protesters, who rallied around a moral cause, not a party or an ideology. In fact, the 1992 student demonstrations remained unusually nonpartisan, and tempered with humor (students recited clever, often bawdy chants during the marches), helping the general public understand and support their cause, and amusing police forces. The students took to the streets not only because their country's leader was caught in a tangle of corruption; the educational system of Brazil had long been suffering extreme economic hardship, and Collor's government had authorized further slashing of funds. However, because of the popularity of the students' central issue, because both the media and labor raised the same call for impeachment, and because Collor was strongly opposed by the congress, the student-led drive resulted in the president's impeachment and his subsequent resignation. Following the success of the demonstration and the loss of the movement's central issue, student political activism predictably dropped off, but it did not return to the low levels prior to 1992—student interest stayed focused on political and university issues.[1]

Brazil's successful student demonstrations were unique to Latin America in the 1990s. Although many other Latin American countries suffered economic hardship—their fiscal difficulties especially evident in their education budgets and programs—generating student demonstrations, few were as effective in bringing about reform as Brazil's. In Chile, for example, in 1992, students occupied administration buildings and held demonstrations at many universities to protest financial aid policies that forced lower-income students out. No novices at power games, the administrations of Chile's universities neither encouraged nor suppressed the students' actions, choosing to play both sides of the dispute: they chastised the students (without employing violence) while simultaneously using their demonstrations to ask the government for more funds. Since the fall of General Augusto Pinochet's regime in 1990, Chile's studentry slowly, but increasingly, became more politically active, with demonstrations sporadically flaring up over educational issues, including financial aid policies, tuition increases, and university appointments, with limited success.[2]

Many student educational reform protests in other countries did not fare as well. In Nicaragua, for example, police troops fired on demonstrators demanding more money for public universities in December 1995, injuring students and killing a professor. In a move calculated to defuse the situation, the government blamed the police involved and began an investigation to head off any potentially large student uprising. The tactic worked, and the incident did not spark a greater student response.[3] Nevertheless, students continued to protest for more money for higher education. As some Latin American countries continued to suppress student demonstrations, radical students characteristically turned to acts of terrorism, which promoted more police violence. In Managua, for example, students seeking more government funding for education took over the Foreign Ministry Building and held hostages for one day early in 1996, though they were subsequently overrun by police troops. And in the Dominican Republic, students at the Autonomous University of Santo Domingo demonstrating against university over-crowding clashed with police; when militant students started throwing firebombs, officers opened fire. Such radical acts occurred sporadically throughout the 1990s in Latin America, generally precipitating heavier government control of universities.

In Peru student politics, like the country itself, underwent a dramatic evolution in the 1990s; students launched their own campaigns for gov-ernment seats in Peru's 2000 elections.[4] The New Republic Movement began as a grassroots student organization that sought to replace Peru's established politicians, who according to the movement refused to look toward the future. Claiming that the president was a tyrant and his gov-ernment corrupt, in 1999 Peruvian students held massive demonstra-tions against him; in Lima students staged sit-down strikes in the city streets, condemning the presence of police troops on major campuses and the government's decision to appoint officials to lead and thus con-trol universities. The students' pressure was enough to make the gov-ernment remove troops from Peru's campuses; in subsequently forming the New Republic Movement, students hoped to partake directly in gov-ernment decisions through their candidates for the nation's congress, with the reform of Peru's shaky economy and the reversal of Peru's sky-rocketing unemployment rate as their platform.[5]

The battle over Mexican educational reforms and the future of the National Autonomous University of Mexico (UNAM) continued into the 1990s. In 1990 three years after the student strikes forced the university rector to back down and abandon his attempts to raise tuition and impose degree time limits, UNAM had a new rector and a university commission with significant student representation (achieved by stu-dent lobbying efforts) to address the need to reform the university.

Although teacher and researcher representatives agreed to institute tougher faculty evaluations, the students refused to budge on corresponding student issues; they blocked attempts by the administration's representatives to institute entrance examinations, to increase tuition, and to set any time-to-degree limits. The commission thus could not produce a viable plan for saving UNAM, and so the responsibility for suggesting and implementing reforms rested, once again, on the office of UNAM's rector. By June 1992, the new rector bit the bullet and announced that tuition would be increased at UNAM but that extremely low-income students would be exempt from paying the fees, while financial aid would be offered to others to meet the new costs.[6] Students immediately threatened a strike if any attempt was made to raise fees, forcing the university to back down once again. In 1994 UNAM's rector again attempted to raise fees, and students went on strike for several weeks, shutting down the institution until the rector again scrapped the proposal. UNAM's administration made some progress in the mid-1990s, however, as it attacked the reform problems in small pieces, managing to set time-to-degree limits and to eliminate guaranteed admission for all university-affiliated high school graduates in 1997.

In 1999 a new UNAM rector made another push for reform after oil prices fell. Heavily dependent for revenues on the sale of oil, the Mexican government was prompted by the drastic drop in oil value to slash UNAM's budget (to which it contributed 90 percent). The attempt met with the usual student resistance, demonstrations, and a threatened strike, as students poured off Mexico City's largest campus, clogging the city's streets; this time, however, the rector refused to back down, and the students responded by occupying the campus, even though a majority of students did not actively support striking. The strikers contended that the issue was the infringement on the constitutional right of all citizens to a free education, and that the increase only marked a first step toward the privatization of Mexico's public school system. The administration argued that UNAM simply could no longer operate without increasing tuition. Supported by labor unions and the Party of Democratic Revolution (PRD), which saw in the strike an opportunity for its candidates to exploit in the upcoming national elections, the students centered their resistance around UNAM's main campus in Mexico City. Fearing another '68-like incident, and benefiting from the leftist agitation, the mayor of Mexico City, PRD member, and presidential hopeful Cuauhtemoc Cárdenas publicly supported the students' actions and ordered the police not to become involved in the dispute under any circumstances, thus putting more pressure on UNAM's rector to handle the crisis. Hoping to end the strikes and demonstrations, the rector subsequently announced that paying the new tuition fee would be voluntary, but the students, interpreting this as a sign of weakness, raised their demands to include rescinding UNAM's entrance exams and the recently adopted time-to-degree limits. The university refused, and the strike and occupation continued; students fortified the buildings they held against police attack.

Despite its internationally recognized stadium and colorful library murals by Juan O'Gorman, UNAM's main campus was by the beginning of 1999 an eyesore—physically falling apart, with plaster routinely dropping from classroom ceilings and plumbing so deteriorated that many toilets on campus could no longer flush. By the end of the year, the dilapidated and still striker-occupied main campus had been abandoned by the majority of students, who were completing courses off campus, or who had simply given up on the semester (remarkably, almost 200,000 students kept up with their work for the semester, took off-campus finals, and were credited for their classes).[7] The campus remained occupied for the following semester. But the atmosphere had changed; the general public, as well as students trying to finish their degrees, had become frustrated with the demonstrators, and the popularity of the PRD party, as well as Cárdenas, correspondingly suffered. Everyone involved was frustrated that the only architectural additions made to UNAM's main campus in 1999 came in the form of shoddily erected student barricades, which did not aid students attempting to earn enough credits to graduate or help in getting the toilets to flush. The Marxist rhetoric of the occupiers of UNAM began to wear thin by the end of 1999, even on Cárdenas and the PRD, as the increasingly frustrated radicals began to turn on the politician and the party.

In practical terms, as Mexico entered the new millennium, there was neither enough public money available nor enough room for the country's college-age population to attend existing institutions of higher education; at the beginning of 2000, Mexico's public universities could serve less than 20 percent of those eligible to attend, and many more students were destined to graduate from high school in the upcoming decade. The radical students holding the university claimed that the answer was more government funding and more democracy—that the university was unconstitutionally turning toward privatization and elitism, but Mexico's government simply claimed empty pockets.[8]

Late in January 2000, UNAM's administration, which had long given up on its plans for reforms and tuition increases, called for a university-wide student vote to gauge student support for the strike; in a highly publicized vote, the students overwhelmingly chose to end the strike. Thus backed by both public and student opinion, the government could move against the protesters, who could no longer claim to represent the student body. The government of President Ernesto Zedillo and UNAM university authorities thus carefully broadcast both to the strikers and to Mexico's general population that an end to the nine-month strike was forthcoming, and that it was the will of the people. On the first of February, strikers violently attacked a group of custodians, an event captured on video and broadcast on the national news, creating in its wake a favorable moment, if ever there was one, for government intervention. In February, hundreds of federal police troops in riot gear, carrying sticks and shields but no firearms, swarmed onto the campus and surrounded the barricaded buildings; under heavy media coverage the radical students voluntarily marched out of the buildings and into the hands of the police, who arrested them. While the student activists claimed victory and railed against what they perceived as continued government oppression, the government was busily engaged in controlling the media spin on the police action, pointing out that neither the president nor the university had ordered the police action, but that a federal judge had issued arrest warrants for the strikers for illegal seizure of property. In addition to destroyed university property and many Che Guevera posters, police discovered homemade bombs and potted marijuana plants in the occupied buildings. By showing restraint and patience, the government and the university administration avoided a potentially fatal situation and defused the student strike, without bloodshed or public outrage.

The Rebirth of Student Activism in the United States

In the United States in the 1990s, student resistance actions were issue-based rather than ideologically based, and since the issues tended to be of limited national appeal, student demonstrators received little media coverage.[9] Although students participated in anti–Gulf War demonstrations early in the decade, most protests concerned local issues, ranging from limits set on alcohol consumption by universities and townships to the establishment of ethnic studies programs in universities or health-care benefits for graduate students.

In January 1991 thousands of students joined in a demonstration across from the White House to protest the Persian Gulf War; protesters ranged from Vietnam veterans to students concerned about conscription, and many waved signs with antiwar slogans such as "No Blood for Oil." The demonstrators found themselves opposed not by police or military but by pro–Persian Gulf demonstrators, including members of SMASH, or Students Mobilized against Saddam Hussein. Smaller antiwar demonstrations occurred on U.S. campuses throughout the war, but the war failed to generate a massive student movement because of the conservative climate on U.S. campuses, the war's general popularity, and the extremely few American casualties incurred in the conflict.[10]

Following the 1992 verdict in Los Angeles acquitting white police officers of beating motorist Rodney King, African-American students protested at campuses across the United States. In Atlanta students from a number of colleges—Spelman, Morehouse, Morris Brown, Clark Atlanta University—marched downtown, where, joined by other demonstrators, they clashed with police troops after protesters started attacking white-owned businesses and white pedestrians. Riots also broke out for several days following the verdict at the Atlanta University Center, the combined area of the individual colleges. Students vandalized area businesses before police troops overwhelmed the rioting demonstrators with tear gas. The unpopular King verdict briefly reenergized African-American political organizations on U.S. campuses in the 1990s.[11]

Many acts of student protests in the 1990s were generated not out of moral outrage, but from defense of students' right to consume alcohol. Much to the embarrassment of administrators, students at a number of schools violently clashed with police over "the right to party"—indeed, many U.S. demonstrations in the 1990s had more in common with medieval European town-and-gown riots than with twentieth-century political activism. At the University of Hartford, approximately one thousand students battled police in March 1991 after officers attempted to impound a beer keg at a student party.[12] At Ohio University, several thousand students rioted in April 1998 for a second annual violent protest over the loss of an hour of drinking when clocks were officially set back at the beginning of daylight savings time; forced out of area bars, upset students hurled rocks and bottles at police, who knew to show up in full riot gear after the previous year's riot. The troops finally resorted to shooting wooden "knee-knocker" bullets at the rioters to suppress them. Alcohol-related issues caused uprisings at numerous universities, including Miami University in Ohio, Michigan State, the University of Connecticut, and Washington State.

Although such apolitical demonstrations often made newspaper headlines, by far the majority of student protests were highly political, and involved activist commitment and personal risk. Fasting tactics came to the fore of student political protests for a brief time in 1994, as students found hunger strikes to be an extremely effective means of protest. A wave of such strikes occurred on a number of campuses, including Columbia, Sarah Lawrence College, Stanford, UCLA, UC Santa Barbara, the University of Colorado, and the University of Hawaii at Manoa, over such issues as the establishment of multicultural courses or the need for ethnic studies programs. A novel and extremely effective strategy for garnering short bursts of media attention, hunger strikes successfully furthered already strong campus movements regarding multicultural, ethnic, and racial issues.[13]

Indeed, throughout the mid- to late 1990s, students at many campuses across the nation took administrations to task over the lack of ethnic studies programs or their hiring and tenuring practices. At Princeton, students occupied the administration building in 1995, demanding the establishment of Latino and Asian-American studies programs; protesters at Columbia did the same with their university's admissions building in 1996 to draw attention to the same issue on their campus. In California, students at Berkeley seized the campus's administration building in 1997 when Berkeley conformed with California's state-ratified Proposition 209, which made it illegal for state agencies to grant preferences based on gender or race (209 ended affirmative-action practices at public colleges and universities in California). And in May 1999 five students at Berkeley mounted a hunger strike linked to a larger demonstration protesting budget cuts in the university's ethnic studies program. Except in cases concerning state or federal mandates (such as Proposition 209), hunger strikes were generally successful.

Another issue fueling student protest on U.S. campuses in the late 1990s was universities' patronizing of clothing manufacturers that relied on sweatshop labor for their products. In 1998, students protesting at Duke University demanded that the university raise its standards for allowing clothing manufacturers to use the university's name and logo on their products; Duke students wanted full disclosure of where and under what conditions workers produced clothing bearing Duke's name.[14] Students at numerous other U.S. universities launched similar protests in an attempt to force logo-licensing companies to raise their licensing standards. Antisweatshop demonstrations, which in some cases including sit- and knit-ins, occurred at Georgetown, University of Wisconsin at Madison, Cornell, Princeton, Harvard, and Yale, among dozens of other universities in 1998 and 1999, and many were successful.[15]

As U.S. studentry began to recognize the power of their own civil rights—and of media publicity—they increasingly turned to legal measures to ensure that their voices be heard and to check universities in their employment of power. Students began launching successful lawsuits against universities when police used excessive force to disperse demonstrations, sending a clear message to universities that they would be held responsible for calling in police troops.[16] And a series of court decisions upheld the rights of graduate students as employees to organize unions, and thus to demand employee benefits and compensation. Although graduate unions had existed in the United States since 1969, they made headlines in the 1990s when they raised issues concerning the U.S. university as an unfair work environment. University administrations from Yale to the University of Georgia fought graduate students' efforts to organize and to unionize, fearing that if they succeeded, the universities' source of relatively cheap labor would demand increased benefits packages, health care, and even higher wages. The unionization drives concerned official recognition of the status of graduate instructors as part-time labor; such an admission would underscore graduate teaching assistants' legal rights as employees and their concomitant exploitation. Although students achieved unionization at a significant number of universities, many graduate students remained apathetic or uninterested in unionizing, dooming to failure many drives taking place on individual campuses or within individual systems. Nonetheless, the mere presence of unions on campuses, and even of unionization drives that failed, opened up dialogues with administrators and encouraged universities to institute fairer employment practices.

European University Reforms and New Student Demonstrations

By the mid-1990s, the German educational system was in dire need of reform, primarily because of the massive overcrowding of university classrooms and severe economic strain on the campus system. With an infrastructure designed to support barely half of almost 2 million students at its universities, a significant lack of technical schools, a lack of funds, and a guarantee of free education to all high school graduates, the public university system could not continue functioning as it had. By the mid-1990s university officials, students, and government officials, including Chancellor Helmut Kohl, were holding meetings in efforts to resolve the crisis. University officials sought the creation of more facilities, the streamlining of programs, and the imposition of time-to-degree limitations on students, many of whom, they argued, were simply never going to stop using their student status to access health-care benefits. Students, by contrast, opposed such limitations, although they supported the streamlining of educational programs. Wishing to avoid the inevitable firestorm, Germany's government began maneuvers to shift the responsibility for legislating reforms, and the authority to design new degrees, to Germany's sixteen states.[17]

Students all over Germany went on strike to protest the impending and potentially costly reforms, arguing that the government should pick up the tab for upgrading the school system; large numbers of students occupied campuses and protested at more than a quarter of the country's universities. Many university officials supported the students' efforts to get more funds out of the government (some even facilitated the strikers), and opportunistic politicians publicly sided with the students as well, but Germany was severely depressed economically and could do little to alleviate the situation. Faced with little alternative and opposed by a vocal but relatively weak student movement with only limited public support, a number of German universities began charging tuition.[18]

In Britain thousands of students took to the streets in 1997, protesting the decision to bring to an end the university tuition waiver for all British citizens, except those below the poverty level. Britain was the first European country to abandon across the board a free education policy for public university students. As in Germany, overcrowding and a need to modernize university facilities in the face of the global economy and a decline in international competitiveness precipitated the reform. Significant numbers of British students protested the tuition increase, but the activists demonstrating could not muster the national resistance needed to fight the reforms.[19]

By the mid-1990s, France's universities also experienced massive overcrowding problems, and desperately sought increased government aid; since the early 1980s, the number of students attending French universities had doubled, and the infrastructure of the school system simply had not kept pace. Thousands of students demonstrated for government funds and university reforms at universities in Paris, Bordeaux, Nantes, and Rouen. Citing that France was in the midst of a recession and could do nothing to alleviate the problem, government education officials pleaded with students not to escalate the situation or resort to violence. Nevertheless, in November 1995, over 50,000 students at French universities declared a strike to protest the conditions of France's higher education; tens of thousands of students marched in Paris alone. Although minor scuffles broke out and police arrested a number of unruly protesters, the demonstrations remained on the whole peaceful and controlled. The government responded with a pledge to commit more funds to revamp the system, but the demonstrating students rejected that offer and a subsequent one. By the end of 1995 over half of the nation's universities were hosting strikes. In early 1996 students voted to end their strikes, primarily so they could still receive credit for the academic year.[20]

In other countries, such as Greece and Spain, intense but isolated student protests occurred sporadically in the last decade of the millennium. Students in Greece, for example, violently rioted in December 1997 over university reforms that attempted to set higher entrance requirements. In Athens, National University students took to the streets in protest, burning parked cars and firebombing local businesses and a bank. Students assaulted police attempting to quell the riot with rocks and paving stones. And in Spain, near the Autonomous University of Barcelona, police troops wielding batons attacked unruly students demonstrating against Spain's monarchy in 1997. Protesting on the eve of Princess Cristina's wedding, angry pro-Catalonia nationalists hanged life-size dolls of the bride and groom from a street sign.[21]

More Flashes of Resistance in Eastern Europe

Following the Velvet Revolution, the Czechoslovakian university system underwent tremendous retooling; the Soviet-style Communist government of Czechoslovakia had severely crippled the nation's institutions of higher learning, eradicating theoretically oriented and broad-based humanities programs or turning them into technical training mills. Czechoslovakia's new government granted universities autonomy, giving them wide latitude in governing and restructuring themselves, and in the early 1990s, foreign corporations extended loans to universities in Czechoslovakia, as well as in Hungary and in Poland. Repairs to the facilities, however, came slowly, simply because the governments of the individual nations that faced radical political and governmental reform had few, if any, funds available for their systems of higher education: universities, including those in Czechoslovakia, were, for the most part, on their own. For the next few years, activist Czech students focused on education reform and stayed out of the political scene, but in November 1991 they were back on the streets of Prague supporting President Václav Havel's emergency efforts to keep a Slovakian independence movement from splitting the nation.[22]

In all three countries, university financial difficulties raised the specter of tuition fees, which did not exist under Communism. In 1995 the Czech Republic asked students capable of contributing to do so; and after much debate, the country's students agreed. In Hungary and Poland, however, suggested reforms, such as tuition and time-to-degree limitations, led to massive student demonstrations. Although desired, westernization would not come easy. Foreign companies nevertheless invested in the hitherto untapped markets, and the universities and the studentry of Eastern Europe all changed radically over the next decade—students attending universities in Prague, who ten years earlier would have gathered to discuss democracy in dimly lit and unheated coffeehouses, were at the turn of the millennium grabbing a Big Mac and fries and eyeing sports cars between classes, discussing postmodernism in hip Internet bars.

In Albania, students successfully pressured the Communist government into instituting reforms to the university system in 1990, and then demonstrated for major government reforms, such as a multiparty system and freedom of the press. Student-led riots in major cities kept pressure on the government, which feared the potential turn to violence, and by the end of December 1990 the government drafted a new constitution that allowed for more civil freedoms, permitted foreign investment, and opened a door for a parliamentary democracy. But what appeared to be the beginning of a relatively peaceful revolution for democracy ended in 1991 with the scripted reelection of the Communist government. In a move to preempt massive student demonstrations, the government suspended nearly all university classes immediately following the election and sent students home. Despite the campus closing, students demonstrated and rioted in university cities, although the government brutally and effectively suppressed them.[23]

In Yugoslavia students protested for university autonomy throughout the 1990s, but most of their energies were directed against President Slobodan Milosević, who in 1991 easily crushed student demonstrations with police troops. But by early 1992 Milosević's power showed signs of waning; in March 1992 hundreds of students from Belgrade University, occupied Terazije Square and called for the president's resignation and for the removal of government representatives on campus.

The students were emboldened by the absence of immediate police suppression, and their ranks swelled into the thousands during the day, though many feared to stay on the square overnight. Publicly decrying the leader of the socialist government, the students directly blamed their president for the rampant inflation and mass hunger facing Yugoslavia; Milosević was not amused, but he also was not secure enough politically to risk the public backlash or larger student uprising that suppressing the students might provoke. Relying on cold weather and general student apathy, the president simply chose to lie low and wait out the students. His strategy worked.[24] In June, however, the students renewed their efforts and upped the ante by calling a strike at Belgrade University—over ten thousand students participated. The students occupied the campus and again called for the president's resignation; opposition party members echoed the students' demands and held massive demonstrations of their own.[25] Economic sanctions against Yugoslavia by the United Nations contributed to social unrest as goods became scarce and unaffordable for most people. Milosević's patience again paid off, however, for when Belgrade students temporarily halted their strikes, the president of Yugoslavia had the government legislate that henceforth the university would be under government ownership and control. Under the new laws, universities were no longer autonomous, and students could legally demonstrate only on sanctioned protest sites.

Students immediately demonstrated against the new legislation, but they had lost their momentum and were unprepared to fight the new measures; indeed they had trouble organizing an effective large-scale counterattack. In December 1992 they trained their sights on the upcoming elections, but conventional efforts to oust Milosević failed. Returning to the streets in demonstrations, students generated a sustained protest movement that Milosević restrained himself from violently crushing, as he feared martyring students might cause workers to join the demonstrations. By the mid-1990s, demonstrating students were part of the everyday political and social landscape. The demonstrations did not always occur without violence. Police were often accused of beating, arresting, and torturing dissidents, even if they were not attacking demonstrations in force. The isolated acts of oppression did not deter the students, however. Calling for the president's resignation, for university autonomy, and for social reforms, students continued to demonstrate both in large and small numbers in Yugoslavia's cities until the NATO bombing campaign began in the spring of 1999. During the bombings student dissent continued, but understandably could not capture the nation's attention. Following the end of NATO military actions and the separation of Kosovo, students resumed the fight against Milosević in Belgrade and held a massive demonstration in November 1999 outside the parliament building, at a time when opposition parties were calling for early elections. No longer in a patient mood, Milosević unleashed stick-and-shield-wielding Serb police, who mercilessly beat the demonstrators. In 2000, the national student movement called Otpor (which means "resistance") stepped up its program of defiance, holding demonstrations and strikes. The population of Serbia rose in defiance as well, and elected a new president within the year.

In Bucharest, Romania, students demonstrated in massive numbers for democracy in 1990, but they lost momentum when Ion Iliescu and his party won Romania's national elections on May 20. In June, however, students began protesting again and held a hunger strike on Bucharest's University Square. When police moved in on the students with clubs and attempted to arrest them, the square erupted into a full-scale riot, and a pitched battle ensued in which police killed a number of demonstrators and arrested several hundred. Joined by massive numbers of supporters, students repelled the police troops and reclaimed the square. Police released the arrested students to defuse the situation, but the momentum was with the demonstrators, who began setting fire to city vehicles and government buildings. When army units ignored the government's demand to quell the rioters, the government resorted to busing in thousands of miners, who, hired for the occasion and directed by police, ruthlessly attacked the demonstrators with clubs. Overrunning the university during the morning of June 14, the miners demolished everything in their path, brutally beating students and faculty trying to save the university from being destroyed. Following the suppression of the students and the demolition of Bucharest University at the hands of the miners, however, the government reimbursed the university for damages and, notably, began major governmental reforms, such as decentralization. During the remainder of the decade student protests continued to flare up, but for the most part they were aimed at instituting university reforms, rather than at the government. The country itself underwent tremendous changes in the 1990s, actively seeking foreign investment and westernizing, and even courting the protective arm of NATO. Students worked for reforms, but would not risk harming the precarious political situation. Reform efforts included liberalizing Romania's universities—even to the extent that multicultural, affirmative action efforts were attempted in several universities.[26]

Students of the Former Soviet Union

For the most part, the various instances of student resistance flaring up in the former Soviet Union were sporadic and of limited duration during and following the breakup of the nation. Russia saw relatively little student resistance. The political apathy of Soviet studentry in Moscow continued through the end of the century, even during the hard-line Communist coup attempt against Mikhail Gorbachev in 1991. The coup occurred while most students were on break, but the Defense Ministry also announced that students henceforth would be exempt from being drafted into the military, in an effort to divide, if not preempt, a united student response when students returned to campus. By contrast, in the Ukrainian Republic, thousands of students demonstrated for Gorbachev and Boris Yeltsin in Kiev.

In Soviet Georgia, students joined opposition parties in 1991 to protest against the breakaway republic's government, which they accused of sabotaging democracy, exacerbating ethnic divisions within the country, and supporting the attempted coup on Gorbachev. After police began shooting demonstrators in September, military officials interceded on the students' behalf, reminding the government that the military had its own political agenda. The move by the military was not so much an endorsement of the students as it was a display of power. Fearing bloodshed anyway, the Ministry of Education suspended classes until the student turbulence ceased. In Central Asian nations—Kazakhstan, Kyrgyzstan, Tajikistan, Turkmenistan, and Uzbekistan—the student activism that had flourished under Gorbachev's reform efforts withered following the breakup of the Soviet bloc. There are a number of reasons for the vacuum in student resistance efforts in these areas. Most of them have to do with the radical changes sweeping the various countries—a confusing, sudden influx of Western ideas, money, corporations, and materials, and a sudden outflow of many liberal university professors who emigrated west; severely depressed national economies; the sudden release from Communist dogma and the appearance of new curriculum choices; and the necessity of national unity for the survival of the nations' independence. But perhaps most importantly, the individual governments did not tolerate dissent. After Uzbekistan's independence, for example, university students protesting against the country's president were immediately and brutally suppressed by troops who did not hesitate to kill. Although democratic efforts within universities and among studentry of the various Central Asian nations were beginning to show by the mid-1990s, for the most part, the visible lack of student resistance continued throughout the decade in the former Soviet bloc Central Asia nations.[27]

Student Resistance Continues in the Middle East

The Persian Gulf conflict began while many universities in the Middle East were on break; to avoid student-sparked conflicts, many universities postponed the beginning of the next semester until after the conflict ended. Students, nevertheless, protested against both Iraq and the United States in 1991 at universities in Egypt, though most students supported Egypt's endorsement of the coalition forces. In Algeria and Jordan, thousands of students demonstrated against U.S. involvement, and Jordanian students publicly burned U.S. flags. Protests also occurred on campuses in the Sudan and in Yemen. But as the Gulf War demonstrations largely fell along government-supported political lines in the various area nations, the students did not meet with much opposition, and indeed often were supported by the ruling powers.

Fearing student uprisings, terrorism, and even a second Intifada, the Israeli government, however, forced many universities to suspend classes, and curfews halted the activities of students. Following the Gulf War, universities and colleges in the West Bank and Gaza Strip began to reopen—they had been closed since 1988, in response to antioccupation student activities and the Palestinian Intifada. At first the campuses remained relatively quiet; students were glad to be back at university facilities, where the majority of them focused their attentions on academic issues, but conflict between students and the occupational forces was inevitable. In July 1995, Palestinian students at the West Bank University of An-Najah marched to protest the incarceration of Palestinians suspected of terrorism. Israeli troops blocked the marchers as they approached the prison holding the suspects; the standoff turned into a battle between armed troops and rock-wielding students, and Israeli troops killed three Palestinian students. Each side blamed the other for starting the fight, and the incident only added to the tensions, sparking subsequent protests and similar sporadic conflicts between students and troops in the occupied area.[28] As peace negotiations disintegrated in 2000, student resistance again dramatically increased.

In the late 1990s a rash of student protests at Turkish universities broke out after school officials complied with a government ban that outlawed the wearing of head scarves by women—a blatant attempt to contain Islamic fundamentalism. The government also forbade men to wear traditional Islamic beards. The bans had been instituted nationwide to stem a growing fundamentalist tide, but their actual enforcement had been left up to university officials; while many university administrations strictly enforced the policies, calling in police and ejecting students who appeared at lectures with head cloths or facial hair, others took a more tolerant stance, wishing above anything to avoid bloodshed over the issue. Protests against the bans drew thousands of students, but they were neither forcefully suppressed nor effective at getting the ban repealed.

Following the cultural revolution in Iran, with its purges of moderates and pro-Westerners, acts of student resistance in the 1980s against the new regime were virtually nonexistent. Iran's new theocracy wanted a new generation of citizens trained to be loyal to the new government, and to achieve that quickly, they officially lowered the maturity age for female citizens to the age of nine.[29] By the beginning of the new millennium, the population of Iran had increased by over 35 million people. The massive shift in population age demographics would eventually work against the fundamentalists as the increase in younger voters would subsequently fuel the liberalization of the political sphere; inevitably, the new generation would grow older, and many would rebel against the conservatives. The explosion in population—and students—

generated tremendous problems as unemployment rates soared in the 1990s. The bleak employment future of students, the high level of literacy, and the increased exposure to outside sources of information added to students' level of discontent; more and more frustrated Iranian students, who saw the potential strength of their numbers, began voicing a need for democracy, freedom of the press, and civil rights.[30]

Not surprisingly, a new phase of student activism in Iran began in the late 1990s. In May 1997 Iran elected a new and moderate president, Mohammed Khatame. Nonetheless, fundamentalists in the government continued to control Iran's military and police forces. With Khatame's election, student supporters of the president stepped up their prodemocracy activities and launched a series of public demonstrations, which ended by being brutally suppressed by both police and civilian vigilantes.[31] Still, students at Iranian universities continued to demonstrate for the liberalization of their institutions and country, firmly and nonviolently refusing to end their prodemocracy actions. Their efforts were slowly rewarded, and over the next few years Iran became more open to Western ideas and accepted more freedom of the press. In July 1999 the student resistance movement heated up to a level unprecedented since the 1979 revolution. At the University of Tehran, a small number of students protesting the government closing of a liberal newspaper caused a reactionary conservative backlash in which police and vigilantes stormed a student dormitory and beat students. In response, massive numbers of students rioted and attacked police and hard-liners; the streets around the University of Tehran erupted into pitched battles between armed riot police and prodemocracy students for weeks, sparking protests and violence at other universities. Police eventually quelled the riots and arrested well over one thousand students. To defuse the situation, the government singled out Tehran's chief of police as the scapegoat for the police brutality. Prodemocracy students continued to demonstrate for liberalization, however, and focused their immediate attention on freeing the students arrested during and after the riots. These demonstrations were surpassed, however, in November 1999, by a massive student march through the streets of Tehran celebrating the twentieth anniversary of the seizure of the U.S. embassy; once again, students shouted slogans such as "Death to

America" and burned effigies of U.S. leaders.[32] At the turn of the century, Iran's studentry once again asserted its power and complicated centrality in the evolution of the nation. Yet with a dramatic shift toward supporting increased personal freedoms, social liberalization, and international participation, Iran's studentry was on a collision course with the hard-liners and conservative forces that students had helped put in power decades before.

Student Protest and State Violence in Africa

The last decade of the millennium was a turbulent one for many African universities. In the wake of Eastern European revolutions against Communism, and rampant local economic difficulties, many African students increased prodemocracy efforts and campaigned for the establishment of multiple-party political systems; student protests were on the rise in many countries, including Angola, Ethiopia, Ghana, Kenya, Mozambique, Nigeria, South Africa, Togo, Zaire, Zambia, and Zimbabwe. In the majority of these nations, student demonstrations for multiple-party systems or other government reforms often met with violent government suppression, though in some instances, internal and external political pressures forced previously single-party African nations to hold multiparty elections, as in the case of the Ivory Coast. Nevertheless, in the majority of instances, governments greeted student liberalization efforts with brutal force, often at the behest of corrupt government-appointed university officials.

At the University of Lubumbashi, Zaire's government unleashed the military on students in retaliation for the beating of government officials by prodemocracy students demonstrating for liberalization. In May 1990 government-sponsored machete-and-club-wielding men overran the campus; the marauding forces ostensibly targeted dissidents for assassination, but once on the campus, they went berserk, killing a still undisclosed number of students. The university was irreparably destroyed during the Lubumbashi massacre, and the military subsequently removed the bodies of those slain. The attack sparked massive student demonstrations at the country's other universities, and the government repeatedly closed them in response to the protests during the following years. Such violent suppression of student dissent was nothing new to Zaire, however; President Mobutu Sese Seko had often used brutal measures against the nation's studentry since ascending to power in 1965.[33]

Zaire was not the only country suppressing student activists. At the beginning of the decade, the University of Zimbabwe repeatedly hosted prodemocracy demonstrations that riot police violently dispersed. In 1992 a government increase in tuition sparked demonstrations by Zimbabwe University students that culminated in a massive march on the Ministry of Education, where club-wielding police repulsed students; the angry students turned their attention to downtown Harare, where they burned cars and vandalized businesses. In response, the university expelled all of its students, and forced them to reapply for admission. Student demonstrations, riots, and conflicts with police also caused university closings in Nigeria and Zambia throughout the decade.[34]

In South Africa, student unrest in the 1990s focused on segregation, racism, democratization, overcrowding, and lack of funds—all issues related to years of apartheid. The nation's apartheid laws were repealed in 1991, but the country still had a rough road to travel to reach democracy. The sites of most of the acts of student resistance were the nation's colleges and universities initially established in the outlying and independent "homeland" nations as black or mixed-race schools—institutions created following the government's passing of legislation in 1959 forbidding almost all blacks to attend the county's white institutions. In 1992 and 1993 universities repeatedly closed down after prodemocracy student demonstrations rocked campuses. Following Nelson Mandela's election to the presidency of South Africa, student activists lost their antiapartheid focus and unifying moral thunder; consequently many students turned away from political activism, although a number of radicals continued to agitate for changes that they perceived were not happening fast enough. Sporadic and often violent acts of student resistance, demanding university and government reforms, continued to occur with the same tenor as before the free elections, as if aimed at the same repressive government.

In Kenya, student demonstrations against the government of President Daniel Arap Moi were nothing peculiar to the 1990s, but the deplorable state of the corrupt university system was. Moi, who also served as the university chancellor, appointed university administrators, and funds and materials ostensibly aimed at relieving the dreadful conditions of Kenya's schools disappeared, turning what was one of Africa's best educational systems in the 1970s into one of the worst in the 1990s. Students and faculty protested the corruption in demonstrations and strikes, which Kenya's government suppressed through intimidation, arrests, and the physical occupation of the nation's campuses. The government incorporated campus purging into its national student loan applications by channeling disbursements through local, government-appointed officers who denied loans to suspected dissidents. At Kenyatta University and Egerton University students rioted in the mid-1990s over mismanaged loan payments and the exorbitant costs of university room and board, and police arriving on the scene crushed the student uprising.[35]

At the University of Nairobi, where educational materials such as chalk had become scarce by 1995, roofs leaked, and very few toilets flushed, students demonstrated and then rioted in 1997 over increases in tuition and government efforts to collect on student loans. Armed riot police arrived on the campus and attacked the students with clubs, whips, and guns while the protesters fought back with stones. The police rampage left several students dead. In Nairobi in the late 1990s the school system was too corrupt and too destitute to run smoothly; many of its once prestigious faculty had long fled the country, or been fired or jailed. Although arrests and purgings of universities weakened student activism on Kenya's campuses, students continued to speak out against the corruption of the state and ethnic violence. The University of Nairobi was again closed by authorities in February 1999 after students rioted for several days following the government sale to developers of one of Nairobi's few remaining clumps of virgin forests, lying just outside the city. Police and students battled through the streets of Nairobi, but neither the forest, nor the students, stood a chance.[36]

The Threat of Student Activism in India and Violence in Bangladesh

India witnessed sporadic and generally isolated instances of student resistance in the 1990s. Students went on a hunger strike in May 1992 at a Muslim university in New Delhi, for example, to demand the firing of a teacher who publicly stated that the ban on Salmon Rushdie's *Satanic Verses* should be lifted; when the strike failed to attract university authorities' attention, students rioted on the campus, destroying property and attacking faculty. The administration responded, immediately closing the university and ejecting all the students from the campus. But whether they actually took place or not, the very threat of massive student uprisings served as an effective tool for Indian students, one that students used to their advantage. In 1997, for example, students forced University of Delhi administrators to abandon attendance policies by taking over administration offices; the university refrained from using police force, for when force was used against India's students activists, the numbers did not favor the universities, as violence often led to massive campuswide protests and demonstrations.[37]

Politically motivated students in Bangladesh expended the majority of their energies against rival campus groups in the 1990s, killing close to one hundred students a year. For decades, student-on-student violence—beatings and assassinations—were relatively commonplace at Bangladeshi colleges and universities, and fear and intimidation were the order of the academic day. In the late 1990s, the government of Bangladesh made an effort to curb the violence on its campuses, arresting and prosecuting students involved in politically motivated fights or caught on campus with weapons.

Radical Resistance in South Korea

In South Korea, student resistance forces began the decade with little momentum, primarily because the government appeared to be pursuing goals that the majority of student radicals supported. But by 1993 activist student groups articulated a clear antigovernment, prodemocracy stance, pushing for reunification with North Korea and demanding national labor reform; the platform attracted a significant number of adherents.[38] Demonstrations in Seoul, in which helmeted students carried sticks, evolved into ferocious riots and bloody clashes with police, culminating in the beating death of a police officer in 1993. Following the death, government repression and student defections weakened the radical movement, but in August 1996 thousands of students again violently demonstrated for unification with North Korea, battling with police and destroying private property. Determined to end the radical student movement, the government made mass arrests, charged hundreds of students with assaulting officers and civilians, and held student leaders responsible for the several deaths that had occurred; the government also banned the student organizations involved in the protests.

The brutality of the students, combined with nationwide trepidation over a possible North Korean invasion, made the activists generally unpopular. Radical students saw their strength diminish further when, in 1998, Kim Dae Jung, an advocate of liberalization and labor reform and a person widely known to be sympathetic to student causes, became president of South Korea, an event that took yet more thunder out of the student movement. Radical students continued to protest, in some cases violently, but they could only field limited numbers in their demonstrations; by the end of the decade, student radicals often abandoned attempts to start their own protests, opting instead to join and to radicalize larger labor demonstrations.[39]

A New Wave of Student Demonstrations Breaks Out over Indonesia

Since the suppression of student demonstrations in 1978 and the imprisonment of the leaders of those protests, Indonesian universities strictly observed a governmental policy that banned political activism on campuses and eliminated student councils. The government chokehold on campuses proved highly effective; schools that once sustained lively political debate became hauntingly quiet for almost two decades. Fear held students in check, and those who did agitate did so off campus or faced arrest; in 1990, for example, a student on the Gadjah Mada campus who voiced a need for critical thinking received a prison term of eight years.[40] Indonesia's military, which was repeatedly condemned internationally for human rights violations, kept all forms of political dissension under tight control. In February 1998, however, Indonesia's campuses erupted in waves of student protests, which threatened to spill over into city streets. The country's plummeting economy, which among other things raised the possibility of widespread hunger among the general population, sparked the initial protests; they quickly turned from demonstrations against the government's handling of the economy to demonstrations against President Suharto, who had been in power since a student-sparked rebellion toppled Sukarno's regime in 1966.

Students in Jakarta began testing the government's ban on off-campus demonstrations by holding antigovernment marches through the city's streets; they were brutally attacked by club-wielding police in March. In the midst of the protests, the government assembly elected Suharto to a seventh term as president; the intensity of the student demonstrations, as well as the violence with which they were dispersed, escalated. In May, thousands of protesting students in Yogyakarta engaged police troops in violent battles on the campus and in surrounding neighborhoods. At Trisakti University in Jakarta, army troops opened fire with automatic rifles on student demonstrators on May 12, killing six and wounding dozens of others; far from quelling Indonesia's student uprising, however, the violence galvanized student resistance to government forces throughout the country. Following the massacre at Trisakti University, students rioted through the streets of Jakarta for three days, burning cars and businesses, attacking any government officials or troops they found. Students in other cities stepped up their protests as well, and continued to face off with police and government forces, waging war with troops, fighting tear gas, truncheons, and guns with stones, bottles, and fire. In Jakarta alone, over one thousand people died in the general mayhem, and thousands of houses were ransacked or burned. Realizing that the country had become uncontrollable, Suharto resigned from the office he'd held for over thirty years.[41]

But the students were not finished; they continued to demonstrate for democracy and government reform, squaring off with Indonesia's powerful military. By November violent battles in Jakarta were commonplace, and while the military suppressed demonstrations and arrested students, soldiers kept turning up brutally beaten and, occasionally, murdered. On November 13, however, the military took decisive action: on the campus of Atma Jaya University, troops opened fire with automatic weapons on a massive demonstration, killing over a dozen demonstrators and wounding hundreds of others. This marked the beginning of a brutal military crackdown, and the beginning of the end of Indonesia's student movement. Violent suppression by Indonesia's military, followed by government reforms, took the steam out of the riot-ing students. Following an interim government headed by B. J. Habibie, Abdurrahman Wahid became president, balancing Indonesia's powerful military with a civilian-led government; student demonstrations contin-ued to occur on a lesser scale throughout the remainder of the decade, reflecting among other issues the conflict over the breakaway province of East Timor in 1999. Internal social pressure for liberalization and external international monetary incentives that came with increased democracy, combined with a leader open to tolerance and claiming the law of the land came before his own interests, finally put Indonesia on a path that appeared to lead beyond autocratic rule.[42]

The Shattered State of Student Resistance in China

Following the Tiananmen Square uprising, the government continued to crack down on the student movement in China, hunting down stu-dent leaders involved in the prodemocracy demonstrations of 1989 who remained at large and immediately suppressing political movements on campuses as they formed; under government pressure universities expelled large numbers of political students and outlawed demon-strations. The suppression had an extremely sobering effect on pro-democracy students, and heavy government surveillance and party propaganda campaigns on campuses effectively kept the movement from building momentum again. Students daring to criticize the gov-ernment's actions in Beijing in 1989, or current government policies, found themselves immediately arrested. On the anniversaries of the Tiananmen Square massacre, severe warnings, troops, and police kept commemorative demonstrations from occurring, although students throughout China signaled their resentment of Deng Xiaoping by break-ing thousands of bottles on campuses and squares (the word for "little bottle" in Chinese is *xiaoping*). The government released one of the leaders of the student movement, Wang Dan, in 1993, along with others arrested following the massacre (Wang was again subsequently arrested for agitating for democracy). Only a few times in the 1990s did Chinese students witness any large protests; the first occurred following Hong Kong's return to China on July 1, 1997, when Hong Kong university students protested restrictions on their civil liberties. Student demonstrations in Hong Kong began immediately following the transfer. The students did not protest alone, however; thousands of residents also marched in Hong Kong's streets during the first days of July. Although firm, China showed extreme care in its handling of the situation, leaving city officials to resolve the crisis, which they did with tolerance and tact; both the Chinese government and Hong Kong officials publicly acknowledged the former colony's "special status."[43]

China's management of the transfer of Hong Kong was part of a larger public relations effort by the government seeking to counter the effects of the Tiananmen Square massacre (which had led to international economic sanctions and sharp criticisms of the country). As part of that effort, in April 1999 China signed a United Nations declaration announcing that human rights were universal; the country made limited internal liberalizing efforts in the 1990s as well. On the tenth anniversary of the massacre, however, certain areas of Tiananmen Square were, coincidentally, under renovation, and for safety reasons blocked off to the public by large metal fences. The government nevertheless continued to arrest prodemocracy student dissidents and to sentence students to prison for setting up prodemocracy Internet information sites or distributing opposition literature in more conventional ways.[44]

One massive student demonstration that did occur in China in the 1990s happened in November 1999, when tens of thousands of students briefly returned to the streets of Beijing and China's other major cities to join civilians in protesting the NATO bombing of the Chinese embassy building in Belgrade. In China's capital, anti-Western demonstrators, including many students, attacked the British and U.S. embassies; although China's government did not officially sanction the demonstrations or the attacks on the embassies in Beijing, universities did facilitate the student protests in limited ways by busing student representatives to approved demonstration sites. After several days of protesting, however, students were reminded to observe government policies regarding demonstrations strictly, to remain on campuses, and to focus on campus activities, not political ones.[45]

Epilogue
Whither Student Resistance?

This book has sought to describe a history of student resistance, from the formation of medieval student collectives wielding economic power over local towns to protests against sweatshop labor in the United States at the turn of the millennium, in terms of how students throughout the world have used, and in some cases lost, their power. Students—and student actions—are a salient feature of the modern world; and acts of student resistance throw social, economic, and political powers into relief.

Students throughout the world continue to rely on centuries-old strategies of defying authority. Disruptions in individual classrooms, demonstrations on campuses, marches in city streets, economic boycotts, and even armed defiance to state authority are now all part and parcel of student resistance actions. Nevertheless, as the new millennium begins, students are also developing new strategies and new ways to resist. Students now, for example, communicate internationally through the Internet, sharing tactics, legal advice, encouragement, and slogans—and the Web's full potential as a power source has only begun to be tapped. Nonviolent tactics continue to be refined, and, more and more, students turn to legal measures and to the media for aid.

While student resistance actions blossomed—often with violence—in many countries over the last decade, in other countries student resistance largely appears to have become a thing of the past. In France, the United States, Germany, and China, student activist levels are clearly not what they once were, and students in these countries who attempt to agitate for change suffer comparisons with their historical predecessors that generally belittle their efforts, denigrate their generation, and bemoan the current political environment.

What armchair appraisers of current student resistance levels do not generally take into account, however, is the extent of student activism elsewhere in the world (in many countries students are engaged in life and death struggles for freedoms and reforms) and that in any case, student activism depends to a great extent on a country's current cultural and political context; critics need to understand that resistance serves an important function in all societies, and that relative levels of activism indicate much about existing sociopolitical power structures. We must also realize that the nature of student resistance in a given nation evolves continually: the history of student resistance suggests that just as oppression is omnipresent in the world, so too is resistance to oppression. Although a generation of activists may be suppressed by a powerful government in one country or simply lack organization or a cause against which to organize a struggle, as the future brings with it political and sociological changes and new generations of students, resistance will inevitably rise again.

We must also remember that when resistance erupts, it often does so quickly and in unexpected ways. Empowered through collective action, unruly students can challenge their institutions, societies, and governments; they can be tremendous catalysts for change. Given that the outcomes of student-led uprisings remain unpredictable and that students themselves can rarely control the powers they unleash, acts of student resistance—in all forms—must be considered seriously. Simply put, in the modern world, student resistance efforts are one of the key forces in social power dynamics. "Whither student resistance?" It's a good question to ask.

Notes

Introduction

1. One cannot discuss history in terms of power without addressing the work of Michel Foucault, who argues that individuals are always caught in and manipulated by systems of power, whether they know it or not. Particularly relevant to this study of student resistance are his discussions on how the individual in modern societies internalizes societal rules and thus monitors and disciplines him- or herself. Foucault's historical studies suggest that social acts are the effect of institutionalized power, and thus they discuss human behavior in terms of the exercising of forces of power, rather than in terms of, say, individual acts of free will. While not strictly Foucauldian, my approach is indebted to Foucault's insights regarding power relations. For discussions of power relevant to student resistance, see Michel Foucault, *Discipline and Punish: The Birth of the Prison,* trans. Alan Sheridan (New York: Pantheon, 1977); and *Power/Knowledge: Selected Interviews and Other Writings, 1972–1977* (New York: Pantheon, 1980).

Chapter 1

1. An earlier and small organization of medical students and scholars existed in Salerno, but it was very narrowly focused. As noted in the introduction, this study has its limits, which preclude a lengthy discussion of the varied educational systems throughout the world that the modern Western university largely replaced or modified. And, of course, the Western system had roots elsewhere. Although other ancient educational systems are relatively well documented, unfortunately acts of student resistance in them are not.

Many civilizations, from Asia to the New World, had well-developed systems of education long before the rise of medieval European universities, and many allowed secular as well as religious training, but as much as universities are influenced by local traditions, it is a reality that the majority of modern universities throughout the world, as organizations of power, are descendants of or heavily influenced by those founded in medieval Europe. On ancient non-Western educational systems, see Carlton Beck, ed., *Perspectives on World Education* (New York: Wm. C. Brown, 1970); Edward D. Myers, *Education in the Perspective of History* (New York: Harper and Brothers, 1960). On medieval universities, see Nicholas Orme, *Education and Society in Medieval and Renaissance*

England (London: Hambledon Press, 1989); William J. Courtenay, *Schools and Scholars in Fourteenth-Century England* (Princeton, N.J.: Princeton University Press, 1987); and Charles H. Haskins, *The Rise of the Universities* (Ithaca, N.Y.: Cornell University Press, 1957).

2. Willis Rudy chronicles the rise of the medieval university in his very readable *The Universities of Europe, 1100–1914* (Rutherford, N.J.: Associated University Presses, 1984).

3. Evidence exists that shows thirty-six locations in England having a school between 1066 and 1200, and more than seventy in the thirteenth century. For details of early European schools and school life, see Orme, *Education and Society.*

4. As a rule, attending medieval universities was a male prerogative, though there are exceptions to this. Some female students did attend the University of Bologna during the Middle Ages. Novella and Bettina Calderini were two such early students, though the historical accounts of them focus not on their intellects but on their appearances; Novella, for example, was reputedly so beautiful that she had to veil her face to keep from distracting the male students. See Rudy, *Universities of Europe.*

5. Masters often banded together for protection into their own "colleges" to protect their interests, instituting professional guidelines, policies, certificates, and teaching licenses; they endeavored to create both a need for their services and trade protection. See Orme, *Education and Society.*

6. Rudy, *Universities of Europe,* 24–25.

7. The king also saw a chance to display power, and indeed used this and subsequent student uprisings to do so.

8. The University of Paris was actually organized and incorporated by masters, not students (unlike the university at Bologna), but this was done to generate the collective bargaining power of students and masters over the townspeople around them.

9. See Charles H. Haskins, "The Earliest Universities," in *Student Activism: Town and Gown in Historical Perspective,* ed. Alexander DeConde (New York: Charles Scribner's Sons, 1971), 19–32.

10. On the formation of early European universities and the regulation of student life, see Robert S. Rait, *Life in the Medieval University* (Cambridge: Cambridge University Press, 1931). Of course the students of medieval Europe were often from a privileged economic class, and thus already held a certain amount of power. See also Haskins, "The Earliest Universities."

11. See Rait, *Life.*

12. Antony Wood, quoted in Rait, *Life,* 124.

13. From Antony Wood, *Antony's History and the Antiquities of the University of Oxford,* ed. J. Gutch, 1792–96; quoted in Christopher Hibbert and Edward Hibbert, eds. *The Encyclopedia of Oxford* (London: Macmillan, 1988), 424.

14. Wood, *Antony's History*, quoted in Rait, *Life*, 125.
15. Wood, *Antony's History*, quoted in Rait, *Life*, 125.
16. See Hibbert, *Encyclopedia of Oxford*, 120.
17. See Annie Dunlop, "Scottish Student Life in the Fifteenth Century," *Scottish Historical Review* 26 (1947): 47–63.
18. In 1636, for example, in an effort to control student unruliness Oxford adopted the Laudian Code, written in Latin by the archbishop of Canterbury and chancellor of Oxford, William Laud (1573–1645). The code regulated everything from the length of hair permissible at Oxford to conduct beyond the halls of the university, predictably forbidding gambling, drinking, smoking, and visiting harlots; it also contained some curiosities, such as the exclusion of rope-dancers from university grounds.

Chapter 2

1. The church lost ground on a variety of fronts as governments, scholars, and laymen increasingly challenged its authority. The willingness to defy church doctrine by political leaders only encouraged secular scholars in their own defiance. For example, Philip IV of France was bold enough to have Pope Boniface VIII (1294–1303) imprisoned and to remove the papacy to Avignon in southern France, which caused the Great Schism (1378–1417), making European countries choose obeisance between a pope at Avignon and a pope in Rome. Such actions underscored the political facets of the church, showing that, like the various governments challenging it, it was an organization of power.
2. Early advocates of reformation at universities took great risks in voicing their views. It was not until a political climate came about that could support attempts at reformation that people such as Luther could voice their views with a relative amount of personal security; even then they often hired their own security forces.
3. Roland Bainton, *Here I Stand: A Life of Martin Luther* (New York: Abingdon, 1970), 106.
4. For the conversion of Oxford into a military barracks and royal court during the civil war, see Christopher Hibbert and Edward Hibbert, eds., *The Encyclopedia of Oxford* (London: Macmillan, 1988), 91–93.
5. Antony Wood, quoted in Hibbert and Hibbert, *Encyclopedia of Oxford*, 424.
6. Luther was fortunate in his protection by Frederick of Saxony, but he was also favored by a political situation in which the Holy Roman Emperor, Charles V, needed the cooperation of German Protestants to stop the advance of the Turks up the Danube Valley; and thus there is a further twist in the power relations surrounding Luther's rebellious actions.
7. Thomas Lacqueur, *Religion and Respectability: Sunday Schools and Working Class Culture, 1780–1850* (New Haven: Yale University Press, 1976).

8. Many groups owe their existence to the early Turnvereins, which by World War I had hundreds of thousands of student participants. The stress on physical fitness and nationalism in the German schools contributed greatly to the popular discourses surrounding the appearance and behavior of the ideal German man and woman under Hitler. See George Mosse, *The Image of Man: The Creation of Modern Masculinity* (New York: Oxford University Press, 1996), 41–55.

9. See Lewis Feuer, *Conflict of Generations: The Character and Significance of Student Movements* (New York: Basic Books, 1969); Heinrich von Trietschke, *History of Germany in the Nineteenth Century,* vol. 3, trans. Eden Paul and Cedar Paul (New York: McBride, Nast, 1915).

10. K. H. Jarausch, "The Sources of German Student Unrest, 1815–1848," in *The University in Society,* ed. Lawrence Stone (Princeton, N.J.: Princeton University Press, 1974), 537–38; Trietschke, *History of Germany.*

11. Priscilla Robertson, "Students on the Barricades: Germany and Austria, 1848," in *Student Activism: Town and Gown in Historical Perspective,* ed. Alexander DeConde (New York: Charles Scribner's Sons, 1971), 59–71.

12. Koppel Pinson, *Modern Germany* (New York: Macmillan, 1966), 63–65.

13. Their self-definitions were anti-Semitic at times, and much of their eventual success and popularity was due to a growing popularity of such anti-Semitic sentiments, which, although unpalatable, certainly served to help define the group. One of the most important operations key to forming a powerful organization is the process of self-definition, usually achieved by identifying an enemy.

14. Trietschke, *History of Germany,* 58.

15. See Willis Rudy, *The Universities of Europe, 1100–1914: A History* (Rutherford, N.J.: Associated University Presses, 1984), 105–7. After Carl Sand assassinated Kotzebue, Follen moved to France; he ended up teaching at Harvard in the United States in 1825 under the name of Charles Follen, eventually became a Unitarian minister, and was an avid member of the American Anti-Slavery Society. See David F. Burg, *The Encyclopedia of Student and Youth Movements* (New York: Facts on File, 1998), 75; Feuer, *Conflict of Generations,* 59–68.

16. On Follen's rise to power, see Edmund Daniel Spevack, *Charles Follen's Search for Nationality and Freedom in Germany and America, 1795–1840,* (Ph.D. diss., Johns Hopkins University, 1993).

17. Hajo Holborn, *A History of Modern Germany, 1648–1840* (New York: Knopf, 1964), 465–66.

18. See Frank Thackeray, *Antecedents of Revolution: Alexander I and the Polish Kingdom, 1815–1825* (New York: Columbia University Press, 1980).

19. See Feuer, *Conflict of Generations,* 266–67.

20. Sheldon S. Cohen, "The Turkish Tyranny," *New England Quarterly* 47, no. 4 (1974): 564–83.

21. Lowell H. Harrison, "Rowdies, Riots, and Rebellions," *American History Illustrated* 7, no. 3 (1972): 18–29; James R. McGovern, "The Student Rebellion

in Harvard College, 1807–1808," *Harvard Library Bulletin* 19, no. 4 (1971): 341–55.

22. Oberlin College in Ohio, for example, had a reputation for antislavery sentiment before the Civil War and saw a number of abolitionist student demonstrations, but it also suffered from discriminatory practices well into the twentieth century. See David Diepenbrock, "Black Women and Oberlin College in the Age of Jim Crow," *UCLA Historical Journal* 13 (1993): 27–59.

23. See Donald L. Huber, "The Rise and Fall of Lane Seminary: An Antislavery Episode," *Timeline* 12, no. 3 (1995): 2–19.

24. Indeed many of the resistance actions occurring on campuses were more akin to unruly medieval uprisings; John F. Marszalek argues that U.S. universities sanctioned annual "rush weeks" on campuses in the eighteenth, nineteenth, and twentieth centuries to let such uprisings occur in semicontrolled fashion. John F. Marszalek, "The Class Rush—A Description," *Journal of Sports History* 17, no. 3 (1990); 366–68.

25. Kenneth Porter, "The Oxford-Cap War at Harvard," *New England Quarterly* 14 (1941): 77–83.

Chapter 3

1. Gustav Adolf Schoffel was one such student. Ejected from the University of Heidelberg for giving Communist tracts to peasants and trying to start a popular revolt, Schoffel nevertheless continued to agitate, this time for the Berlin uprising, in part by publishing an inflammatory paper and giving public speeches. After the initial uprising was smashed, he continued to agitate, for which he was arrested and jailed. After gaining his freedom, Schoffel became involved in the uprising in Baden and was killed. See Priscilla Robertson, "Students on the Barricades: Germany and Austria, 1848," *Student Activism: Town and Gown in Historical Perspective*, ed. Alexander DeConde (New York: Charles Scribner's Sons, 1971), 59–71.

2. Lola Montez was as notorious for her dancing as for her scandals: in her "spider dance" (a rendering of the Tarantella), she would spin sensually and gyrate while dropping artificial spiders from her petticoats, stamping on them.

3. Of course, not all student movements in the German states were so idealistic or political in nature, and not all German student groups radical or socially reformist. Following the revolution, students continued to form collectives, and fraternities sprang up throughout the confederation; some, like the *Burschenschaften*, were explicitly politically oriented, but many were not, and many were simply drinking clubs or dueling societies: the Korps, for example, which had existed prior to the revolution, was the elitest of the elite dueling fraternities; during the 1848 uprisings it defended conservative views.

4. The German and Austrian student involvement in the revolutions of 1848 were unique, but student involvement in politics was not unique to those countries.

Small groups of students agitated throughout Europe in other countries before the revolutions, such as in Italy and Switzerland. In the latter country, a movement of students and intellectuals called the Radicals had been openly fighting against Switzerland's cantons since 1839.

5. For an in-depth discussion of the Vienna Revolution, see R. J. Rath, *The Viennese Revolution of 1848* (Austin: University of Texas Press, 1957).

6. The students turned the great hall of the university into their political headquarters, and there they rested from their patrols, ate, and drank; they also threw parties in the hall and entertained women. See Priscilla Robertson, "Students on the Barricades," 59–71.

7. In 1894 Alfred Dreyfus was court-martialed for treason against France and sent to Devil's Island. Information later surfaced that another individual was responsible for the crimes ascribed to Dreyfus (giving military information to Germany), but a military trial of the man, Ferdinand Esterhazy, resulted in a verdict of not guilty in 1898. Riots broke out as the public split over the issue, with those supporting Dreyfus charging the military with anti-Semitism.

8. This idea would later find adherents in other cultures: John Locke formalized it into a contract theory of government; Montesquieu developed it in France; and it was incorporated into the American Declaration of Independence. It would be used time and again by revolutionaries in France and America. See E. H. Gwynne-Thomas, *A Concise History of Education to 1900 A.D.* (Washington, D.C.: University Press of America, 1981).

9. Willis Rudy, *The Universities of Europe, 1100–1914: A History* (Rutherford, N.J.: Associated University Presses, 1984), 24–25.

10. Although known earlier as "Peking," in keeping with recent historical trends and to convey continuity in the city's history of student actions, "Beijing" is used throughout. Cf. Jeffrey Wasserman, *Student Protests in Twentieth-Century China: The View from Shanghai* (Stanford, Calif.: Stanford University Press, 1991).

11. See Leslie Roos Jr., Noralou Roos, and Gary Field, "Students and Politics in Turkey," in DeConde, *Student Activism*, 144–46.

12. Cf. "The Bombay Students' Brotherhood," *Modern Review* 14 (March 1914): 264. See also Philip G. Altbach, *Student Politics in Bombay* (New York: Asia Publishing House, 1965).

13. See Joel Rosenthal, "Southern Black Student Activism: Assimilation vs. Nationalism," *Journal of Negro Education* 44, no. 2 (1975): 113–29.

14. See David Skilles Bogen, "The First Integration of the University of Maryland School of Law," *Maryland Historical Magazine* 84, no. 1 (1989): 39–49.

15. In the mid-seventeenth century, academies modeled on Jesuit schools were founded in Kiev and in Moscow, but these were primarily theologically oriented. The University of Moscow was founded in 1755, but it was not a center of scholarship until the nineteenth century.

16. This demanded an immediate reform of Russia's lower educational system: not

only did Latin suddenly need to be taught, but education in Latin demanded shifts in perception, with the classical language reorganizing how students thought; it also demanded educational materials be imported or produced, such as texts written in Latin.

17. See Abraham Kreusler, "U.S.S.R.," *Perspectives on World Education*, ed. Carlton Beck (Milwaukee: University of Wisconsin, 1970); Samuel D. Kassow, *Students, Professors, and the State in Tsarist Russia* (Berkeley and Los Angeles: University of California Press, 1989).

18. See Avram Yarmolinsky, *Road to Revolution: A Century of Russian Radicalism* (New York: Macmillan, 1962).

19. On the self-destructive cycle of repression and retaliation in Russia at the time and its effect on Karakozov's assassination attempt, see Lewis Feuer, *Conflict of Generations* (New York: Basic Books, 1969), 128–29.

20. See Feuer, *Conflict of Generations*, 93.

21. See Daniel Brower, *Training the Nihilists: Education and Radicalism in Tsarist Russia* (Ithaca, N.Y.: Cornell University Press, 1975).

22. For a detailed account of the evolution of the radical Russian revolutionary groups of the time, see Yarmolinsky's *Road to Revolution: A Century of Russian Radicalism*.

23. Feuer, *Conflict of Generations*, 136.

24. Russia eventually instituted some limited reforms following a government report by a special state investigative commission that the students indeed had valid complaints (some apolitical organizations were subsequently allowed, but students were warned against joining political groups).

Chapter 4

1. On the many organizations for European youth during this time, see Walter Laqueur, *Young Germany: A History of the German Youth Movement* (New York: Basic Books, 1962).

2. By 1927, over half of the male youth of Germany and over one quarter of the female youth belonged to youth organizations. See Laqueur, *Young Germany.*

3. On the early-twentieth-century German studentry and its evolution into National Socialism, see Michael Stephen Steinberg, *Sabers and Brown Shirts: The German Students' Path to National Socialism* (Chicago: University of Chicago Press, 1977).

4. Toller's plays include *Transfiguration* (1919) and *Masses and Man* (1922); his autobiography, *I Was a German*, was published in 1933. On Toller and the Munich uprising, see M. J. Bonn, *The Wandering Scholar* (New York: Day: 1948).

5. For example, Peter Karpovich made an appointment to see Education Minister Nicholas Bogolepov in his office, where Karpovich shot and killed him. Avrahm Yarmolinsky, *Road to Revolution: A Century of Russian Radicalism* (New York: Macmillan, 1962).

6. For example, after the attack on and sentencing of the Moscow students in 1902, a student assassinated Minister of the Interior Dmitri Sipyagin and was apprehended and hanged. In protest, students at several Russian universities called a strike, which was summarily suppressed, and arrested members were shipped off to Siberia by Vyacheslav Plehve, Sipyagin's replacement. In 1904 Plehve was assassinated by a student, and the wheel of destruction began yet another revolution (Yarmolinsky, *Road to Revolution*).

7. See Abraham Ascher, *The Revolution of 1905: Russia in Disarray* (Stanford, Calif.: Stanford University Press, 1988).

8. Thousands of students and workers met at a political rally at St. Petersburg University in October, for instance, where students not only encouraged revolution but raised money to buy arms.

9. Ascher, *The Revolution of 1905.*

10. Of course the students countered with strikes, including a nationwide protest in 1908, but without popular issues they could not generate the power needed to seriously threaten the state, and they found themselves in a desperate situation without allies. Samuel Kassow, *Students, Professors, and the State in Tsarist Russia* (Berkeley: University of California Press, 1989).

11. See Isaac Steinberg, *Spiridonova: Revolutionary Terrorist* (Freeport, N.Y.: Books for Libraries Press, 1971).

12. On student resistance in Hungary, see Ferenc Vali, *Rift and Revolt in Hungary* (Cambridge: Harvard University Press, 1961); and Hans-Georg Heinrich, *Hungary: Politics, Economics, and Society* (Boulder, Colo.: Lynn Rienner, 1986).

13. Princip and a colleague both died in prison while serving their twenty-year sentences. For a psychological analysis of Gavrilo Princip, including excerpts from the notes made by his psychiatrist, Martin Pappenheim, see Lewis Feuer, *Conflict of Generations* (New York: Basic Books, 1969), 82–87.

14. Chou Tse-tsung, *May Fourth Movement* (Cambridge: Harvard University Press, 1960).

15. On the Shanghai Protests and the May Fourth Movement, see Jeffrey N. Wasserstrom, *Student Protests in Twentieth-Century China: The View from Shanghai* (Stanford: Stanford University Press, 1991), 41–71.

16. See Chou, *The May Fourth Movement*; Wen-Lan Kiang, *The Chinese Student Movement* (New York: King's Crown, 1948).

17. Mao Zedong would later call the May Fourth Movement the "June Third Movement" in an effort to downplay the students and stress the role of workers in the victory (it was on June 3 that workers backed the demonstrating students by going on strike).

18. See Frank Bonilla and Myron Glazer, *Student Politics in Chile* (New York: Basic Books, 1969).

19. See Richard J. Walter, *Student Politics in Argentina: The University Reform and Its Effects, 1918–1964* (New York: Basic Books, 1968).

20. David F. Burg, *Encyclopedia of Student and Youth Movements* (New York: Facts on File, 1998), 175–76.

21. Max Horn, *The Intercollegiate Socialist Society, 1905–1921: Origins of the Modern American Student Movement* (Boulder, Colo.: Westview Press, 1979).

22. In 1902 student activists openly defied a Board of Health quarantine at the University of Nevada at Reno during a smallpox epidemic (Sally Springmeyer Zanjani, "George Springmeyer and the Quarantine Rebellion of 1902: Student Revolt Reaches the University of Nevada," *Nevada Historical Society Quarterly* 23, no. 4 [1980]: 283–89).

Chapter 5

1. See Harry Kantor, *The Ideology and Program of the Peruvian Aprista Movement* (New York: Octagon, 1966).

2. Judith Ewell, *Venezuela: A Century of Change* (Stanford: Stanford University Press, 1984).

3. See Richard J. Walter, *Student Politics in Argentina: The University Reform and Its Effects, 1918–1964* (New York: Basic Books, 1968).

4. On social movements in individual countries and the effect of students on them, see Arturo Escobar and Sonia El Alvarez, eds., *The Making of Social Movements in Latin America* (Boulder, Colo.: Westview Press, 1992).

5. At the same time, Chinese students studying abroad formed Communist groups of their own, organizations that would have a subsequent impact on China. Students from the foreign-based Communist groups who returned to China to play key roles in China's future included Chou En-lai and Deng Xiaoping.

6. Jeffrey N. Wasserstrom, *Student Bodies in Twentieth-Century China: The View from Shanghai* (Stanford, Calif.: Stanford University Press, 1991), 27–50.

7. On the relationship between the May Thirtieth Movement and the development of the Chinese Communist Party, see James P. Harrison, *The Long March to Power: A History of the Chinese Communist Party, 1921–1972* (New York: Praeger, 1972).

8. See A. Richard Rigby, *The May 30th Movement* (Canberra, Australia: Griffin, 1980).

9. The majority of students supported the government, but many of course did not. Hsi-nan University, for example, incited Communist-backed student protests in the province before the government closed it down. Students who resisted were imprisoned, and police brutally terrorized students throughout the province.

10. In the 1930s, an extremist group of Chiang Kai-shek followers formed called the Blue Shirts, with members placed in key positions in school military programs; they recruited many students and were fervently anti-Communist. See Maria Hsia Chang, *The Chinese Blue Shirts: Fascism and Developmental Nationalism* (Berkeley and Los Angeles: University of California Press, 1985).

11. On the proliferation of underground student groups in China, see Jean Chesneaux, ed., *Popular Movements and Secret Societies in China, 1840–1950* (Stanford: Stanford University Press, 1972).

12. John Israel and David Klein, *Rebels and Bureaucrats: China's December 9ers* (Berkeley and Los Angeles: University of California Press, 1976).

13. See John Israel, *Student Nationalism in China, 1927–1937* (Stanford: Stanford University Press, 1966).

14. See Harrison, *Long March to Power.*

15. Gregory Henderson argues that student activism has played a greater role in Korea's national politics than in any other country's. For a discussion of the history of this role, see his *Korea: The Politics of the Vortex* (Cambridge: Cambridge University Press, 1968).

16. See Michiya Shimbori, "Comparison between Pre- and Post-War Student Movements in Japan," *Sociology of Education* 37 (fall 1963): 59–70.

17. Harsja Bachtiar, "Indonesia," in *Student Political Activism: An International Reference Handbook*, ed. Philip G. Altbach (New York: Greenwood Press, 1989), 106–7.

18. For a discussion of pre- and post-independence student movements in India, see Reavathi Narsimhan, "Student Movements in India: A Post-Independence Survey," *Indian Journal of Youth Affairs* 2, no. 1 (1980): 37–48.

19. See Philip Altbach, *Student Politics in Bombay* (Bombay and New York: Asia Publishing House, 1965).

20. See Donald K. Emmerson, "Africa Student Organizations: The Politics of Discontent," *African Report* 10 (May 1965).

21. See Konrad Jarausch, *Students, Society, and Politics in Imperial Germany: The Rise of Academic Illiberalism* (Princeton, N.J.: Princeton University Press, 1982).

22. See Michael Stephen Steinberg, *Sabers and Brown Shirts: The German Students' Path to National Socialism, 1918–1935* (Chicago: University of Chicago Press, 1977).

23. See Karl Stern, *The Pillar of Fire* (Garden City, N.Y.: Image Books, 1951); Lewis Feuer, *Conflict of Generations* (New York: Basic Books, 1969), 288.

24. In addition to organizing the National Socialist German Student Union in 1929 and being appointed the Nazi Party youth leader in 1931, Schirach became the leader of the Hitler youth. Schirach published a number of books, including *Hitler, wie ihn Keiner Kent* (1932), and *Triumph des Willens* (1932), as well as a collection of poems (1934). As a soldier he was awarded the German Iron Cross, and in 1940 was made governor of Vienna. Shirach repudiated Hitler following the war, however; nevertheless he was sentenced to prison and served twenty years for war crimes.

25. Other fraternities, especially the right-wing dueling fraternities, embraced Nazi principles, excluding Jews and Freemasons, for example, long before the Nazi union dominated university organizations.

26. Germany and France were not alone in hosting a trend toward fascism among large portions of its studentry, and in some European countries the success of student fascist organizations more closely paralleled Germany's. In Italy, for example, the Gruppi Universitaria Fascisti (formed in 1920) became a prominent national student organization promoting fascism. See Tracy H. Koon, *Believe, Obey, Fight: Political Socialization of Youth in Fascist Italy, 1922–1943* (Chapel Hill: University of North Carolina Press, 1985).

27. In *Conflict of Generations* (271–73), Lewis Feuer suggests that Etudiants Action Française members were rebelling against their Republican, liberal fathers, becoming self-proclaimed royalists in a national oedipal drive; he suggests that UNEF was right in viewing right-wing student activists as pawns of larger powers, though Feuer suggests those powers were psychosociological rather than political.

28. See Belden A. Fields, *Student Politics in France: A Study of the Union Nationale des Etudiants de France* (New York: Basic Books, 1970).

29. The striking students were reacting to more issues than those concerning Professor Scelle, many of which revolved around the government at the time. Premier Edouard Herriot, already beset by greater difficulties than those concerning education, however, also resigned during the student strikes. He would return to power in 1932, but not last the year out as premier.

30. Right-wing students also supported Mussolini's invasion of Ethiopia; many of the activists saw fascism as the quickest way to overthrow the bourgeoisie and introduce socialism. See Feuer, *Conflict of Generations*, 270–75.

31. Intercollegiate right-wing and leftist organizations existed, but even they fought primarily localized battles; it was not until the 1920s that students began national organization efforts, though most continued to fight local battles. See, for example, Marcia Lynn Johnson, "Student Protest at Fisk University in the 1920s," *Negro History Bulletin* 33, no. 6 (1970): 137–40.

32. See Robert Paul Cohen, *Revolt of the Depression Generation: America's First Mass Student Protest Movement, 1929–1940.* (Ph.D. diss., University of California, Berkeley, 1987).

33. The evolution of Agnes Ryan's activist efforts mirror the transformations of those occurring across the United States in the 1920s and '30s. The suffragist and pacifist began meeting with students locally and formed a peace group in the 1920s, and by the '30s she was participating in a national disarmament tour. In 1939 she sponsored the New Hampshire Student Peace Service and later founded a school for nonviolence. See Marcia R. Rollison, "Agnes Ryan and the New Hampshire Peace Movement," *Historical New Hampshire* 50, nos. 3–4 (1995): 184–212.

34. See Robert Cohen, *When the Old Left Was Young: Student Radicals and America's First Mass Student Movement* (New York: Oxford University Press, 1993).

35. On the development of U.S. student peace movements, see Patti M. Peterson,

"Student Organization and the Anti-War Movement in America, 1900–1960," *American Studies* 13, no. 1 (1972): 131–47.

36. The National Student League and the Student League for Industrial Democracy continued to fight locally as well: in 1935, for example, they successfully campaigned against a New York bill that would have forced students to take loyalty oaths. See Cohen, *When the Old Left Was Young.*

37. Ralph S. Brax, "When Students First Organized against the War," *New-York Historical Society Quarterly* 63, no. 3 (1979): 228–55.

38. The cooperation among student groups with various and often hostile ideologies under the auspices of organizations such as the American Student Union during the 1930s was referred to as the Student United Front, which lasted until Germany invaded Poland and a world war became imminent; as more and more countries were drawn into the conflict, the U.S. student factions increasingly resumed their previous antagonisms.

39. For an in-depth discussions of the major student organizations and actions occurring during the 1930s, see Ralph S. Brax, *The First Student Movement: Student Activism in the United States during the 1930s* (Port Washington, N.Y.: Kennikat Press, 1981); and Cohen, *When the Old Left Was Young.*

40. On these various organizations, see David F. Burg, *The Encyclopedia of Student and Youth Movements* (New York: Facts on File, 1998).

Chapter 6

1. A number of students voiced opposition to the Nazis, and many demonstrated at the outset of the war, but they were quickly silenced. Groups such as White Rose in Munich protested fascism as long as they could, but during the war students suspected of resistance faced arrest, probable torture, and, often, execution.

2. According to Jean-Pierre Worms, in 1940 the university enrollment in France was at 55,000 (down from 80,000 the year before), but in 1943 the figure rose to 106,000. Worms, "The French Student Movement," in *Student Activism: Town and Gown in Historical Perspective,* ed. Alexander DeConde (New York: Charles Scribner's Sons, 1971), 72–86.

3. See A. Belden Fields, *Student Politics in France: A Study of the Union Nationale des Étudiants de France* (New York: Basic Books, 1970).

4. For more on the Algerian student independence movement, see Donald K. Emmerson, ed., *Students and Politics in Developing Nations* (New York: Praeger, 1968).

5. For a detailed description of the revolt, see Ferenc Vali, *Rift and Revolt in Hungary* (Cambridge: Harvard University Press, 1961).

6. Hans-Georg Heinrich, *Hungary: Politics, Economics, and Society* (Boulder, Colo.: Lynne Rienner, 1986).

7. George Z. F. Bereday, "Social Cleavage: Warsaw," in DeConde, *Student Activism,* 135–42.

8. See Stuart J. Dowsey, ed., *Zengakuren: Japan's Revolutionary Students* (Berkeley, Calif.: Ishi Press, 1970).

9. Japan's protesting studentry received international attention and condemnation from the press when they attacked the car of Eisenhower's press secretary, James Hagerty, upon his arrival in Tokyo on June 10; Hagerty had to be rescued by helicopter.

10. See John Israel, "Reflections on the Modern Chinese Student Movement," in DeConde, *Student Activism*, 165–89.

11. See Suzanne Pepper, *Civil War in China: The Political Struggle, 1945–1949* (Berkeley and Los Angeles: University of California Press, 1978).

12. See Jeffrey Wasserstrom, *Student Protests in Twentieth-Century China: The View from Shanghai* (Stanford, Calif.: Stanford University Press, 1991), 149–239.

13. For an overview of student actions during the civil war, see Jessie Lutz, "The Chinese Student Movement of 1945–1949," *Journal of Asian Studies* 31, no. 1 (1971): 89–110; Pepper, *Civil War in China*.

14. At the University of Rangoon, for example, Burmese students went on strike repeatedly in the 1950s, protesting against university reforms. Prime Minister U Nu originally permitted the strikers to assemble before sending police troops to disperse them. In what became a cycle of protest and suppression, the leaders were arrested, which sparked protests for their release.

15. N. Jayaram, "India," in *Student Political Activism: An International Reference Handbook*, ed. Philip G. Altbach (New York: Greenwood Press, 1989), 92.

16. Philip G. Altbach, "The Transformation of the Indian Student Movement," *Asian Survey* 6, no. 8 (August 1966): 448–60.

17. For a general survey of African organizations and the roles of their leaders, see Donald K. Emmerson, "African Student Organizations: The Politics of Discontent," *African Report* 10 (May 1965): 6–12.

18. Many leaders of African independence movements and independent African governments received their political training in student resistance organizations. Following the Ivory Coast's 1960 independence from France, the government was, for instance, filled with men who had at one time been student leaders. Cf. Emmerson, *Students and Politics*.

19. Emmerson, "African Student Organizations."

20. Student activists at the Jewish Theological Seminary in New York City pressured the Synagogue Council of America to begin a nationwide program in 1943 to educate U.S. citizens about the ongoing Holocaust and the moral need for U.S. intervention. See Rafael Medoff, "'Retribution Is Not Enough': The 1943 Campaign by Jewish Students to Raise American Public Awareness of the Nazi Genocide," *Holocaust and Genocide Studies* 11, no. 2 (1997): 171–89.

21. Rodolph Leslie Schnell, *National Activist Student Organizations in American Higher Education, 1905–1944* (Ann Arbor: University of Michigan Press, 1976).

22. Some socialist groups survived the winter of the Cold War. The Young Socialist

Alliance, for example, was founded in 1959 as a federation of weakened and highly factionalized socialist organizations. In the 1960s the alliance would rise again to protest war.

23. Amy F. Pfeiffenberger, "Democracy at Home: The Struggle to Desegregate Washington University in the Post-War Era," *Gateway Heritage* 10, no. 3 (1989–90): 14–25.

24. See Arthur Liebman, *The Politics of Puerto Rican University Students* (Austin: University of Texas Press, 1970).

25. Hugh Thomas, *The Cuban Revolution* (New York: Harper and Row, 1977).

26. Philippe Schmitter, *Interest, Conflict, and Political Change in Brazil* (Stanford, Calif.: Stanford University Press, 1971), 206–7.

27. Jim Handy, *Gift of the Devil: A History of Guatemala* (Boston: South End Press, 1984).

28. See Judith Ewell, *Venezuela: A Century of Change* (Stanford, Calif.: Stanford University Press, 1984).

29. Paul H. Lewis, *Socialism, Liberalism, and Dictatorship in Paraguay* (New York: Paragon, 1982). In Chile, students led by the Federación de Estudiantes de Chile also protested against an increase in transportation fares and were temporarily successful in obtaining lower rates from the government; after a series of demonstrations in which one student was killed, bus fares were reduced; but once the students calmed down, the rates were again raised. See Frank Bonilla and Myron Lazer, *Student Politics in Chile* (New York: Basic Books, 1970).

30. In 1945 the Agrupación Feminina Universitaria formed as one of the first Argentinean women's political organizations. David F. Burg, *The Encyclopedia of Student and Youth Movements* (New York: Facts on File, 1998), 35.

31. But in 1958 the new president, Arturo Frondizi, saw the opportunity to increase his favor among powerful Catholics if he allowed the founding of private Catholic universities; students held huge demonstrations that temporarily blocked the establishment of private colleges. Nevertheless, Argentina's Congress did subsequently pass a bill granting legitimacy to private colleges. Burg, *The Encyclopedia of Student and Youth Movements,* 15; Richard J. Walter, Student *Politics in Argentina: The University Reform and Its Effects, 1918–1964* (New York: Basic Books, 1964).

Chapter 7

1. The student groups targeted for destruction by the military after 1961 included those that were politically radical, like the socialist or anti-imperialist groups that advocated the rejoining of North and South Korea.

2. For in-depth discussions of Korea's student uprisings, see William Douglas, "Korean Students and Politics," *Asian Survey* 3, no. 12 (December 1963): 584–95; and Andrew C. Nahm, *Korea: Tradition and Transformation* (Elizabeth, N.J.: Hollym International, 1988).

3. See Stuart J. Dowsey, ed., *Zengakuren: Japan's Revolutionary Students* (Berkeley, Calif.: Ishi Press, 1970).

4. Ellis S. Krauss, *Japanese Radicals Revisited: Student Protest in Postwar Japan* (Berkeley and Los Angeles: University of California Press, 1974); Dowsey, ed., *Zengakuren.*

5. Michael Howard and Wm. Roger Louis, *Oxford History of the Twentieth Century* (New York: Oxford University Press, 1998), 222–24.

6. Jeffrey Wasserstrom, *Student Protests in Twentieth-Century China: The View from Shanghai* (Stanford, Calif.: Stanford University Press, 1991), 296, 302–6. See also Jeffrey Wasserstrom and Elizabeth Perry, eds., *Popular Protest and Political Culture in Modern* China (Boulder, Colo.: Westview Press, 1992); Hong Yung Lee, *The Politics of the Chinese Cultural Revolution: A Case Study* (Berkeley and Los Angeles: University of California Press, 1978).

7. Before 1965 Indonesian Communist student groups had attempted to ban oppositional groups from university campuses.

8. Harsja W. Bachtiar, "Indonesia," in *Students and Politics in Developing Nations,* ed. Donald K. Emmerson (New York: Praeger, 1968), 180–214.

9. Arief Budiman, "Student Movement in Indonesia," *Asian Survey* 18, no. 6 (June 1978): 614–25.

10. The demonstrations only delayed the nationalization of Hindi; they did not prevent it. Philip G. Altbach, "The Transformation of the Indian Student Movement," *Asian Survey* 6, no. 8 (August 1966): 448–60.

11. For an evolution of Indian student movements, see Reavathi Narsimhan, "Student Movements in India: A Post-Independence Survey," *Indian Journal of Youth Affairs* 2 (March 1980): 37–48.

12. One reason the union took so long to take a stand was the fear of its own subsequent disintegration. Although many student groups left the Union Nationale over the Algerian issue, others remained, though they publicly voiced dissent. See A. Beldon Fields, *Student Politics in France: A Study of the Union Nationale Etudiants de France* (New York: Basic Books, 1970).

13. Cyril Levitt, "Federal Republic of Germany," in *Student Political Activism,* ed. Philip G. Altbach (Westport, Conn.: Greenwood Press, 1989), 212.

14. See Cyril Levitt, *Children of Privilege: Student Revolt in the Sixties, a Study of Student Movements in Canada, the United States, and West Germany* (Toronto: University of Toronto Press, 1984).

15. Levitt, "Federal Republic of Germany." On medical student actions, see Uta Gerhardt, "The Sociology of Health/Medical Sociology in the Federal Republic of Germany," *Research in the Sociology of Health Care* 8 (1989): 275–88.

16. Eva Weller and Willfried van der Will, *Protest in Western Germany,* ed. Julian Nagel (London: Merlin Press, 1969), 49–52.

17. On the following day, April 6, 1967, Commune students and the SDS held a widely publicized demonstration against Humphrey in Berlin.

18. Russian students sympathetic to those in Czechoslovakia actually demonstrated in Red Square following the 1968 invasion of Czechoslovakia, though they suffered greatly for it.

19. See Leslie L. Roos Jr., Noralou P. Roos, and Gary R. Field, "Students and Politics in Turkey," *Daedalus* 97, no. 1 (winter 1968): 184–200.

20. See Ben Magubane, "Before Soweto and After: The Struggle for Liberation," *Christianity and Crisis* 38, no. 3 (1978): 41–44.

21. Cf. Colin J. Bundy, "South Africa," in Altbach, *Student Political Activism*, 23–36; Martin Murray, *South Africa: Time of Agony, Time of Destiny* (London: Verso, 1987); and Mokubung O. Nkomo, *Student Culture and Activism in Black South African Universities* (Westport, Conn.: Greenwood Press, 1984).

22. See Emmerson, *Students and Politics.*

23. For interviews with activists involved in the Greensboro sit-ins, see Eugene Pfaff, "Greensboro Sit-Ins," *Southern Exposure* 9, no. 1 (1981): 23–28.

24. For a study of the sit-in movement, see Aldon Morris, "Black Southern Student Sit-In Movement: An Analysis of Internal Organization," *American Sociological Review* 46, no. 6 (1981): 744–46. For an analysis of a specific sit-in movement, see David E. Sumner, "The Nashville Student Movement," *American History Illustrated* 23, no. 2 (1988): 28–31.

25. Students employed direct-action tactics aimed at desegregation all over the United States, not just in the South. Particularly effective nonsouthern campaigns were fought in California and Texas. See Henry J. Gutierrez, "Racial Politics in Los Angeles: Black and Mexican American Challenges to Unequal Education in the 1960s," *Southern California Quarterly* 78, no. 1 (1996): 51–86; Martin Kuhlman, "Direct Action at the University of Texas during the Civil Rights Movement, 1960–65," *Southwestern Historical Quarterly* 98, no. 4 (1995): 550–66.

26. Julian Bond, one of the participants of the Atlanta actions of March 15, would gain national notoriety for his subsequent role in the civil rights struggle.

27. Clayborne Carson, *In Struggle: SNCC and the Black Awakening of the 1960s* (Cambridge: Harvard University Press, 1981).

28. On the 1960–61 student tactics, see David J. Garrow, ed., *Atlanta, Georgia, 1960–1961: Sit-ins and Student Activism* (Brooklyn, N.Y.: Carlson, 1989). For a personal narrative of a 1960 sit-in, see Merrill Proudfoot, *Diary of a Sit-In* (Urbana: University of Illinois Press, 1990).

29. SNCC's success was in large part due to the work of its female members, although the male members often received the lion's share of the publicity and much of the credit. On the work of Ruby Doris Smith Robinson and other women activists associated with the organization, see Cynthia Griggs Fleming, "Black Women Activists and the Student Non-Violent Coordinating Committee: The Case of Ruby Doris Smith Robinson," *Journal of Women's History* 4, no. 3 (1993): 64–82.

30. James Farmer, president of CORE, organized the Freedom Riders, and the first

two buses began their ill-fated journey across the South in May 1961 with Farmer among the passengers; after the destruction of the buses (one was burned and the other overrun by racists with clubs), CORE stopped its support of the effort. SNCC continued the campaign and provided support and future participants. The Freedom Riders were eventually effective, and reluctantly the Interstate Commerce Commission banned segregated travel and facilities. See Robert Weisbrot, *Freedom Bound: A History of America's Civil Rights Movement* (New York: Penguin, 1991); and Doug McAdam, *Freedom Summer* (New York: Oxford University Press, 1988).

31. The integration of public schools, especially elementary and secondary schools, in the United States had tremendous effects politically, socially, and culturally. Not only did it contribute to the "white flight" phenomenon in U.S. cities, but it also sparked a significant rise in private schools catering to white students, which reinforced class distinctions in higher education.

32. In 1970 students at the University of Mississippi formed the Black Student Union to organize further campaigns for student equality; in protests held almost a decade after integration they claimed African-American students still had second-class status on the Oxford campus. See Anthony W. James, "A Demand for Racial Equality: The 1970 Black Student Protest at the University of Mississippi," *Journal of Mississippi History* 57, no. 2 (1995): 97–120. For an analysis of an African-American student movement on a typical U.S. campus (University College, New York) during the 1960s and '70s, see William H. Exum, *Paradoxes of Protest: Black Student Activism in a White University* (Philadelphia: Temple University Press, 1985).

33. For an analysis of the social influences that determine the likelihood of a U.S. student becoming an activist in the 1960s, see Darren E. Sherkat and T. Jean Blocker, "The Political Development of Sixties Activists: Identifying the Influence of Class, Gender, and Socialization on Protest Participation," *Social Forces* 72, no. 3 (1994): 821–42. On the impact of gender on the activist process, see Doug McAdam, "Gender as a Mediator of the Activist Experience: The Case of Freedom Summer," *American Journal of Sociology* 97, no. 5 (1991): 1211–40.

34. James Chaney, Andrew Goodman, and Michael Schwerner were the murdered students.

35. See McAdam, *Freedom Summer.*

36. See Emily Stoper, "The Student Nonviolent Coordinating Committee: Rise and Fall of a Redemptive Organization," *Journal of Black Studies* 8, no. 1 (1977): 13–34.

37. After traveling through the South with SNCC during the start of the decade, Hayden gained some notoriety after writing about his experiences, which included his arrest in 1961 and the violent reactions he witnessed to SNCC; see Ronald Fraser, *1968: A Student Generation in Revolt* (New York: Pantheon, 1988), 61. On Hayden's political evolution and career, see Jonathan Weiss, "Tom

Hayden's Political Evolution during the New Left Years: Rebel without a Theory," *Michigan Journal of Political Science* 5 (1984): 1–38.

38. See James Miller, *"Democracy in the Streets": From Port Huron to the Siege of Chicago* (New York: Simon and Schuster, 1987).

39. For an early discussion of the New Left's development, see Staughton Lynd, "The New Left," *Annals of the American Academy of Political and Social Science* 382 (1969): 64–72.

40. See Martha Webb Carithers, "A Social Movement Career: National SDS" (Ph.D. diss., University of Kansas, 1982).

41. See Mark Reed Stoner, "The Free Speech Movement: A Case Study in the Rhetoric of Social Intervention" (Ph.D. diss., Ohio State University, 1987).

42. The arrested student was Jack Weinberg. On the evolution and the social importance of the Berkeley student uprisings see W. J. Rorabaugh, *Berkeley at War: The 1960s* (New York: Oxford University Press, 1989).

43. See Janet Harris, "Berkeley," in *Students in Revolt*, ed. Janet Harris (New York: McGraw-Hill, 1970), 25–42.

44. For an analysis of how the media reacted to the Berkeley movement, see Susan Saunders, *Berkeley's Free Speech Movement: A Study in Press Reaction to First Amendment Issues* (Ph.D. diss., University of Washington, 1989).

45. After the Berkeley revolt, SDS membership across the country soared. For a variety of contemporary accounts and analyses of the Berkeley revolt, see Seymour Lipset and Sheldon Wolin, eds. *The Berkeley Student Revolt* (Garden City, N.Y.: Doubleday, 1965).

46. In 1969 the Young Lords seized and occupied a neighborhood church for over a week, calling for space in the church from which free food could be distributed to ghetto children. Surrounded by police and the press, the Young Lords finally surrendered and were arrested. They were released when the church, the city, and the students negotiated the establishment of a church day-care center. David Burg, *Encyclopedia of Student and Youth Movements* (New York: Facts on File, 1998), 227.

47. In 1965 an antiwar demonstration organized by the Vietnam Day Committee held at the University of California at Berkeley campus drew over two thousand participants; the committee almost immediately fell prey to factionalism and self-destructed after the event, however. See Gerard J. DeGroot, "The Limits of Moral Protest and Participatory Democracy: The Vietnam Day Committee," *Pacific Historical Review* 64, no. 1 (1995): 95–119.

48. See Marialyce O'Connor Gottschalk, *The Student Power Movement at the UW-Madison Campus, 1966–1968* (Ph.D. diss., University of Wisconsin, 1987).

49. Some campus antiwar efforts were effective. Students and faculty effectively protested against the University of Pennsylvania's contracts with the U.S. Defense Department and convinced the administration to end its sponsorship of government chemical and biological weaponry research and development for

the Vietnam War effort. Jonathan Goldstein, "Vietnam Research on Campus: The Summit/Spicerack Controversy at the University of Pennsylvania, 1965–67," *Peace and Change* 11, no. 2 (1986): 27–43.

50. In 1967 the International Student Conference, which was formed as the Western opponent to the International Union of Students in 1950, suffered a similar fate as it was rumored that the CIA also funded them.

51. See Lewis Feuer, *Conflict of Generations* (New York: Basic Books, 1969), 239–40.

52. Potential student revolutionaries took note when Castro acknowledged his indebtedness to students in his "I am a Marxist-Leninist" speech (December 2, 1961). Feuer, *Conflict of Generations*, 249.

53. See Arturo Escobar and Sonia El Alvarez, *The Making of Social Movements in Latin America* (Boulder, Colo.: Westview, 1992); James R. Whelan, *Out of the Ashes: Life, Death, and Transfiguration in Chile, 1833–1988* (Washington, D.C.: Regency, 1989); Harry Kantor, *The Ideology and the Program of the Peruvian Aprista Movement* (New York: Octagon, 1966); and Judith Ewell, *Venezuela: A Century of Change* (Stanford, Calif.: Stanford University Press, 1984).

Chapter 8

1. Greil Marcus, *Lipstick Traces: A Secret History of the Twentieth Century* (London: Secker and Warburg, 1989), 426–29. The Situationists were a volatile group of anarchists who had a great influence on European urban activists and the intellectual and artistic avant-garde. They published their ideas in their journal *Situationist International,* and sought the destruction of all bourgeois enterprises, including those associated with publishing (one of their publications, for example, was bound in sandpaper so that it would destroy whatever books it had the fortune to be shelved between). For a comprehensive collection of Situationist writings and concepts, see *Situationist International Anthology*, ed. Ken Knabb (Berkeley, Calif.: Bureau of Public Secrets, 1981).

2. Marcus, *Lipstick Traces*, 427.

3. Cited in ibid, 427.

4. On Cohn-Bendit's relationship to the Paris revolt, see Ronald Fraser et al., *1968: A Student Generation in Revolt* (New York: Pantheon, 1988), 203–30; Marcus, *Lipstick Traces*, 426–29.

5. See George Ross and Laura Frader, "The May Generation from Mao to Mitterand," *Socialist Review* 18, no. 4 (1988): 105–16.

6. See Bernard E. Brown, *Protest in Paris: Anatomy of a Revolt* (Morristown, N.J.: General Learning Press, 1974).

7. Frustrated in France, Cohn-Bendit traveled to and unsuccessfully agitated in Germany for two years for labor reform. He retired from activism in 1970 to run a bookstore in Frankfurt, and in 1975 he published his autobiography, *Le Grand Bazar.*

8. Fraser, *1968*, 233–34.

9. Devlin served a six-month sentence for her role in the Derry riots; she was reelected to Westminster in 1970, and expressed the view that the turn from defensive actions to active terrorism was, among other things, a strategic mistake for the reform movement. In 1981 she and her husband were wounded and very nearly assassinated by a Protestant extremist.

10. Fraser, *1968*, 274–76.

11. See also Colin Crouch, *The Student Revolt* (London: Bodley Head, 1970).

12. See Students and Staff of Hornsey College of Art, *The Hornsey Affair* (Harmondsworth, England: Penguin, 1969).

13. The rage for large-scale demonstrating among university students even spread to Denmark, a nation not known for its student uprisings; in 1968 students peacefully protested for university reforms at Copenhagen University and occupied some of the university buildings.

14. On the Baader-Meinhof Gang, see Jillian Becker, *Hitler's Children: The Story of the Baader-Meinhof Terrorist Gang* (Philadelphia: Lippincott, 1977).

15. For a discussion of the Italian student-worker unions constructed from student veterans of the movement, see Fraser, *1968*, 248–60.

16. Fear of Soviet aggression played a big part in political power struggles in Eastern Europe. See Seymour Martin Lipset, "The Possible Effects of Student Activism on International Politics," *Students In Revolt*, ed. Seymour Martin Lipset and Philip G. Altbach (Boston: Beacon Press, 1969), 495–521.

17. On the evolution of the Ethiopian student movement, see Alem Asres, "History of the Ethiopian Student Movement (in Ethiopia and North America): Its Impact on Internal Social Change, 1960–1974" (Ph. D. diss., University of Maryland, 1990).

18. See William John Hanna, *University Students and African Politics* (New York: Africana, 1975), 15–16.

19. David Burg, *Encyclopedia of Student and Youth Movements* (New York: Facts on File, 1998), 124.

20. Burg, *Encyclopedia of Student and Youth Movements*, 11.

Chapter 9

1. See Michiya Shimbori, "Japan," in *Student Political Activism*, ed. Philip G. Altbach (New York: Greenwood Press, 1989), 137–55.

2. See Stuart J. Dowsey, ed., *Zengakuren: Japan's Revolutionary Students* (Berkeley, Calif.: Ishi Press, 1970).

3. Shimbori, "Japan," 143.

4. See Arturo Escobar and Sonia E. Alvarez, eds., *The Making of Social Movements in Latin America* (Boulder, Colo.: Westview Press, 1992).

5. See Julio Scherer and Carlos Monsiváis, *Parte de Guerre: Tlatelolco 1968* (Mexico City: Aguila, 1999).

6. The government has historically borne the blame for the event, and has often

been accused of orchestrating the crackdown. In 1999 excerpts of the private papers of General Garciá Barragán, secretary of defense in 1968, were published; the papers, released by Barragán's grandson, more explicitly implicate the presidential guard and President Diáz Ordaz. Scherer and Monsiváis, *Parte de Guerre: Tlatelolco 1968.*

7. See Evelyn P. Stevens, *Protest and Response in Mexico* (Cambridge, Mass.: MIT Press, 1974).

8. William C. Hine argues that much of the student discontent that led up to the 1967–68 conflicts and casualties centered around the policies and behavior of the college's president, Benner C. Turner, whom legislators loved but students and faculty resented. William C. Hine, "Civil Rights and Campus Wrongs: South Carolina Sate College Students Protest, 1955–1968," *South Carolina Historical Magazine* 97, no. 4 (1996): 310–31.

9. Many of the colleges spotlighted by the media already had extensive histories of activism; see, for example, Marcia Lynn Johnson, "Student Protest at Fisk University in the 1920s," *Negro History Bulletin* 33, no. 6 (1970): 137–40.

10. See Donald Cunnigen, "Malcolm X's Influence on the Black Nationalist Movement of Southern Black College Students," *Western Journal of Black Studies* 17, no. 1 (1993): 32–43.

11. See John S. Kunen, "The Strawberry Statement: Notes of a College Revolutionary," *Vietnam Generation* 3, no. 1 (1991): 48–57.

12. See Stephen Donadio, "Black Power at Columbia," *Commentary* 46, no. 3 (1968): 67–76.

13. An early member of SNCC, Tom Hayden worked for the organization in 1961 in Georgia and Mississippi. The principal author of the Port Huron Statement, Hayden was president of SDS during the academic year of 1962–63, and as an anti–Vietnam War activist, he subsequently made several journeys to Vietnam. He was also involved in the demonstrations during the 1968 Democratic Convention, and was subsequently tried for his involvement and participation in the Chicago riots. In 1971 he surfaced at the Berkeley People's Park protests. A decade later, however, the politically savvy Hayden was a representative in the state government of California.

14. See James Samuel Bowen, *Black Student Militance: Campus Unrest among Black Students, 1968–1972* (Ph. D. diss., Columbia University, 1982).

15. Ronald Fraser et al., *1968: A Generation in Revolt* (New York: Pantheon, 1985), 195–202.

16. For a narrative of the Columbia student revolts and an excerpt of Taylor's speech, see Janet Harris, *Students in Revolt* (New York: McGraw-Hill, 1970), 77.

17. For a history of Columbia student unrest and a discussion of university administration and student negotiations and strategies employed during the 1968 uprising, see Ellen Kay Trimberger, "Why a Rebellion at Columbia Was Inevitable," *Trans-action* 5, no. 9 (1968): 28–38.

18. See, for example, Diana Trilling, "On the Steps of Low Library: Liberalism and the Revolution of the Young," *Commentary* 46, no. 5 (1968): 29–55.

19. Joanne Grant, *Confrontation on Campus: The Columbia Pattern for the New Protest* (New York: Signet, 1969).

20. Pennsylvania's governor (1967–1971), Raymond P. Shafer, for example, ascribed the scarcity of similar student demonstrations in Pennsylvania (and the fact that when they did occur, no students were killed) to the state's policy of immediate and decisive use of overwhelming force to suppress demonstrations and occupations (personal interview, November 13, 1999).

21. See Fraser, *1968*, 286. As a graduate student, Jerry Rubin (1938–1994) had been a leader of the student uprising at Berkeley in 1964, and he was tried and convicted for inciting a riot during the 1968 Democratic Convention. Rubin would later make his fortune in stock market investments. Abbie Hoffman (1936–1989) received an M.A. in psychology at Berkeley in 1960, and subsequently spent his life working for a variety of social causes and marginalized people—in the early '60s he worked for civil rights; in the late '60s in New York City he established a hippie commune in the East Village; and finally, he agitated for environmental awareness in New York State. Wanted by state authorities on drug charges, he went into hiding during the 1970s, eventually giving himself up to police in 1980.

22. On the effects of such anti-war student activism on U.S. foreign policy, see Benjamin T. Harris, "Impact of Public Opposition on American Foreign Policy with Vietnam," *Conflict* 11, no. 1 (1991): 41–52.

23. See James Miller, *"Democracy Is in the Streets": From Port Huron to the Siege of Chicago* (New York: Simon and Schuster, 1987).

24. David Burg, *Encyclopedia of Student and Youth Movements* (New York: Facts on File, 1998), 56–57. African-American student demonstrations occurred all over the country; at the University of Wyoming, black football players refused to play against Brigham Young University because Mormons denied blacks the priesthood. For well over a decade following the players' ejection from Wyoming's team, the university had trouble attracting quality black athletes. Clifford A. Bullock, "Fired by Conscience: The 'Black 14' Incident at the University of Wyoming and Black Protest in the Western Athletic Conference, 1968–70," *Wyoming History Journal* 68, no. 1 (1996): 4–13.

25. The use of force by police on campuses only increased in prevalence as the decade wore on, despite outcry by university students and faculty; see, for example Elizabeth Tornquist's article on the suppression of black student demonstrations at Duke, "Tear Gas Blurs the Image as Duke Opts for 'Law and Order,'" *New South* 24, no. 2 (1969): 21–29.

26. Student uprisings of this sort were not restricted to universities and colleges; in Burlington, North Carolina, for example, a student protest at a local high school led to a large off-campus riot in which businesses were burned and gunfire

between police and a gunman left a teenage boy dead. See Burg, *Encyclopedia of Student and Youth Movements*, 36.

27. Abraham H. Miller, "People's Park: Dimensions of a Campus Confrontation," *Politics and Society* 2, no. 4 (1972): 433–58.

28. Gerard DeGroot discusses how Ronald Reagan used the student demonstrations in California during the 1960s to demonstrate decisive leadership, a populist morality, and a "commitment to law and order," thus enabling him to build a constituency and a career that eventually would land him in the White House. Gerard DeGroot, "Reagan's Rise," *History Today* 45, no. 9 (1995): 31–36; "Ronald Reagan and Student Unrest in California, 1966–70," *Pacific Historical Review* 65, no. 1 (1996): 107–29.

29. Sara Evans, *Personal Politics: The Roots of Women's Liberation in the Civil Rights Movement and the New Left* (New York: Alfred Knopf, 1979); Evans, "Tomorrow's Yesterday: Feminist Consciousness and the Future of Women," in *Women of America*, ed. Carol Ruth Berkin and Mary Beth Norton (Boston: Houghton Mifflin, 1979): 330–417.

30. See Harold Jacobs, ed., *Weathermen* (Berkeley: Ramparts, 1970).

31. As the Black Panthers evolved into a militant and openly revolutionary group, they found that their suppression increased. From 1968 to 1970, the FBI and state police forces began aggressively campaigning to eliminate the Panthers; coming down hard on the group in numerous raids, shoot-outs, and arrests, they simply and effectively eliminated the militant side of the group. Arrested, many of the group's members faced conspiracy charges and prison terms, and police and federal agents killed a number of the Panthers outright in raids. In the early 1970s, the group turned away from advocating violence and focused on social programs. Leaders of the Black Panthers included Bobby Seale, Huey Newton, and Eldridge Cleaver.

32. Burg, *Encyclopedia of Student and Youth Movements*, 126. Antiwar demonstrations were taking place on every major U.S. campus by 1969; over four hundred student protesters occupied Harvard's University Hall that year, for example, an action that ultimately strengthened the institution by provoking an administrative reorganization and a redefinition of the school's mission. See Archie C. Epps, "The Harvard Rebellion of 1969: Through Change and Through Storm," *Proceedings of the Massachusetts Historical Society* 107 (1995): 1–15.

33. Burg, *Encyclopedia of Student and Youth Movements*, 122.

Chapter 10

1. Cyril Levitt, "Federal Republic of Germany," in *Student Political Activism: An International Reference Handbook*, ed. Philip G. Altbach (New York: Greenwood Press, 1989), 217–18.

2. See L. Becker, *Hitler's Children: The Story of the Baader-Meinhof Gang* (Philadelphia: Lippincott, 1977); A. D. Moses, "The State and the Student Movement in

West Germany, 1967–77," in *Student Protest: The Sixties and After,* ed. Gerard J. Degroot (New York: Longman, 1998), 139–49.

3. See Andrei S. Markovits and Philip S. Gorski, *The German Left: Red, Green, and Beyond* (New York: Oxford University Press, 1993), 73–75.

4. Levitt, "Federal Republic of Germany"; see also A. D. Moses, "The State."

5. On the birth, life, and death of Students for a Democratic Society, see Kirkpatrick Sale, *SDS* (New York: Random, 1973).

6. For a discussion of the Santa Barbara revolt and rioting in nearby Isla Vista, see Jack Whalen and Richard Flacks, "The Isla Vista 'Bank Burners' Ten Years Later: Notes on the Fate of Student Activists," *Sociological Focus* 13, no. 3 (1980): 215–36.

7. For a discussion of the fallout from the events at U.C., Santa Barbara, see Jack Whalen and Richard Flacks, "Echoes of Rebellion: The Liberated Generation Grows Up," *Journal of Political and Military Sociology* 12, no. 1 (1984): 61–78.

8. See David Burg, *The Encyclopedia of Student and Youth Movements* (New York: Facts on File, 1998), 38.

9. In "Four Dead in Ohio," Lesley Wischam analyzes how the events unfolded and offers suggestions as to how the events could have otherwise turned out had both sides tried different tactics at key moments. *American History Illustrated* 25, no. 2 (1990): 24–33.

10. Jim Lewis offers his eyewitness account of the incident in "Black Day in May," *American History Illustrated* 25, no. 2 (1990): 34–35.

11. Eight of the guardsmen were tried, but found not guilty of manslaughter; the state of Ohio was forced to pay restitution to the dead students' families. See Peter Davies, *The Truth about Kent State: A Challenge to the American Conscience* (New York: Farrar, Straus and Giroux, 1973).

12. See Tim Spofford, *Lynch Street: The May 1970 Slayings at Jackson State College* (Kent, Ohio: Kent State University Press, 1988).

13. On blue-collar workers' responses to student antiwar demonstrations, see Kenneth Heineman, "The Silent Majority Speaks: Antiwar Protest and Backlash, 1965–1972," *Peace and Change* 17, no. 4 (1992): 402–33.

14. See Tom Bates, *RADS: The 1970 Bombing of the Army Mathematics Research Center of the University of Wisconsin and Its Aftermath* (New York: HarperCollins, 1992).

15. A gun battle with police in May 1974 left most of the SLA dead, and almost all SLA members who remained at large were tracked down by FBI over the next few years. One member, Kathleen Soliah, avoided arrest until 1999.

16. Although a few state governments received substantial negative publicity over their handling of student activists in the 1970s, public opinion on the whole favored low-tolerance policies, and governors increasingly used physical suppression to end demonstrations. See James L. Gibson, "The Policy Conse-

quences of Political Intolerance: Political Repression during the Vietnam War Era," *Journal of Politics* 51, no. 1 (1989): 13–35.

17. Eugene Genovese, "On Black Studies: Academic Discipline and Political Struggle," *Proceedings and Papers of the Georgia Association of Historians* (1981): 1–10.

18. Women involved in Chicano student organizations made similar liberation efforts; see Adelaida R. DelCastillo and Magdelena Mora, eds., *Mexican Women in the United States: Struggles Past and Present* (Los Angeles: University of California Chicano Studies Center, 1980).

19. See Valerie Solanis, "SCUM Manifesto," *Berkeley Barb,* June 7–13, 1968; cited in Judith Albert and Stewart Albert, *The Sixties Papers: Documents of a Rebellious Decade* (New York: Praeger, 1984), 463–64.

20. *off our backs* appeared for the first time in 1970.

21. In April 1970, students at Uvalde, Texas, went on strike to protest racist practices and the firing of a Hispanic teacher. See Juan O. Sanchez, "Walkout Cabrones! The Uvalde School Walkout of 1970," *West Texas Historical Association Yearbook* 68 (1992): 122–33.

22. In "Reforming the University: Student Protests and the Demand for a 'Relevant' Curriculum," Julia A. Reuben outlines the various ways in which curriculum changes and new studies programs were adopted by institutions in the U.S. during the late 1960s and early 1970s. See DeGroot, *Student Protest,* 153–68.

23. See Carol A. B. Warren and Joann S. DeLora, "Student Protest in the 1970s: The Gay Student Union and the Military," *Urban Life* 7, no. 1 (1978): 67–90.

24. A number of participants in the occupation documented their experiences in essays or books on the Alcatraz action. LaNada Boyer, a former University of California student, contributed to the public relations of the demonstration and describes the key players in her "Reflections on Alcatraz," *American Indian Culture and Research Journal* 18, no. 4 (1994): 75–92; Edward D. Castillo, an instructor of Indian students at UCLA, joined the occupation, and he details its demise due to internal factionalism and anarchy on the island in "A Reminiscence of the Alcatraz Occupation," *American Indian Culture and Research Journal* 18, no. 4 (1994): 111–22.

25. This was not the first attempt at capturing the island; in 1964 a group of local Native Americans made a similar attempt, but the political and cultural environment was not conducive to a successful protest. The occupiers were unable to grab and hold the attention of national media.

26. The Alcatraz Proclamation was delivered by Adam Nordwall, a business owner and leader of the Bay Area Native American movement; quoted in Paul Chaat Smith and Robert Allen Warrior, *Like a Hurricane: The Indian Movement from Alcatraz to Wounded Knee* (New York: New Press, 1996), 28–29.

27. For an analysis of the occupation and the role students played in the action, see

Steve Talbot, "Indian Students and Reminiscences of Alcatraz," *American Indian Culture and Research Journal* 18, no. 4 (1994): 93–102.

28. After the Alcatraz occupation, Oakes organized a traveling college, a bus-based institution that traveled to reservations; his influence in the Native American movement continued to wane when he was paralyzed in a barroom brawl.

29. In "Why Terrorism Subsides: A Comparative Study of Canada and the United States," *Comparative Politics* 21, no. 4 (1989): 405–26, Jeffrey Ian Ross and Ted Robert Gurr trace the evolution of student antiwar activism in terrorist groups and their eventual suppression from 1960 to 1985.

30. Miriam R. Jackson, "Vietnam War Refought: Kent State, 1977," *Vietnam Generation* 4, nos. 3–4 (1992): 110–18.

31. Burg, *Encyclopedia of Student and Youth Movements*, 90.

32. For a discussion of the phases of student activism in Japan in the 1970s, see Michiya Shimbori, "Japanese Student Activism in the 1970s," in *Student Politics: Perspectives for the Eighties*, ed. Philip G. Altbach (Metuchen, N.J.: Scarecrow Press, 1981), 119–36; Simbori, "Japan," in Altbach, *Student Political Activism*, 137–44.

33. For a discussion of student activism in Thailand in the late 1960s and '70s, see Chai-Anan Samudavanija, "Thailand," in Altbach, *Student Political Activism*, 185–96.

34. Burg, *Encyclopedia of Student and Youth Movements*, 106–7.

35. Stanley Rosen, "China," in Altbach, *Student Political Activism*, 76–79.

36. On the development of South Korea's student movements in the 1970s, see Jaeho Lee, *A History of Korean Student Movements after Liberation* (Seoul: Hongsungsa, 1984). Burg, *Encyclopedia of Student and Youth Movements*, 13.

37. A. S. Malambo, "Student Protest and State Reaction in Colonial Rhodesia: The 1973 Chimukwembe Student Demonstration at the University of Rhodesia," *Journal of Southern African Studies* 21, no. 3 (1995): 473–90.

38. See Ngoni Chideya, "Zambia," in Altbach, *Student Political Activism*, 57–72.

39. See Behrooz Ghamari-Tabrizi, "Between the Shah and the Imam: The Students of the Left in Iran, 1977–81," in DeGroot, *Student Protest*, 232–47.

40. On the capturing of the U.S. embassy, see Parviz Daneshvar, *Revolution in Iran* (New York: St. Martin's Press, 1996), 145–74.

41. Robin Wright, "Letter from Teheran: We Invite the Hostages to Return: The Extraordinary Changing View of Iran's Revolution," *New Yorker,* November 8, 1999, 38–47.

42. G. Sick argues that more than fear of the new U.S. president influenced the decision to release the hostages within an hour of Reagan's assuming office, citing among other things the antagonism between the leaders of Iran's revolution and Carter's administration. *October Surprise: America's Hostages in Iran and the Election of Ronald Reagan* (London: I. B. Taurus, 1991).

Chapter 11

1. See Pamela Constable and Arturo Valenzuela, *A Nation of Enemies: Chile under Pinochet* (New York: Norton, 1991).
2. Cristina Bonasegna and Tim Frasca, "Students and Faculty End 11–Week-Old Stint at U. of Chile after Rector's Replacement, But They Seek More Changes," *Chronicle of Higher Education*, November 11, 1987.
3. Iván Jaksič and Sonia Nazario discuss the turning away from political party struggles and toward university reform in the late 1970s and early 1980s by Chile's studentry in their essay "Chile," in *Student Political Activism: An International Reference Handbook*, ed. Philip G. Altbach (New York: Greenwood, 1989), 359–70.
4. Mike Tangeman, "Mexico's National Autonomous University Hopes to Settle Long-Standing Controversy over Academic Reforms," *Chronicle of Higher Education*, January 24, 1990.
5. Simon Rottenberg, "The Universities and South Africa: The Campaign for Divestment," *Minerva* 24, nos. 3–4 (1986): 223–41; Marc Fisher, "The Second Coming of Student Activism," *Change* 11, no. 1 (1979): 26–30.
6. See Eric L. Hirsch, "Sacrifice for the Cause: Group Processes, Recruitment, and Commitment in a Student Social Movement," *American Sociological Review* 55, no. 2 (1990): 243–54.
7. Philip Altbach and Robert Cohen discuss apartheid and the state of post-1960s student activism in "American Student Activism: The Post-Sixties Transformation," *Journal of Higher Education* 61, no. 1 (1990): 32–49.
8. In her article on the proliferation of shantytown protests on campuses from 1985 to 1990, Sarah A. Soule discusses both the development of the anti-apartheid tactic and its speed in terms of lateral diffusion theory ("The Student Divestment Movement in the United States and Tactical Diffusion: The Shantytown Protest," *Social Forces* 75, no. 3 [1997]: 855–883).
9. See Altbach and Cohen, "American Student Activism," 467–68.
10. Philip G. Altbach and Robert Cohen's analysis ("American Student Activism," 457–73) of the U.S. divestment movement foregrounds the dedication and passion of the student activists involved but also suggests an extreme myopia and the limited interest of many of the activists, as most abandoned the anti-apartheid cause once their individual universities divested; South Africa, however, remained under apartheid.
11. Taking the student South African divestment movement as a model, Students for a Free Tibet formed in 1994 and quickly spread to hundreds of U.S. campuses; by 1995 SFT had become an international organization and began boycotts and lobbying efforts against corporations they perceived as supporters of China's occupation of Tibet. In 1996 Holiday Inn pulled out of Tibet under heavy activist pressure.

12. For an extremely detailed account of the Gallaudet demonstrations, see John B. Christiansen and Sharon N. Barnartt, *Deaf President Now! The 1988 Revolution at Gallaudet University* (Washington, D.C.: Gallaudet University Press, 1995).

13. See Harold Orlans, "The Revolution at Gallaudet," *Change* 21, no. 1 (January 1989): 8–18.

14. Nevertheless, such programs were not unilaterally supported. Ohio students protested the implementation of a women's studies program at Kenyon College. See Elizabeth Lilla, "Who's Afraid of Women's Studies?" *Commentary* 81, no. 2 (1986): 53–57.

15. See Marion Lloyd, "Violence Recedes at U. of Karachi, But Pakistani Politics Persists," *Chronicle of Higher Education,* March 26, 1999.

16. Established in 1964, the PLO has since served as the official voice of Palestinians seeking to throw off the Israeli occupation. From the PLO's perspective, Israel was, and continues to be, an imperialist power, but the organization's early endorsement of violence and sabotage and its involvement with the late 1980s Intifada, as well as Israel's favor among Western nations, led to its condemnation by Western powers. In the 1990s, however, both the PLO and Israel sought political means for resolving the future governance of Palestine, and as a result the PLO made tremendous leaps both in its power and in its political program, and was officially recognized as a legitimate force and entity by Western nations. In 2000, the PLO sought to politically use its new legitimacy in its struggle with Israel. On the development of the Palestinian liberation movement through the 1980s, see Don Peretz, *Intifada: The Palestinian Uprising* (Boulder, Colo.: Westview Press, 1990).

17. For a concise discussion of the Intifada, see David Burg, *Encyclopedia of Student and Youth Movements* (New York: Facts on File, 1998), 105.

18. Burton Bollag, "Czech Students' Protest over Crackdown by Police Leads to Biggest Demonstration in 20 Years," *Chronicle of Higher Education,* November 29, 1989.

19. Students were in for a tough lesson, however, if they thought the new government would allow student dissent; almost immediately President Ion Iliescu's government began suppressing student demonstration. See Colin Woodard, "Brutal Attack on Romanian Students Casts Doubt about Government," *Chronicle of Higher Education,* July 25, 1990; Burg, *Encyclopedia,* 194.

20. In 1989 the country's name was officially changed to Myanmar. Although restricted in her movements by the government, Aung San Suu Kyi was awarded the Nobel Peace Prize in 1991. See: "Burma Hints That It Will Reopen Universities Closed since 1996," *Chronicle of Higher Education,* March 6, 1998.

21. Park was assassinated under the direction of the Korean Central Intelligence Agency.

22. Foon Rhee draws parallels between the South Korean students demonstrating in the 1980s and U.S. student protesters in the 1960s and also analyzes their differ-

ences in "Vanguards and Violence: A Comparison of the U.S. and Korean Student Movements," *Korean Studies* 17 (1993): 17–38.

23. David N. Clark, ed., *The Kwangju Uprising: Shadows over the Regime in South Korea* (Boulder, Colo.: Westview Press, 1988); Chung-in Moon and Kang Mun-gu, "Democratic Opening and Military Intervention in South Korea," in *Politics and Policy in the New Korean State: From Roh Tai-Woo to Kim Young-sam*, ed. James Cotton (New York: St. Martin's Press, 1995).

24. Cited in Shinil Kim, "South Korea," in Altbach, *Student Political Activism*, 174; for a brief discussion of self-immolation, students, and Korean labor movements in the 1980s, see ibid., 173–78. Alan R. Kluver treats the history and use of self-immolation by Korean reformers in more depth in "Student Movement in Confucian Societies," in *Student Protest: The Sixties and After*, ed. Gerard J. DeGroot (London: Addison Wesley, 1998), 219–31.

25. Cited in Jeffrey Wasserstrom, *Student Protests in Twentieth-Century China: The View from Shanghai* (Stanford, Calif.: Stanford University Press, 1991), 298. Wasserstrom is careful to note that what democracy signified for the Chinese student in the 1980s was not necessarily what it signified in the West at that time; Wasserstrom claims that "democracy" was used in an elitist sense (in that students wanted more of a voice in government for themselves, but did not necessarily want the same rights extended to, say, workers or peasants) or in a vague way to mean the "loosening of political and cultural constraints." Wasserstrom also notes that women were a conspicuous minority in leadership positions in the democracy movement.

26. At the time, Deng Xiaoping was a leader of the reform movement.

27. For an extensive treatment of the Shanghai protests in the 1980s, see Wasserstrom, *Student Protests in Twentieth-Century China*, 295–327.

28. For a discussion of the student activists' point of view, see Craig Calhoun, "Revolution and Repression in Tiananmen Square," *Society* 26, no. 6 (September–October 1989): 21–38.

29. On the strategies used by the student leaders of the People's Movement to keep it alive, see Frank N. Pieke, "The 1989 Chinese People's Movement in Beijing," in DeGroot, *Student Protest*, 248–63.

30. On the issues involved in the movement leading up to June 3, see Craig Calhoun, "Protest in Beijing: The Conditions and Importance of the Chinese Student Movement of 1989," *Partisan Review* 56, no. 4 (1989): 563–80.

31. A similar sculpture, though a smaller and closer replica of the Statue of Liberty, appeared in the May–June prodemocracy marches in Shanghai. Wasserstrom notes (*Student Protests*, 318–19) that such Western icons have a long history in Chinese student demonstrations.

32. Autonomous workers' groups sprang up at this time in cities all over China. In "Remembering Tiananmen Square: Who Died in Beijing, and Why," Robin Munro, a journalist who witnessed the Tiananmen Square uprising and the

subsequent suppression on the night of June 3, argues that the birth of the autonomous groups posed the threat that brought Deng's fist down on Beijing (*Nation*, June 11, 1990, 811–22).

33. Antony J. Taylor uses an eyewitness account of the Beijing demonstrations and government suppression to illustrate, among other things, the difficulties of emotional objectivity in such phenomena in "The 1989 Student Protest in Beijing," *International Journal of Mass Emergencies and Disasters* 12, no. 3 (November 1994): 357–68.

34. Pieke ("1989 Chinese People's Movement," 261) notes reports of soldiers being hanged from trees and lightposts.

35. See Munro, "Remembering Tiananmen Square," 814-15. Munro also quotes the following note written by journalist Richard Nations: "Approximately 1:00 A.M.: Southwest corner, on Qianmen West street in front of Kentucky Fried Chicken. Barricade of burning buses blocks the intersection. Riot police are forced into the street under a shower of rocks and glass. Student pickets or organizers seem to intervene to evacuate the 20-odd unarmed police/soldiers with shields and staves caught near burning buses" (816).

36. The many U.S. newspaper and journal articles attacking China's "brutal suppression of the students on Tiananmen Square" that appeared following China's suppression of workers and rioters in the streets of Beijing attest to, among other things, the pervasiveness of the student martyr myth in the United States and the nostalgia for student activism in the popular cultural milieu. See, for example, Ken Hammond, "From Kent State to Tiananmen: Some Personal Reflections," *Vietnam Generation* 2, no. 2 (1990): 127–31.

37. Although Munro is careful to say that it's possible some students were killed in the clearing of the square after the students abandoned the monument, the journalist quotes a number of sources present throughout the incident that claimed not to have seen a single dead student on the square; the only video recording of the evacuation of the square, made by a crew from Televisión Española, showed the several thousand students gathered around the Monument, then in an orderly way abandoning the structure. See Munro, "Remembering Tiananmen Square," 814–15, 82. For other testimonials regarding the student retreat, see Amnesty International, China, *The Massacre of June 1989 and Its Aftermath* (London: Amnesty International, 1990).

38. Heading China's most wanted list, Wang Dan, Wuer Kaixi, and Chai Ling separately went into hiding and attempted to flee the country. Wuer Kaixi and Chai Ling were successful, but Wang Dan, the most visible of the student leaders of the People's Movement, was not. Arrested, he served over three years in prison, but upon his release, he immediately set about agitating and was again arrested in 1995 and reimprisoned until 1998.

39. On the CCP's exploitation of the unreliable reporting of the Tiananmen Square massacre see Munro, "Remembering Tiananmen Square," 822.

40. On the decade leading up to the 1989 suppression, see Ai Wei, "Economic and Trade Relations between the United States and Mainland China in the Past Decade," *Issues and Studies* 26, no. 4 (1990): 63–82. On the fallout of the massacre, see Wasserstrom, *Student Protests,* 297–327; Taylor, "The 1989 Student Protest," 357–68.

Chapter 12

1. See Daniela Hart, "Students in Brazil Take to Streets against President, *Chronicle of Higher Education,* September 23, 1992.
2. In 1997 thousands of students from public universities marched for educational reform in Santiago, which focused international media attention on Chile; the protest was, however, only a part of a more sustained student movement, which included sit-ins and boycotts among its other strategies for regaining public attention.
3. "Nicaragua," *Miami Herald,* December 22, 1995.
4. Coletta Youngers, "The Peru We Built Is Fighting Back," *Washington Post,* April 23, 2000.
5. See Lucien Chavvin, "Students in Peru Channel Protests into a New Political Party," *Chronicle of Higher Education,* June 25, 1999.
6. "Mexico City," *Houston Chronicle,* June 14, 1992.
7. Rhona Statland de Lopez, "Mexico's Largest University Ends Semester amid Student Occupation of the Campus," *Chronicle of Higher Education,* July 23, 1999.
8. "Recovering from Strike: Concerns about UNAM's Future Raised," *Boston Globe,* March 1, 2000.
9. An example of an issue-related demonstration that did spark national media interest, however, was the 1990 Wellesley student petition and campaign against the choice of Barbara Bush as commencement speaker. See Rosanna Hertz and Susan M. Reverby, "Gentility, Gender, and Political Protest: The Barbara Bush Controversy at Wellesley," *Gender and Society* 9, no. 5 (1995): 594–611.
10. Susan Dodge, "Thousands of College Students Protest Persian Gulf War in Rallies and Sit-Ins; Others Support Military Action," *Chronicle of Higher Education,* January 30, 1991.
11. John Blake, "Students Return to AU Center," *Atlanta Journal and Constitution,* August 26, 1992.
12. Kimberley B. Babu, "Arrests End Riot in Hartford," *Boston Globe,* March 4, 1991.
13. At the University of California at Los Angeles (UCLA), for example, students effectively demonstrated for the establishment of a Chicano studies department in 1993. See Christopher Shea, "Hunger Strikes on the Rise," *Chronicle of Higher Education,* May 25, 1995; Raoul Contreras, "Chicano Movement, Chicano Studies: Social Science and Self-Conscious Ideology," *Perspectives in Mexican American Studies* 6 (1997): 20–51. For a theoretical and general historical context

for the study of Latino ethnicity, see Juan Flores, "Latino Studies: New Contexts, New Concepts," *Harvard Educational Review* 67, no. 2 (1997): 208–21.

14. See Martin Van der Werf, "Sweatshop Issue Escalates with Sit-Ins and Policy Shifts," *Chronicle of Higher Education*, March 10, 2000.

15. For a discussion of protests at Duke, see Denise K. Magner, "Duke Agrees to Student Demands on Code of Conduct for Clothing Manufacturers," *Chronicle of Higher Education*, February 12, 1999.

16. Eleven students sued the University of Southern California in 1990 for $2 million, for example, alleging that campus and city police beat them while they tried to peacefully submit a protest letter urging divestment in South African–affiliated companies (*Chronicle of Higher Education*, April 4, 1990).

17. Tom Little, "Adviser Warns That Funding Crisis Could Ruin Universities," *Scotsman* 5 (June 23, 1998): 8.

18. Katherine A. Schmidt, "Germans Fight for College Funds," *USA Today*, December 18, 1997; Burton Bollag, "German Higher Education Faces a Period of Tough Transitions," *Chronicle of Higher Education*, January 16, 1998.

19. Little, "Adviser Warns."

20. Julie Street, "Talking about Revolution," *Real Life*, December 18, 1995.

21. "Wedding Joy Marred by Catalan Resentment," *Herald* (Glasgow), October 4, 1997.

22. See Burton Bollag, "Eastern Europe Finds University Reform Is a Long, Hard Task," *Chronicle of Higher Education*, July 31, 1991.

23. Philip Dine, "Albanian Rebel Lives through 'Miracle': Professor Astonished by All the Changes—and to Be Alive!" *St. Louis Post-Dispatch*, December 16, 1991.

24. Dusko Doder, "Students Demonstrate in Belgrade," *Chronicle of Higher Education*, March 18, 1992.

25. Ira Traynor, "Belgrade Rally Says Milosevic Must Go," *Guardian*, June 29, 1992.

26. See Colin Woodard, "Brutal Attack on Romanian Students Casts Doubt about Government," *Chronicle of Higher Education*, July 25, 1990; Andrei Codrescu, "The Year of Living Illusorily," *St. Louis Post-Dispatch*, December 21, 1990.

27. Igor Greenwald, "Central Asia's Universities Face Challenges in Post-Soviet Era," *Chronicle of Higher Education*, March 22, 1996.

28. Jon Immanuel, "Third Shooting Victim from Nablus March Dies," *Jerusalem Post*, June 27, 1995; Herbert M. Watzman and Issam Ramzi, "3 West Bank Students Killed in Clash with Israeli Troops," *Chronicle of Higher Education*, July 7, 1995.

29. Robin Wright, "Letter from Teheran: We Invite the Hostages to Return," *New Yorker*, November 8, 1999, 42.

30. Ibid., 41.

31. See Burton Bollag, "20 Years after the Islamic Revolution, Iran's Campuses Begin to Loosen Up," *Chronicle of Higher Education*, March 10, 2000.

32. "Anti-U.S. March in Teheran," *New York Times*, November 5, 1999.

33. Peter Guilford, "Belgian Warning to Zaire," *Times of London*, June 26, 1990.

34. Southam News, "Zimbabwe Expels 10,000 Students from University," *Gazette,* June 8, 1992.

35. See Louise Tunbridge, "Kenyan Higher Education Faces Collapse Due to Repression," *Chronicle of Higher Education,* April 5, 1996.

36. Louis Tunbridge, "Kenyan University Closes after Clashes," *Daily Telegraph,* February 2, 1999.

37. "Dispute on Rushdie Closes Campus in India," *New York Times,* May 1, 1992.

38. "Thousands Protest in South Korea," *Phoenix Gazette,* December 1, 1993.

39. For a description of the trends in activist activities and politics, see Colin Woodard, "Student Movement in South Korea Becomes Quiescent under New Government," *Chronicle of Higher Education,* April 17, 1998.

40. Margot Cohen, "Indonesian Students Defy a Legacy of Limits on Student Activism," *Chronicle of Higher Education,* May 15, 1991.

41. Joseph Saunders, "Jakarta Diary: Signs of Intellectual Freedom Begin to Emerge in Indonesia," *Chronicle of Higher Education,* April 17, 1998; David Cohen, "Indonesian Forces Kill 6 Students at Jakarta Protest," *Chronicle of Higher Education,* May 22, 1998.

42. David Cohen, "Indonesian Students Debate Tactics as Protests Become More Violent," *Chronicle of Higher Education,* December 18, 1998. On Wahid's reforms and other bizarre political tactics, see Seth Mydans, "Zigzag in Jakarta: General Is Suspended," *New York Times,* February 14, 2000.

43. Matt Forney and Marcus W. Brauchli, "A Democracy Party Rises from the Ashes of Tiananmen Square," *Wall Street Journal,* May 12, 1999; James Hertling, "Students Join Protests as Hong Kong Returns to Chinese Control," *Chronicle of Higher Education,* July 11, 1997.

44. David Rennie, "Two Solo Protests Mark Tiananmen 10th Anniversary," *Daily Telegraph,* June 5, 1999.

45. Ben Fenton and David Rennie, "CIA Officers Sacked over Bombing of Chinese Embassy," *Daily Telegraph,* April 10, 2000; Paul Desruisseaux, "Anti-American Protests in China Prompt Several Colleges to Cancel Student Trips," *Chronicle of Higher Education,* May 21, 1999.

Bibliography

Albert, Judith, and Stewart Albert. *The Sixties Papers: Documents of a Rebellious Decade*. New York: Praeger, 1984.

Altbach, Philip G., ed. *Student Political Activism: An International Reference Handbook*. Westport, Conn.: Greenwood Press, 1989.

———, ed. *Student Politics: Perspectives for the Eighties*. Metuchen, N.J.: Scarecrow Press, 1981.

———. *Student Politics in America: A Historical Analysis*. New York: McGraw-Hill, 1973.

———. *Student Politics in Bombay*. Bombay and New York: Asia Publishing House, 1965.

———. "The Transformation of the Indian Student Movement." *Asian Survey* 6, no. 8 (August 1966): 448–60.

Altbach, Philip G., and Norman T. Uphoff. *The Student Internationals*. Metuchen, N.J.: Scarecrow Press, 1973.

Altbach, Philip, and Robert Cohen. "American Student Activism: The Post-Sixties Transformation." *Journal of Higher Education* 61, no. 1 (1990): 32–49.

Amnesty International, China. *The Massacre of June 1989 and Its Aftermath*. London: Amnesty International, 1990.

"Anti-U.S. March in Teheran." *New York Times,* November 5, 1999.

Ascher, Abraham. *The Revolution of 1905: Russia in Disarray*. Stanford, Calif.: Stanford University Press, 1988.

Asres, Alem. "History of the Ethiopian Student Movement (in Ethiopia and North America): Its Impact on Internal Social Change, 1960–1974." Ph.D. diss., University of Maryland, 1990.

Babu, Kimberley B. "Arrests End in Riot in Hartford." *Boston Globe,* March 4, 1991.

Barlow, William. *The San Francisco State Student Movement in the '60s*. New York: Pegasus, 1971.

Bates, Tom. *RADS: The 1970 Bombing of the Army Mathematics Research Center of the University of Wisconsin and Its Aftermath*. New York: HarperCollins, 1992.

Beck, Carlton E., ed. *Perspectives on World Education*. New York: Wm. C. Brown, 1970.

Becker, Jillian. *Hitler's Children: The Story of the Baader-Meinhof Terrorist Gang*. Philadelphia: Lippincott, 1977.

Blackstone, Tessa, ed. *Students in Conflict*. London: Weidenfeld and Nicolson, 1970.

Blake, John. "Students Return to AU Center." *Atlanta Journal and Constitution,* August 26, 1992.

Bogen, David Skilles. "The First Integration of the University of Maryland School of Law." *Maryland Historical Magazine* 84, no. 1 (1989): 39–49.

Boggs, Carl. *Social Movements and Political Power: Emergence of Forms of Radicalism in the West.* Philadelphia: Temple University Press, 1986.

Bollag, Burton. "Czech Students' Protest over Crackdown by Police Leads to Biggest Demonstration in Twenty Years." *Chronicle of Higher Education,* November 29, 1989.

———. "Eastern Europe Finds University Reform Is a Long, Hard Task." *Chronicle of Higher Education,* July 31, 1991.

———. "20 Years after the Islamic Revolution, Iran's Campuses Begin to Loosen Up." *Chronicle of Higher Education,* March 10, 2000.

"The Bombay Students' Brotherhood." *Modern Review,* March 1914, 264.

Bonasegna, Cristina, and Tim Frasca. "Students and Faculty End 11–Week-Old Stint at U. of Chile after Rector's Replacement, but They Seek More Changes." *Chronicle of Higher Education,* November 11, 1987.

Bonilla, Frank, and Myron Glazer. *Student Politics in Chile.* New York: Basic Books, 1969.

Bonn, M. J. *The Wandering Scholar.* New York: Day, 1948.

Bowen, James Samuel. "Black Student Militance: Campus Unrest among Black Students, 1968–1972." Ph.D. diss., Columbia University, 1982.

Boyer, LaNada. "Reflections on Alcatraz." *American Indian Culture and Research Journal* 18, no. 4 (1994): 75–92.

Brax, Ralph S. *The First Student Movement: Student Activism in the United States during the 1930s.* Port Washington, N.Y.: Kennikat Press, 1981.

Brower, Daniel R. *Training the Nihilists: Education and Radicalism in Tsarist Russia.* Ithaca, N.Y.: Cornell University Press, 1975.

Brown, Bernard E. *Protest in Paris: The Anatomy of a Revolt.* Morristown, N.J.: General Learning Press, 1979.

Budiman, Arief. "Student Movement in Indonesia." *Asian Survey* 18, no. 6 (July 1978): 614–25.

Bullock, Clifford A. "Fired by Conscience: The 'Black 14' Incident at the University of Wyoming and Black Protest in the Western Athletic Conference, 1968–'70." *Wyoming History Journal* 68, no. 1 (1996): 4–13.

Burg, David F. *Encyclopedia of Student and Youth Movements.* New York: Facts on File, 1998.

Calhoun, Craig. "Protest in Beijing: The Conditions and Importance of the Chinese Student Movement of 1989." *Partisan Review* 56, no. 4 (1989): 563–80.

Cardozier, V. R. "Student Power in Medieval Universities." *Personnel and Guidance Journal* 46 (June 1968): 944–48.

Carithers, Martha Webb. "A Social Movement Career: National SDS." Ph.D. diss., University of Kansas, 1982.

Carmichael, Stokely, and Charles V. Hamilton. *Black Power: The Politics of Liberation in America.* New York: Vintage, 1967.

Carson, Clayborne. *In Struggle: SNCC and the Black Power Awakening of the 1960s.* Cambridge: Harvard University Press, 1981.

Casale, Ottavio M., ed. *The Kent State Affair: Documents and Interpretations.* New York: Houghton Mifflin, 1971.

Castillo, Edward D. "A Reminiscence of the Alcatraz Occupation." *American Indian Culture and Research Journal* 18, no. 4 (1991): 111–22.

Chang, Maria Hsia. *The Chinese Blue Shirts: Fascism and Developmental Nationalism.* Berkeley and Los Angeles: University of California Press, 1985.

Chavvin, Lucien. "Students in Peru Channel Protests into a New Political Party." *Chronicle of Higher Education,* June 25, 1999.

Cheng, Chu-Yuan. *Behind the Tiananmen Square Massacre: Social Political, and Economic Ferment in China.* Boulder, Colo.: Westview Press, 1990.

Christiansen, John B., and Sharon N. Barnartt. *Deaf President Now! The 1988 Revolution at Gallaudet University.* Washington, D.C.: Gallaudet University Press, 1995.

Clark, David N., ed. *The Kwangju Uprising: Shadows over the Regime in South Korea.* Boulder, Colo.: Westview Press, 1988.

Codrescu, Andrei, "The Year of Living Illusorily." *St. Louis Post-Dispatch,* December 21, 1990.

Cohen, Robert. *When the Old Left Was Young: Student Radicals and America's First Mass Student Movement, 1929–1941.* New York: Oxford University Press, 1993.

Cohen, Sheldon S. "The Turkish Tyranny." *New England Quarterly* 47, no. 4 (1974): 564–83.

Constable, Pamela, and Arturo Valenzuela. *A Nation of Enemies: Chile under Pinochet.* New York: Norton, 1991.

Contreras, Raoul. "Chicano Movement, Chicano Studies: Social Science and Self-Conscious Ideology." *Perspectives in Mexican American Studies* 6 (1997): 20–51.

Cotton, James, ed. *Politics and Policy in the New Korean State: From Roh Tai-Woo to Kim Young-sam.* New York: St. Martin's Press, 1995.

Courteney, William J. *Schools and Scholars in Fourteenth-Century England.* Princeton, N.J.: Princeton University Press, 1987.

Crouch, Colin. *The Student Revolt.* London: Bodley Head, 1970.

Cunnigen, Donald. "Malcolm X's Influence on the Black Nationalist Movement of Southern Black College Students." *Western Journal of Black Studies* 17, no. 1 (1993): 32–43.

Daneshvar, Parviz. *Revolution in Iran.* London: Macmillan, 1996.

Davies, Peter. *The Truth about Kent State: A Challenge to the American Conscience.* New York: Farrar, Straus, and Giroux, 1973.

Davis, Natalie Zimon. "The Reasons of Misrule: Youth Groups and Charivaris in Sixteenth-Century France." *Past and Present* 50 (1971): 41–75.

DeConde, Alexander, ed. *Student Activism: Town and Gown in Historical Perspective.* New York: Scribner's, 1971.

DeGroot, Gerard J. "The Limits of Moral Protest and Participatory Democracy: The Vietnam Day Committee." *Pacific Historical Review* 64, no. 1 (1995): 95–119.

———. "Reagan's Rise." *History Today* 45, no. 9 (1995): 31–36.

———. "Ronald Reagan and Student Unrest in California, 1966–70." *Pacific Historical Review* 65, no. 1 (1996): 107–29.

———, ed. *Student Protest: The Sixties and After.* London: Addison Wesley, 1998.

DelCastillo, Adelaida R., and Magdelena Mora, eds. *Mexican Women in the United States: Struggles Past and Present.* Los Angeles: University of California Chicano Studies Center, 1980.

de Lopez, Rhona Statland. "Mexico's Largest University Ends Semester amid Student Occupation of the Campus." *Chronicle of Higher Education,* July 23, 1999.

Desruisseaux, Paul. "Anti-American Protests in China Prompt Several Colleges to Cancel Student Trips." *Chronicle of Higher Education,* May 21, 1999.

Diepenbrock, David. "Black Women and Oberlin College in the Age of Jim Crow." *UCLA Historical Journal* 13 (1993): 27–59.

Dine, Philip, "Albanian Rebel Lives through 'Miracle': Professor Astonished by All the Changes—and to Be Alive!" *St. Louis Post-Dispatch,* December 16, 1991.

"Dispute on Rushdie Closes Campus in India." *New York Times,* May 1, 1992.

Dix, Robert H. *The Politics of Columbia.* New York: Praeger, 1987.

Dobbs, Archibald. *Education and Social Movements, 1700–1850.* New York: Kelley, 1919.

Doder, Dusko. "Students Demonstrate in Belgrade." *Chronicle of Higher Education,* March 18, 1992.

Dodge, Susan. "Thousands of College Students Protest Persian Gulf War in Rallies and Sit-Ins; Others Support Military Action." *Chronicle of Higher Education,* January 30, 1991.

Donadio, Stephen. "Black Power at Columbia." *Commentary* 46, no. 3 (1968): 67–76.

Doolin, Dennis. *Communist China: The Politics of Student Opposition.* Stanford, Calif.: Hoover Institution, 1964.

Douglas, William. "Korean Students and Politics." *Asian Survey* 3, no. 12 (December 1963): 584–95.

Douglass, Frederick. *The Narrative of the Life of Frederick Douglass, an American Slave* [1845]. New York: Penguin, 1986.

Dowsey, Stuart J., ed. *Zengakuren: Japan's Revolutionary Students.* Berkeley, Calif.: Ishi Press, 1970.

Draper, Hal. *Berkeley: The New Student Revolt.* New York: Grove, 1965.

Dunlop, Annie. "Scottish Student Life in the Fifteenth Century." *Scottish Historical Review* 26 (1947): 47–63.

Eichel, Lawrence, et al. *The Harvard Strike.* Boston: Houghton Mifflin, 1970.

Ehrenreich, Barbara, and John Ehrenreich. *Long March, Short Spring.* New York: Monthly Review Press, 1969.

Emmerson, Donald K. *Students and Politics in Developing Nations.* New York: Praeger, 1968.

Epps, Archie C. "The Harvard Rebellion of 1969: Through Change and through Storm." *Proceedings of the Massachusetts Historical Society* 107 (1995): 1–15.

Epstein, Barbara. *Political Protest and Cultural Revolution: Nonviolent Direct Action in the 1970s and 1980s.* Berkeley and Los Angeles: University of California Press, 1991.

Ericson, Edward. *Radicals in the University.* Stanford, Calif.: Hoover Institution Press, 1975.

Escobar, Arturo, and Sonia El Alvarez, eds. *The Making of Social Movements in Latin America.* Boulder, Colo.: Westview Press, 1992.

Evans, Sara. *Personal Politics: The Roots of Women's Liberation in the Civil Rights Movement and the New Left.* New York: Alfred Knopf, 1979.

———. "Tomorrow's Yesterday: Feminist Consciousness and the Future of Women." In *Women of America,* ed. Carol Ruth Berkin and Mary Beth Norton, 330–417. Boston: Houghton Mifflin, 1979.

Ewell, Judith. *Venezuela: A Century of Change.* Stanford, Calif.: Stanford University Press, 1977.

Exum, William H. *Paradoxes of Protest: Black Student Activism in a White University.* Philadelphia: Temple University Press, 1985.

Feuer, Lewis. *Conflict of Generations: The Character and Significance of Student Movements.* New York: Basic Books, 1969.

Fields, A. Belden. *Student Politics in France.* New York: Basic Books, 1970.

Fisher, Marc. "The Second Coming of Student Activism." *Change* 11, no. 1 (1979): 26–30.

Flemming, Cynthia Griggs. "Black Women Activists and the Student Non-Violent Coordinating Committee: The Case of Ruby Doris Smith Robinson." *Journal of Women's History* 4, no. 3 (1993): 64–82.

Flores, Juan. "Latino Studies: New Contexts, New Concepts." *Harvard Educational Review* 67, no. 2 (1997): 208–21.

Foucault, Michel. *Power/Knowledge: Selected Interviews and Other Writings.* New York: Pantheon, 1981.

———. *Discipline and Punish: The Birth of the Prison.* Translated by Alan Sheridan. New York: Pantheon. 1977.

———. *Madness and Civilization.* New York: Random House, 1965.

Fraser, Ronald, et al. *1968: A Student Generation in Revolt.* New York: Pantheon, 1988.

Freud, Sigmund. *The Interpretation of Dreams* [1900]. Vol. 4 of *The Standard Edition of the Complete Psychological Works of Sigmund Freud,* 1–338. London: Hogarth, 1986.

Ganter, Granville. "The Active Virtue of the Columbian Orator." *New England Quarterly* 70, no. 3 (1997): 463–76.

Garrow, David J., ed. *Atlanta, Georgia, 1960–1961: Sit-Ins and Student Activism.* Brooklyn: Carlson, 1989.

Genovese, Eugene. "On Black Studies: Academic Discipline and Political Struggle." *Proceedings and Papers of the Georgia Association of Historians* (1981): 1–10.

Gerhardt, Uta. "The Sociology of Health/Medical Sociology in the Federal Republic of Germany." *Research in the Sociology of Health Care* 8 (1989): 275–88.

Gibson, James L. "The Policy Consequences of Political Intolerance: Political Repression during the Vietnam War Era." *Journal of Politics* 51, no. 1 (1989): 13–35.

Gitlin, Todd. *The Sixties: Years of Hope, Days of Rage.* New York: Bantam, 1987.

Goldstein, Jonathan. "Vietnam Research on Campus: The Summit/Spicerack Controversy at the University of Pennsylvania, 1965–'67." *Peace and Change* 11, no. 2 (1986): 27–43.

Gottschalk, Marialyce O'Connor. "The Student Power Movement at the UW-Madison Campus, 1966–1968." Ph.D. diss., University of Wisconsin, 1987.

Grant, Joanne. *Confrontation on Campus: The Columbia Pattern for the New Protest.* New York: Signet, 1969.

Greenwald, Igor. "Central Asia's Universities Face Challenges in Post-Soviet Era." *Chronicle of Higher Education,* March 22, 1996.

Guilford, Peter. "Belgian Warning to Zaire." *Times,* June 26, 1990.

Gutierrez, Henry J. "Racial Politics in Los Angeles: Black and Mexican American Challenges to Unequal Education in the 1960s." *Southern California Quarterly* 78, no. 1 (1996): 51–86.

Gwynne-Thomas, E. H. *A Concise History of Education to 1900 A.D.* Washington, D.C.: University Press of America, 1981.

Hammond, Ken. "From Kent State to Tiananmen: Some Personal Reflections." *Vietnam Generation* 2, no. 2 (1990): 127–31.

Handy, Jim. *Gift of the Devil: A History of Guatemala.* Boston: South End Press, 1984.

Hanna, William J. *University Students and African Politics.* New York: Africana, 1975.

Harris, Benjamin T. "Impact of Public Opposition on American Foreign Policy with Vietnam." *Conflict* 11, no. 1 (1991): 41–52.

Harris, Janet. *Students in Revolt.* London: McGraw-Hill, 1970.

Harris, Tim. *London Crowds in the Reign of Charles II.* Cambridge: Cambridge University Press, 1987.

Harris, T. J. G. "The Bawdy House Riots of 1668." *Historical Journal* 29 (1986): 537–56.

Harrison, James P. *The Long March to Power: A History of the Chinese Communist Party, 1921–1972.* New York: Praeger, 1972.

Harrison, Lowell H. "Rowdies, Riots, and Rebellions." *American History Illustrated* 7, no. 3 (1972): 18–29.

Harvey, Sylvia. *May '68 and Film Culture.* London: B.F.I., 1980.

Haskins, Charles H. *The Rise of the Universities.* Ithaca, N.Y.: Cornell University Press, 1923.

Heineman, Kenneth. "The Silent Majority Speaks: Antiwar Protest and Backlash, 1965–1972." *Peace and Change* 17, no. 4 (1992): 402–33.

Heinrich, Hans-Georg. *Hungary: Politics, Economics, and Society.* Boulder, Colo.: Lynn Rienner, 1986.

Henderson, Gregory. *Korea: The Politics of the Vortex.* Cambridge: Cambridge University Press, 1968.

Hertling, James. "Students Join Protests as Hong Kong Returns to Chinese Control." *Chronicle of Higher Education,* July 11, 1997.

Hertz, Rosanna, and Susan M. Reverby. "Gentility, Gender, and Political Protest: The Barbara Bush Controversy at Wellesley." *Gender and Society* 9, no. 5 (1995): 594–611.

Heywood, Colin. *Childhood in Nineteenth-Century France.* Cambridge: Cambridge University Press, 1988.

Hibbert, Christopher, and Edward Hibbert. *The Encyclopedia of Oxford.* London: Macmillan, 1988.

Hine, William C. "Civil Rights and Campus Wrongs: South Carolina State College Students Protest, 1955–1968." *South Carolina Historical Magazine* 97, no. 4 (1996): 310–31.

Hirsch, Eric L. "Sacrifice for the Cause: Group Processes, Recruitment, and Commitment in a Student Social Movement." *American Sociological Review* 55, no. 2 (1990): 243–54.

Holborn, Hajo. *A History of Modern Germany, 1648–1840.* New York: Knopf, 1964.

hooks, bell. *Outlaw Culture.* New York: Routledge, 1994.

———. *Teaching to Transgress.* New York: Routledge, 1994.

Horn, Max. *The Intercollegiate Socialist Society, 1905–1921.* Boulder Colo.: Westview Press, 1979.

Howard, Michael, and Wm. Roger Louis. *Oxford History of the Twentieth Century.* New York: Oxford University Press, 1998.

Huber, Donald L. "The Rise and Fall of Lane Seminary: An Antislavery Episode." *Timeline* 12, no. 3 (1995): 2–19.

Immanuel, Jon. "Third Shooting Victim from Nablus March Dies." *Jerusalem Post,* June 27, 1995.

Israel, John, and Donald Klein. *Rebels and Bureaucrats: China's December 9ers.* Berkeley and Los Angeles: University of California Press, 1976.

Jackson, Miriam R. "Vietnam War Refought: Kent State, 1977." *Vietnam Generation* 4, nos. 3–4 (1992): 110–18.

Jacobs, Harold, ed. *Weathermen.* Berkeley: Ramparts Press, 1970.

James, Anthony W. "A Demand for Racial Equality: The 1970 Black Student Protest at the University of Mississippi." *Journal of Mississippi History* 57, no. 2 (1995): 97–120.

Jarausch, Konrad. *Students, Society, and Politics in Imperial Germany: The Rise of Illiberalism*. Princeton, N.J.: Princeton University Press, 1982.

Johnson, Marcia Lynn. "Student Protest at Fisk University in the 1920s." *Negro History Bulletin* 33, no. 6 (1970): 137–40.

Kantor, Harry. *The Ideology and Program of the Peruvian Aprista Movement*. New York: Octagon, 1966.

Kassow, Samuel D. *Students, Professors, and the State in Tsarist Russia*. Berkeley, Calif.: University of California Press, 1989.

Kiang, Wen-Lang. *The Chinese Student Movement*. New York: King Crown's Press, 1948.

Knabb, Ken, ed. *The Situationist International Anthology*. Berkeley, Calif.: Bureau of Public Secrets, 1981.

Krauss, Ellis. *Japanese Radicals Revisited: Student Protest in Post-War Japan*. Berkeley and Los Angeles: University of California Press, 1974.

Kuhlman, Martin. "Direct Action at the University of Texas during the Civil Rights Movement, 1960–65." *Southwestern Historical Quarterly* 98, no. 4 (1995): 550–66.

Kunen, John S. "The Strawberry Statement: Notes of a College Revolutionary." *Vietnam Generation* 3, no. 1 (1991): 48–57.

Laquer, Walter. *Young Germany: A History of the German Youth Movement*. New York: Basic Books, 1972.

Lee, Hong Yung. *The Politics of the Chinese Cultural Revolution: A Case Study*. Berkeley and Los Angeles: University of California Press, 1978.

Lee, Jaeho. *A History of Korean Student Movements after Liberation*. Seoul: Hongsungsa, 1984.

Levitt, Cyril. *Children of Privilege: Student Revolt in the Sixties, a Study of Student Movements in Canada, the United States, and West Germany*. Toronto: University of Toronto Press, 1984.

Levy, Daniel, and Gabriel Szekely. *Mexico: Paradoxes of Stability and Change*. Boulder, Colo.: Westview Press, 1987.

Lewis, Jim. "Black Day in May." *American History Illustrated* 25, no. 2 (1990): 34–35.

Lewis, Paul. *Socialism, Liberalism, and Dictatorship in Paraguay*. New York: Praeger, 1982.

Liebman, Arthur, et al. *Latin American University Students: A Six Nation Study*. Cambridge: Harvard University Press, 1972.

———. *The Politics of Puerto Rican University Students*. Austin: University of Texas Press, 1970.

Lilla, Elizabeth. "Who's Afraid of Women's Studies?" *Commentary* 81, no. 2 (1986): 53–57.

Lipset, Seymour M. *Rebellion in the University: A History of Student Activism in America*. Woodstock, N.Y.: Beekman, 1971.

———, ed. *Student Politics*. New York: Basic Books, 1967.

Lipset, Seymour, and Sheldon Wolin, eds. *The Berkeley Student Revolt.* Garden City, N.Y.: Doubleday, 1965.

Little, Tom. "Adviser Warns That Funding Crisis Could Ruin Universities." *Scotsman* 5 (June 23, 1998): 8.

Lloyd, Marion. "Violence Recedes at U. of Karachi, but Pakistani Politics Persists." *Chronicle of Higher Education,* March 26, 1999.

Lucas, Christopher. *American Higher Education: A History.* New York: St. Martin's Press, 1994.

Lutz, Jessie. "The Chinese Student Movement of 1945–1949." *Journal of Asian Studies* 31, no. 1 (1971): 89–110.

Lynd, Staughton. "The New Left." *Annals of the American Academy of Political and Social Science* 38, no. 2 (1969): 64–72.

McAdam, Doug. *Freedom Summer.* New York: Oxford University Press, 1988.

———. "Gender as a Mediator of the Activist Experience: The Case of Freedom Summer." *American Journal of Sociology* 97, no. 5 (1991): 1211–40.

McGill, William J. The Year of the Monkey: Revolt on Campus, 1968–1969. New York: McGraw-Hill, 1982.

McGovern, James R. "The Student Rebellion in Harvard College, 1807–1808." *Harvard Library Bulletin* 19, no. 4 (1971): 341–55.

McManus, Philip, and Gerald Schlabach, ed. *Relentless Persistence: Nonviolent Action in Latin America.* Philadelphia: New Society Publishers, 1991.

Magner, Denise K. "Duke Agrees to Student Demands on Code of Conduct for Clothing Manufacturers." *Chronicle of Higher Education,* February 12, 1999.

Magubane, Ben. "Before Soweto and After: The Struggle for Liberation." *Christianity and Crisis* 38, no. 3 (1978): 41–44.

Majumdar, Ramesh. *History of the Freedom Movement in India.* Calcutta: Firma K. L. Mukhopadhyay, 1962–63.

Malambo, A. S. "Student Protest and State Reaction in Colonial Rhodesia: The 1973 Chimkwembe Student Demonstration at the University of Rhodesia." *Journal of Southern African Studies* 21, no. 3 (1995): 473–95.

Marcus, Greil. *Lipstick Traces: A Secret History of the Twentieth Century.* London: Secker and Warburg, 1989.

Markovits, Andrei S., and Philip S. Gorski. *The German Left: Red, Green, and Beyond.* New York: Oxford University Press, 1993.

Marszalek, John F. "The Class Rush—A Description." *Journal of Sports History* 17, no. 3 (1990): 366–68

Matthews, Anne. *Bright College Years: Inside the American Campus Today.* Chicago: University of Chicago Press, 1997.

Medoff, Rafael. "'Retribution Is Not Enough': The 1943 Campaign by Jewish Students To Raise American Public Awareness of the Nazi Genocide." *Holocaust and Genocide Studies* 11, no. 2 (1997): 171–89.

"Mexico City." *Houston Chonicle,* June 14, 1992.

Miller, Abraham H. "People's Park: Dimensions of a Campus Confrontation." *Politics and Society* 2, no. 4 (1972): 433–58.

Miller, James. *"Democracy Is in the Streets": From Port Huron to the Siege of Chicago.* New York: Simon and Schuster, 1987.

Minzhu, Han, ed. *Cries for Democracy: Writings and Speeches from the 1989 Chinese Democracy Movement.* Princeton, N.J.: Princeton University Press, 1990.

Mommsen, Wolfgang, and Gerhard Hirschfield. *Social Protest, Violence and Terror in 19th and 20th Century Europe.* New York: St. Martin, 1982.

Morris, Aldon. "Black Southern Student Sit-In Movement: An Analysis of Internal Organization." *American Sociological Review* 46, no. 6 (1981): 744–46.

Mosse, George. *The Image of Man: The Creation of Modern Masculinity.* New York: Oxford University Press, 1996.

Munro, Robin. "Remembering Tiananmen Square: Who Died in Beijing, and Why." *Nation,* June 11, 1990, 811–22.

Murray, Martin. *South Africa: Time of Agony, Time of Destiny.* London: Verso, 1987.

Mydans, Seth. "Zigzag in Jakarta: General Is Suspended." *New York Times,* February 14, 2000.

Myers, Edward D. *Education in the Perspective of History.* New York: Harper and Brothers, 1960.

Nagel, Julian. *Student Power.* London: Merlin, 1969.

Nahm, Andrew C. *Korea: Tradition and Transformation.* Elizabeth, N.J.: Hollym International, 1988.

Narsimhan, Reavathi. "Student Movements in India: A Post Independence Survey." *Indian Journal of Youth Affairs* 2 (March 1980): 37–48.

"Nicaragua." *Miami Herald,* December 22, 1995.

Nkomo, Mokumbung O. *Student Culture and Activism in Black South African Universities.* Westport, Conn.: Greenwood Press, 1984.

Novak, Stephen. *The Rights of Youth: American Colleges and Student Revolt, 1789–1815.* Cambridge: Harvard University Press, 1977.

Orlans, Harold. "The Revolution at Gallaudet." *Change* 21, no. 1 (January–February 1989): 8–18.

Orme, Nicholas. *Education and Society in Medieval ad Renaissance England.* London: Hambledon Press, 1989.

Pepper, Suzanne. *Civil War in China: The Political Struggle, 1945–1949.* Berkeley and Los Angeles: University of California Press, 1978.

Peretz, Don. *Intifada: The Palestinian Uprising.* Boulder, Colo.: Westview Press, 1990.

Peterson, Patti M. "Student Organization and the Anti-War Movement in America, 1900–1960." *American Studies* 13, no. 1 (1972): 131–47.

Pfaff, Eugene. "Greensboro Sit-Ins." *Southern Exposure* 9, no. 1 (1981): 23–28.

Pfeiffenberger, Amy F. "Democracy at Home: The Struggle to Desegregate Washington University in the Post-War Era." *Gateway Heritage* 10, no. 3 (1989–90): 14–25.

Pinson, Koppel, *Modern Germany*. New York: Macmillan, 1966.

Porter, Kenneth. "The Oxford Cap War at Harvard." *New England Quarterly* 14 (March 1941): 77–83.

Proudfoot, Merrill. *Diary of a Sit-In*. Urbana: University of Illinois Press, 1990.

Rait, Robert S. *Life in the Medieval University*. Cambridge: Cambridge University Press, 1931.

Rath, R. J. *The Viennese Revolution of 1848*. Austin: University of Texas Press, 1957.

Ray, Anil B. *Students and Politics of India*. New Delhi: Manohar, 1977.

Rennie, David. "Two Solo Protests Mark Tiananmen 10th Anniversary." *Daily Telegraph,* June 5, 1999.

Rhee, Foon. "Vanguards and Violence: A Comparison of the U.S. and Korean Student Movements." *Korean Studies* 17 (1993): 17–38.

Richie, Gladys Ward. *The Rhetoric of American Students in Protest during the 1960s*. Ann Arbor: University of Michigan Press, 1973.

Rigby, Richard. *The May 30th Movement*. Canberra, Australia: Griffin, 1980.

Rorabaugh, W. J. *Berekeley at War: The 1960s*. New York: Oxford University Press, 1989.

Rollison, Marcia R. "Agnes Ryan and the New Hampshire Peace Movement." *Historical New Hampshire* 50, nos. 3–4 (1995): 184–212.

Roos, Leslie. "Students and Politics in Turkey." *Daedalus* 98 (winter 1968): 184–203.

Rosenthal, Joel. "Southern Black Student Activism: Assimilation vs. Nationalism." *Journal of Negro Education* 44, no. 2 (1975): 113–29.

Ross, Jeffrey Ian, and Ted Robert Gurr. "Why Terrorism Subsides: A Comparative Study of Canada and the United States." *Comparative Politics* 21, no. 4 (1989): 405–26.

Roszak, Theodore. *The Making of a Counter Culture*. Garden City, N.Y.: Anchor Books, 1970.

Ross, George, and Laura Frader. "The May Generation from Mao to Mitterand." *The Socialist Review* 18, no. 4 (1988): 105–16.

Rottenberg, Simon. "The Universities and South Africa: The Campaign for Divestment." *Minerva* 24, nos. 3–4 (1986): 223–41.

Rudy, Willis. *The Universities of Europe, 1100–1914*. Rutherford, N.J.: Associated University Presses, 1984.

———. *The Campus and a Nation in Crisis: From the American Revolution to Vietnam*. Cranbury, N.J.: Associated University Presses, 1996.

Russell, Bertrand. *The Autobiography of Bertrand Russell*. London: Allen and Unwin, 1961.

Sale, Kilpatrick. *SDS*. New York: Random House, 1973.

Sampson, Edward E., and Harold A. Korn. *Student Activism and Protest*. San Francisco: Jossie-Bass, 1970.

Sanchez, Juan O. "Walkout Cabrones! The Uvalde School Walkout of 1970." *West Texas Historical Association Yearbook* 68 (1992): 122–33.

Sanderson, Michael, ed. *The Universities in the Nineteenth Century*. London: Routledge and Kegan Paul, 1975.

Saunders, Joseph. "Jakarta Diary: Signs of Intellectual Freedom Begin to Emerge in Indonesia." *Chronicle of Higher Education,* April 17, 1998.

Saunders, Susan. "Berkeley's Free Speech Movement: A Study in Press Reaction to First Amendment Issues." Ph.D. diss., University of Washington, 1989.

Scherer, Julio, and Carlos Monsivais. *Parte de Guerre: Tlatelolco 1968.* Mexico City: Aguila, 1999.

Schmidt, Katherine A. "Germans Fight for College Funds." *USA Today,* December 18, 1997.

Schmitter, Philippe. *Interest Conflict and Political Change in Brazil.* Stanford, Calif.: Stanford University Press, 1971.

Schnell, Rodolph Leslie. *National Activist Student Organizations in American Higher Education.* Ann Arbor: University of Michigan Press, 1976.

Shepherd, George W. "Seven Days That Shook the Sudan," *Africa Today* 11, no. 10 (December 1964): 10–13.

Sherkat, Darren E., and T. Jean Blocker. "The Political Development of Sixties Activists: Identifying the Influence of Class, Gender, and Socialization on Protest Participation." *Social Forces* 72, no. 3 (1994): 821–42.

Shimbori, Michiya. "Comparison between Pre- and Post-War Student Movements in Japan." *Sociology of Education* 37 (fall 1963): 59–70.

Sick, G. *October Surprise: America's Hostages in Iran and the Election of Ronald Reagan.* London: I. B. Taurus, 1991.

Smith, David Horton. *Latin American Student Activism.* Lexington, Mass.: Lexington Books, 1973.

Smith, Paul Chat, and David Warrior. *Like a Hurricane: The Indian Movement from Alcatraz to Wounded Knee.* New York: New Press, 1996.

Soule, Sarah A. "The Student Divestment Movement in the United States and Tactical Diffusion: The Shantytown Protest." *Social Forces* 75, no. 3 (1997): 855–83.

Southam News. "Zimbabwe Expels 10,000 Students from University." *Gazette,* June 8, 1992.

Spevack, Daniel. "Charles Follen's Search for Nationality and Freedom in Germany and America, 1795–1840." Ph.D. diss., Johns Hopkins University, 1993.

Spofford, Tim. *Lynch Street: The May 1970 Slayings at Jackson State College.* Kent, Ohio: Kent State University Press, 1988.

Stein, Daniel Lewis. *The Yippies in Chicago.* Indianapolis, Ind.: Bobbs-Merrill, 1969.

Steinberg, Isaac. *Spiridonova: Revolutionary Terrorist.* Freeport, N.Y.: Books for Libraries Press, 1971.

Steinberg, Michael Stephen. *Sabers and Brown Shirts: The German Students' Path to National Socialism.* Chicago: University of Chicago Press, 1977.

Stern, Karl. *The Pillar of Fire.* Garden City, N.Y.: Image Books, 1951.

Stevens, Evelyn P. *Protest and Response in Mexico.* Cambridge, Mass.: MIT Press, 1974.

Stone, Laurence, ed. *The University in Society.* Princeton, N.J.: Princeton University Press, 1974.

Stoner, Mark Reed. "The Free Speech Movment: A Case Study in the Rhetoric of Social Intervention." Ph.D. diss., Ohio State University, 1987.

Stoper, Emily. "The Student Nonviolent Coordinating Committee: Rise and Fall of a Redemptive Organization." *Journal of Black Studies* 8, no. 1 (1977): 13–34.

Stratera, Gianni. *Death of a Utopia: The Development and Decline of Student Movements in Europe.* New York: Oxford University Press, 1975.

Street, Julie. "Talking about Revolution." *Real Life,* December 18, 1995.

Students and Staff of Hornsey College of Art. *The Hornsey Affair.* Harmondsworth, England: Penguin, 1969.

Suchlichi, Jaime. *University Students and Revolution in Cuba, 1920–1968.* Coral Gables, Fla.: University of Miami Press, 1969.

Sumner, David E. "The Nashville Student Movement." *American History Illustrated* 23, no. 2 (1988): 28–31.

Talbot, Steve. "Indian Students and Reminiscences of Alcatraz." *American Indian Culture and Research Journal* 18, no. 4 (1994): 93–102.

Tangeman, Mike. "Mexico's National Autonomous University Hopes to Settle Long-Standing Controversy over Academic Reforms." *Chronicle of Higher Education,* January 24, 1990.

Taylor, Antony J. "The 1989 Student Protest in Beijing." *International Journal of Mass Emergencies and Disasters* 12, no. 3 (November 1994): 357–68.

Thackeray, Frank. *Antecedents of Revolution: Alexander I and the Polish Kingdom, 1815–1825.* New York: Columbia University Press, 1980.

Thomas, Hugh. *The Cuban Revolution.* New York: Harper and Row, 1977.

"Thousands Protest in South Korea." *Phoenix Gazette,* December 1, 1993.

Tornquist, Elizabeth. "Tear Gas Blurs the Image as Duke Opts for 'Law and Order.'" *New South* 24, no. 2 (1969): 21–29.

Traynor, Ira. "Belgrade Rally Says Milosevic Must Go." *Guardian,* June 19, 1992.

Trietschke, Heinrich von. *History of Germany in the Nineteenth Century.* Translated by Eden and Cedar Paul. New York: McBride, 1917.

Trilling, Diana. "On the Steps of Low Library: Liberalism and the Revolution of the Young." *Commentary* 46, no. 5 (1968): 29–55.

Trimberger, Ellen Kay. "Why a Rebellion at Columbia Was Inevitable." *Transaction* 5, no. 9 (1968): 28–38.

Tse-tsung, Chou. *The May Fourth Movement.* Cambridge: Harvard University Press, 1960.

Tunbridge, Louise. "Kenyan Higher Education Faces Collapse Due to Repression." *Chronicle of Higher Education,* April 5, 1996.

Valenzuela, Arturo. *A Nation of Enemies: Chile under Pinochet.* New York: W. W. Norton, 1991.

Vali, Ferenc. *Rift and Revolt in Hungary.* Cambridge: Harvard University Press, 1961.

Van der Werf, Martin. "Sweatshop Issue Escalates with Sit-Ins and Policy Shifts." *Chronicle of Higher Education,* March 10, 2000.

Walter, Richard. *Student Politics in Argentina: The University Reform and Its Effects, 1918–1964.* New York: Basic Books, 1968.

Warren, Carol A. B., and Joann S. DeLora. "Student Protest in the 1970s: The Gay Student Union and the Military."*Urban Life* 7, no. 1 (1978): 67–90.

Wasserstrom, Jeffrey. *Student Protests in Twentieth-Century China: The View from Shanghai.* Stanford, Calif.: Stanford University Press, 1991.

"Wedding Joy Marred by Catalan Resentment." *Herald* (Glasgow), October 4, 1997.

Wei, Ai. "Economic and Trade Relations between the United States and Mainland China in the Past Decade." *Issues and Studies* 26, no. 4 (1990): 63–82.

Weisbrot, Robert. *Freedom Bound: A History of America's Civil Rights Movement.* New York: Penguin, 1991.

Weiss, Jonathan. "Tom Hayden's Political Evolution during the New Left Years: Rebel without a Theory." *Michigan Journal of Political Science* 5 (1984): 1–38.

Weller, Eva, and Willfried van der Will. *Protest in Western Germany.* Edited by Julian Nagel. London: Merlin Press, 1969.

Whalen, Jack, and Richard Flacks. "Echoes of Rebellion: The Liberated Generation Grows Up." *Journal of Political and Military Sociology* 12, no. 1 (1984): 61–78.

Whelan, James R. *Out of the Ashes: Life, Death, and Transfiguration in Chile, 1833–1988.* Washington, D.C.: Regency, 1989.

Wischam, Lesley. "Four Dead in Ohio." *American History Illustrated* 25, no. 2 (1990): 24–33.

Wolff, Robert Paul. *The Idea of the University.* Boston: Beacon Press, 1969.

Wood, Antony. *Antony's History and the Antiquities of the University of Oxford.* Edited by J. Gutch. Oxford, England, 1792–96.

Woodard, Colin. "Brutal Attack on Romanian Students Casts Doubt about Government." *Chronicle of Higher Education,* July 25, 1990.

——. "Student Movement in South Korea Becomes Quiescent under New Government." *Chronicle of Higher Education,* April 17, 1998.

Wright, Robin. "Letter from Teheran: We Invite the Hostages to Return: The Extraordinary Changing View of Iran's Revolution." *New Yorker,* November 8, 1999, 38–47.

Yarmolinsky, Avrahm. *Road to Revolution: A Century of Russian Radicalism.* New York: Macmillan, 1962.

Youngers, Coletta. "The Peru We Built Is Fighting Back." *Washington Post,* April 23, 2000.

Zanjani, Sally Springmeyer. "George Springmeyer and the Quarantine Rebellion of 1902: Student Revolt Reaches the University of Nevada." *Nevada Historical Society Quarterly* 23, no. 4 (1980): 283–89.

Index

abolitionist movement. *See* anti-slavery movement

Academic Legion, 40–41

Académie des Sciences, Paris, 28

Action Command of Indonesian Students, 127–128

Africa, 43–44, 110–112; 137–138, 163, 164, 197–198, 240–242. *See also individual countries*

African Resistance Movement, 137

African-American studies, 6, 189

AIM. *See* American Indian Movement

Albania, 233

Alcatraz Occupation, 190–192, 275n.25, 275n.26

Alcatraz Proclomation, 191

Alexander I, 46–47

Alexander II, 48–50

Alianza Popular Revolucionara Americana, 71, 75

Algeria, 237; independence movement, 100–101, 138

Altbach, Philip G., 2

American Association of University Students for Academic Freedom, 113

American Indian Movement, 192

American Student Union, 95–96

Amherst College, 36

Angola, 240

anti-apartheid movement, 111–112, 137, 203–204, 277n.8, 277n.10

anti-nuclear arms protests, 101

anti-slavery demonstrations (U.S.), 36–37, 45

anti-sweatshop-labor movement, 229

anti-Vietnam War protests: English, 156–157; German, 134; Japanese,

166–169; U.S., 145–146, 177–179, 183, 187, 188–189, 273n.32

Aprista. *See* Alianza Popular Revolucionara Americana

Argentina, 69–71, 119–121; educational reform movement, 69–71, 75, 76–77

ARM. *See* African Resistance Movement

Asian-American studies, 228

Association Général des Etudiants, 42

Atlanta University, 227

Aung San, 3, 86

Aung San Suu Kyii, 210, 278n.20

Baader-Meinhof Gang, 3, 159–160, 184–185

Bangladesh, 242–243

Barborossa, Frederick, 10

Barcelona, Autonomous University of, 232

Barry, Marion, 139, 206

Batista, Fulgencio, 115–117

Battle of Leipzig, 29

Bavarian Soviet Republic, 59

Beijing University, 66, 107–108, 214–215

Belgrade University, 62, 233–234

Bella, Ahmed Ben, 138

Berkeley, University of California at, 95–96, 114, 142–144, 181, 229, 268n.45. *See also* Free Speech Movement; People's Park

Berlin revolt, 38

Betancourt, Rómulo, 76

Bismarck, 39

Black Hand, 63–64

Black Panther Party, 179, 183, 273n.31

Black Power, 177

black studies. *See* African-American studies

Blanqui, Louis-Auguste, 35
Bohemia, 32
Bologna, early university at, 8–9, 10–11, 252n.4
Bolivia, 69
Bombay University, 45
Bonaparte, Napoleon, 29
Bosch, Juan, 147
Bosnia, 62–64
Boumedienne, Houari, 138
Bowdoin College, 36
Bowie State College, 172, 173–174
Brandt, Willie, 184
Bravo, Ernesto Mario, 119
Brazil, 69, 117, 221–222
Breslau University, 34
Brigham Young University, 272n.24
Brown, Pat, 143–144
Brown v. Board of Education, 115
Budapest student revolt, 102
Bucharest University, 235–236
Bureau of Indian Affairs, 192
Burg, David, 2
Burma. *See* Myanmar
Burschenschaften, 29, 30–32, 38, 255n.3

Caldera, Rafael, 171
Calvin, John, 26
Cambodia, 197
Cambridge University, 11
Campaign for Nuclear Disarmament, 101
Campos, Pedro Albizu, 115
Caracas Central University, 118–119
Cárdenas, Cuauhtemoc, 225
Carlsbad Decress, 32
Carmichael, Stokeley, 2-3, 140
Carpizo, Jorge, 202
Carter, Jimmy, 200
Casteñeda, Jorge Ubico, 117–118
Castro, Fidel, 116, 148
Catherine the Great, 46
Ceausescu, Nicolae, 209
Central Intelligence Agency, 146
chahuts, 91
Chaikovsky Group, 50
Charles I, 24–25
Chiang Kai-shek, 78–83, 107–108
Chicago riots, 177–179, 182

Chile, 68, 71; 201–202, 222; Communism in, 68; University of, 68
China, 44–45, 77–83, 195–196, 213–220, 246–247, 279n.25; anti-Japanese imperialism protests, 65–66, 72, 77–80, 107–108; anti-Maoism, 195; NATO embassy bombing protests, 247; Western influence on education in, 44–45, 64–65. *See also* Cultural Revolution; December Ninth movement; May Fourth movement; May Thirtieth movement; Tiananmen Square demonstrations
Chinese Communist Party, 67, 78–83, 107–108, 213–220
Chou En-lai, 195
Chun Doo Hwan, 210–214
City College of New York protests, 94–95
Civil War (U.S.), 36, 45
Cohn-Behndit, Daniel, 3, 150
Cold War, 100, 104, 112–115, 121, 131, 186, 263–264n.22
collectives, early student, 8–21
Collor de Mello, Fernando, 221–222
Colombia, 118, 148
Columbia University, 6, 36, 94, 95; student revolt at, 174–176, 179
Comenius. *See* John Amos Komenski
Comité Pro Reforma, 69–70
Commune, the, 134
Congo, 137–138, 164
Congress of Racial Equity, 114, 139–140, 142–143
Contreras, Eleázar Lopez, 76
Cordoba, University of, 69–70
CORE. *See* Congress of Racial Equity
Cornell University protest, 179–180
Cosmopolitan Clubs, 72
Cromwell, Richard, 25
Cuba, 71, 115–117, 147
Cultural Revolution (China) 126–127
Cummings, Harry Sythe, 45–46
Czechoslovakia, 135–136, 208–209, 232–233

Dakar, University of (Senegal), 163–164
Daley, Richard, 178

Dartmouth College, 36
Daytona Beach, 16
December Ninth movement, 82–83
Degroot, Gerard, 2
Deng Xiaoping, 195–196, 215–220,
    246–247
Descartes, René, 26
desegregation movement, 114–115,
    138–140, 266n.25
Deutsch Studentenschaft, 87–88
Devlin, Bernadette, 155–156, 270n.9
Directorio Revolutionario, 116
Dominican Republic, 147, 223
Dorpat, University of, 46
Dreyfus, Alfred, 43, 256n.7
Dubcek, Alexander, 208
Duke University, 229
Dutschke, Rudi, 3, 134, 158–159

East Timor, 246
Echeverría, José, 116
Eck, John, 24
Ecuador, 68–69, 71, 147–148
Edward III, 13
Egypt, 237
Eisenach meeting, 39
Emergency Committee for Direct Action
    Against Nuclear War, 101
End the Draft protests, 145–146
England, 22-25, 92, 231; anti-nulear arms
    protests, 101; anti-Vietnam
    protests, 156–157; early student
    uprisings in, 11–17, 22–25, 28;
    proliferation of student groups in,
    42, 59
Enlightenment, the, 27–28; influence on
    Russian educational system, 49
environmental movment, 185
Essex, University of, 157
Ethiopia, 163, 240
ethnic studies, 5, 190, 205, 227, 228,
    229
Etudiants Action Française, 90–92

Farmer, James, 114
Federal Republic of Germany, 98–99,
    131–135, 158–160, 184–186; anti-
    Vietnam War protests, 133–135

Fédération National des Etudiants de
    France, 130
feminism. *See* women; women's studies
Feuer, Lewis, 2
Follen, Carl, 6, 31, 254n.15
France, 8–10, 35, 129–131, 149–156, 186,
    231–232; Algerian independence
    movement, 100–101, 130; anti-
    Nazi protests, 99–100; prolifera-
    tion of student groups in, 42, 59,
    90–92; Vichy government, 99–100.
    See also May riots
Frankfurt University, 23–24, 32, 159
Frankfurt revolt, 32–33
Freaknik, 16
Free Speech Movement, 142–144
Free Tibet Movement. *See* Tibet
Freedom Ride Bus Campaign, 114,
    139–140
Freedom Summer, 140
Front de Liberation Nationale, 101

Gallaudet University Protests, 204–205
Gandhi, Mohandas, 86–87, 109–110
Gaulle, Charles de, 35, 100, 152–154
gay and lesbian studies, 190, 205
Général Association des Etudiants, 91
Georg August University, 33
George Washington University, 187
Georgia, University of (U.S.), 36, 140
Georgia, Soviet, 236
German Democratic Republic, 98–99, 131
German states, 28–34, 38–42, 58–59; anti-
    Catholicism in, 58; early student
    organizations in, 28–34; student
    anti-Semitism in, 42, 58, 88; stu-
    dents uprisings (1848 revolts),
    38–41; student uprisings in (pre-
    1848), 32–34. *See also* Germany
Germany, 59–60, 98–99, 230–231; anti-
    Nazi demonstrations, 262n.1;
    students and National Socialism,
    88–90; student organizations,
    59–60, 87–90. *See also* German
    Democratic Republic; Federal
    Republic of Germany; German
    states
Gero, Ernö, 102–103

Ghana, 110, 240
Giessen, University of, 30
Gómez, Juan Vincente, 75–76
Gorbachev, Mikhail, 216–217, 236–237
Göttingen rebellion, 32
Green Party, 186
Geuvara, Ernesto ("Che"), 2, 148
Greece, 232
Greensboro protests, 138–139, 180–181
Guomindang, 78–83, 107–108
Guatemala, 117–118
Gulf War demonstrations, 227, 237–238

Han Dynasty, 44
Harvard University, 36, 94; 1842 riots, 37
Havana, University of, 147
Havel, Václav, 208, 232
Hayden, Tom, 6, 141–142, 175
Hearst, Patty, 188
Heidelberg University, 26
Herriot, Eduourd, 91
Hezbollah, 200
Hitler Jugend, 29
Hoffman, Abbie, 177
Holocaust, the, 98–99, 263n.20
Holy Roman Empire, 22–23
Hong Kong, University of, 246–247
Hornsey College, 157
House Un-American Activities Committee, 113–114, 140–141
Howard University, 173, 205–206
Hu Yaobang, 214
Humbolt Univerity, 99
Humphrey, Hubert, 134, 178
Hungary, 1956 Revolution, 102–104, 232–233
hunger strikes, 5, 213, 216, 228, 229, 242–243
Hunter College, 94

Illinois, University of, 36
Imperialism, European, 43–46
India, 45, 86–87, 129, 242–243; student organizations in, 87, 109–110
Indonesia, 85, 195; 244–246; anti-imperialist demonstrations, 85; revolution in, 127–128

Indonesian Communist Party, 85, 127–128
Indonesian National Party, 85
International Congress of American Students, 69
International student organizations, 73, 77, 120
Internet, 247, 248
Intifada, 207–208
Iran, 198–199, 238–240
Iraq, 237
Ireland, 154–156
Irigoyen, Hipolito, 69–70, 76
Irish Republican Army, 155
Israel, 207–208, 237–238
Istanbul University, 45, 136–137
Italy, 8–9, 160–162, 186
Ivory Coast, 240

Jackson, Jesse, 206
Jackson State College, 188
Jahn, Friedrich, 28
Japan, 72, 83–84, 104–107, 193–194; anti-U.S. imperialism, 124–126, 166–169; Chinese student protests in, 72; Communism in, 85, 106; post-World War II, 104–105; student organizations in, 84–85
Japan-U.S. Security Treaty protests, 106–107
Jena, University of, 29
Jewish Theological Seminary, 263n.20
Jiménez, Marcos Perez, 118–119
Johnson, Charles W., 45–46
Jordan, 237
July 26 Movement, 116

Kaliaev, Ivan Platinovitch, 55
KAMI. See Action Command of Indonesian Students
Karachi, University of, 206
Karakozov, Dmitri, 49–50
Kazakhstan, 236
Kazan, University of, 46, 53, 60
Kennedy, Robert, 177
Kent State University, 187–188
Kentucky miners' strike, 94
Kenya, 240, 241

Kharkov, University of, 46, 47, 54
Khartoum, University of, 138
Khatame, Mohammed, 239
Khmer Rouge, 197
Khodynka, 54
Khomeini, the Ayatollah, 198
Kiev protests, 54, 60
Kim Dae Jung, 244
King, Martin Luther, 155, 176–177
King, Rodney, 227
Kohl, Helmut, 230
Komenski, John Amos, 26
Korea, 83–84; anti-Japanese imperialism protests, 84; University of, 122–123. *See also* North Korea; South Korea
Kosovo, 234–235
Kotzebue, Auguste, 6, 31
Kravchinski, Sergei, Mikhailovich, 51
Krleza, Miroslav, 64
Kuby, Erich, 131
Kwanju protests, 84, 196
Kwangju uprising, 211–212
Kyrgyzstan, 236

labor, student alliances with, 18–19
Land and Freedom group, 51–52
Lane Seminary, 36
Latin America, 67–71, 75–77, 115–121, 147–148, 169–171, 201–203, 221–226. *See also individual countries*
Latino studies, 228, 281–282n.13
League of Nations, 73
Lenin, Vladimir Ilyich, 53, 55
Les Enrages, 149–151, 153
Let Us Vote, 183, 186
Lipset, Seymour Martin, 2
Littoral University, 119
Locke, John, 28, 256n.8
London, Jack, 72
Lovanium University, 164
Loyola, Ignatius, 26
Lu Ts'ui, 82–83
Lubumbashi, University of (Zaire), 240–241
Luther, Martin, 22–23, 253n.6
LUV. *See* Let Us Vote

McCarthy, Eugene, 177
Madrid University, 43
Managua, 223
Manchu Dynasty, 65
Mandela, Nelson, 241
Mao Zedong, 65, 78–83, 107–108, 126–127, 195–196
March on Washington to End the War in Vietnam, 142
Maryland, University of, 45–46
May Fourth movement (China), 66–67, 77–78
May riots (France), 35, 149–156
May Thirtieth movement (China), 78–82
Mencius, 44
Menderes, Adnan, 136–137
Meredith, James, 140
Metternich, Klemens, 31–32, 40
Mexico, 71, 77, 169–171, 192–193, 202–203, 223–226. *See also* National Autonomous University of Mexico
Mills, C. Wright, 142
Milosević, Slobodan, 233–235
Mississippi, University of, 140, 267n.32
Mitchell, John
MOBE. *See* National Mobilization Committee to End the War in Vietnam
Mobutu, Joseph, 137–138, 164
Moi, Daniel Arap, 241
Montez, Lola, 38–39, 255n.2
Morningside Heights demonstrations, 174–176
Moscow University, 46–49, 53–55, 60, 256n.15, 258n.6
Mozambique, 240
multiculturalism, 228
Munich, University of, 59
Murrow, Edward R., 93
Myanmar, 85–86, 210

Nagy, Imre, 102–104
Nairobi, 242
National Autonomous University of Mexico, 3, 202–203, 223–226
National Committee for a Sane Nuclear Policy, 114

National Congress Party (India), 45, 109–110

National Mobilization Committee to End the War in Vietnam, 177–179

National Organization for Women, 182, 190

National Student Association (China), 67, 80

National Student Federation, 92–93

National Student League, 93–96

National Students' Association (U.S.), 113, 146, 186

National Union of South African Students, 137

Nationalsozialistischer Deutsche Studentbund, 88–90

Native American Movement, 190–192

Native American studies, 6,

Nehru, Jawaharlal, 109–110

Netherlands, 135

Nevada, University of, at Reno, 259n.22

New Left, 142

New York University, 3, 36

Nicaragua, 222–223

Nicholas I, 47

Nicholas II, 55

Nigeria, 112, 240, 241

Nihon University, 168

Nine to Five, 182

Nixon, Richard M., 169, 178, 179, 187, 188

Nkrumah, Kwame, 110–111

Non-Cooperation Movement (India), 86–87, 109–110

North Carolina, University of, 36

North Korea, 243–244

Northern Ireland Civil Rights Association, 154–156

NOW. See National Organization for Women

Oakes, Richard, 190–192, 276n.28

Oberlin College, 36, 255n.22

October Massacre (Mexico). See Tlatelolco

off our backs, 189–190

Ohio State University, 187

Ohnesorg, Benno, 133–134, 158

Opium War, 44–45

Ordaz, Díaz, 171

Oxford Pledge, 92, 95

Oxford University, 12–15, 17, 24-25, 253n.18, 253n.4

pacifism, student, 92, 95, 114. See also Oxford Pledge

Pakistan, 165, 206

Palestinian Resistance Movement, 207–208, 237–238

Paraguay, 69, 119

Paris Peace Conference, 66

Paris revolts. See May riots

Paris, University of, 8–9; 149–150, 252n.8; Dreyfus demonstrations at, 43. See also May riots

Park Chung Hee, 196–197, 210–211

peace movement, 185. See also anti-Vietnam War protests

Pentagon protests, 146

Peoples Park, 181

Péron, Juan, 119–120

Peru, 69, 70–71, 75, 223

Peter the Great, 46

Petőfi Circle, 102

Pinilla, Gustavo Rojas, 118

Pinochet Ugarte, August, 201–202, 222

Pius IV, Pope, 10

Plaza of the Three Cultures. See Tlatelolco

Poland, 34–35, 104, 162, 232–233

Popish Plot, 25

Port Huron Statement, 3, 141–142

Power, discussion of resistance efforts and, 4-7, 251, 253n.1

Prague Spring, 135–136

Princip, Gavrilo, 63–64, 258n.13

Proposition 209

Provos, 135

Puerto Rico, University of, 115

Pusan demonstrations, 196

Queen's University (Ireland)

Quito demonstrations, 68–69

Rangoon, University of , 86

Reagan, Ronald, 179, 181, 187, 200, 204, 273n.28, 276n.42

Red Guards, 126–127

Reformation, the, 22–27

Reign of Terror, 30

Renaissance, the, 22-27

Reno, University of, 73

Resistance, the (France), 99–100

Revolutions of 1848, 38–41

Rhodes, James, 187–188

Rhodesia (see Zimbabwe)

Rhodesia, University of, 197–198

Robinson, Frederick, 93, 94–95

Romania, 209–210, 235–236, 278n.19

Rome, University of, 186

Royal Society of London, 28

Rubin, Jerry, 177

Rudd, Mark, 174

Russia, 46–56, 60–62, 236–237; Bloody Sunday, 61; Bolshevik Revolution, 55; growth of universities in, 46–47; female students in, 49, 62; Mongol invasion of, 46

St. Andrews University, 15, 18

St. Petersburg, University of, 46–48, 53–55, 258n.8

St. Scholastica's Day Riot, 12–14

Salerno collective, 251

San Carlos University (Guatemala), 117–118

San Francisco State University, 5

San Marcos, University of (U.S.), 70, 75

Sand, Carl, 6, 31, 34

SANE. See National Committee for a Sane Nuclear Policy

Santa Barabara, University of California at, 187

Sarajevo demonstrations, 63

Sato Eisaku, 124–126, 169

SAVAK (Iranian Secret Police), 198

Savio, Mario, 143–144

Scelle disturbances, 91

Schmidt, Helmut, 186

Schwarzen, 30-32

Scotland. See St. Andrews University

SCUM. See Society of Cutting Up Men

SCUM Manifesto, 189

SDS (German). See Sozialistischer Deutscher Studentbund

SDS (U.S.). See Students for a Democratic Society

self-immolation, 212

Senegal, 163–164

Seoul demonstrations, 83, 243–244

Shanghai protests, 67, 78–79; pro-democracy, 213–214, 220

shantytown protests. See anti-apartheid movement

Shirach, Balder von, 89–90

Situationists, 149–150, 153, 269n.1

SLA. See Symbionese Liberation Army

SLATE, 114

SLID (see: Student League for Industrial Democracy)

SMASH. See Students Mobilized against Saddam Hussein

Smith College, 94

SNCC. See Student Nonviolent Coordinating Committee

Society of Jesus, 26

Society for Cutting Up Men, 189

Solanis, Valerie, 189

Solanke, Lapido, 87

Sorbonne, the, 130–131, 151–153

South Africa, 111–112, 137, 197, 198, 240, 241. See also anti-apartheid movement

South Carolina State College, 172, 173

South Korea, 122–123, 196–197, 210–213, 243–244

Sozialistischer Deutscher Studentbund, 131–132, 158–159, 184

Spain, 8, 43; Revolution of 1868, 43; student uprisings in, 43, 232

Spiridonova, Maria, 62

spring break, 16

Springer, Axel, 134; attacks on publishing firm of, 184–185

Student League for Industrial Democracy, 95–96, 114, 141

Student Nonviolent Coordinating Committee, 3, 139–140, 145, 172, 175, 266n.29

Students for a Democratic Society, 141–142, 144–145, 174–175, 177, 180, 182, 186

Students Mobilized against Saddam Hussein, 227

Sudan, 138, 237

Suharto, Gen., 128, 195, 244–245

Sukarno, Achmed, 85, 127–128

Sung Dynasty, 44

Sweden, students groups in, 42

Symbionese Liberation Army, 188, 274n.15

Tajikistan, 236

Taylor, Harold, 176

Tehran, U.S. embassy in, 199–200, 239–240

Terazije Square protests, 233–234

Tetzel, Johann, 23

Thailand, 194

Tiananmen Square demonstrations, 3, 214–220, 247, 280n.35; workers and, 217–219, 279–280n.32

Tibet, 277n.11

Timisoara uprising, 209–210

Tlatelolco massacre, 170–171, 270–271n.6

Togo, 240

Tokyo University, 84–85, 105–107, 167–168

Tolstoy, Leo, 62

Torre, Victor Raúl Haya de la, 75

town-and-gown riots, 9–19

Trento Institute of Social Sciences, 160

Trisakti, University (Jakarta), 245–246

Turgenev, Ivan Sergeyevich, 51

Turin University, 160–162

Turkey, 45, 136–137, 238

Turkmenistan, 236

Turnverein, 28–29

Tuskegee, 6

U Nu, 86

Ulyanov, Alexander, 53

UNAM. See National Autonomous University of Mexico

UNEF. See Union Nationale des Etudiants de France

Unionization efforts (U.S.), 3, 229–230

Union Nationale des Etudiants Algériens, 101

Union Nationale des Etudiants de France, 59, 91–92, 100–101, 129–131, 151–152

United States, 36-37, 72, 138–146, 171–183, 186–192, 227–230; anti-communism in, 112–115; anti-Gulf War protests, 227; anti-slavery demonstrations, 36; Civil Rights Movement, 114–115, 171; desegregation actions, 138–140; proliferation of student organizations in, 92; racial equity actions, 97; Socialist Party, 72. See also anti-Vietnam War protests

Universities, formation of, 8–11; medieval, 8–21

Uzbekistan, 236–237

Velvet Revolution, 208–209

Venezuala, 75–76, 118–119, 147–148, 171

Versailles Treaty, 83

Vetrova, Maria Fedoyseyevna, 54

Vienna, University of, 11, 39–41, 62–63

Vienna revolt, 39–41

Vietnam War. See anti-Vietnam War protests

Vilna, University of, 46

Virginia, University of, 36

Wang Dan, 215, 246

Warsaw Riots of 1957, 104

Warsaw University, 162

Wartburg, 29

Waseda University, 84–85, 124

Weather Underground, 182, 188

Weathermen, 182

Wellesley anti-Barbara Bush protests, 281

Whampoa Military Academy, 78, 79

Williams College, 36

Wisconsin, University of, 94, 146; bombing at, 188
women, 6, 8; activist efforts of, 189, 266n.29, 275n.18; early universities and, 8; status of in Indian universities, 45; status of in Russian universities, 49, 62. *See also* National Organization for Women; Society for Cutting Up Men; women's liberation movement; women's studies
women's liberation movement, 189
women's studies, 6, 189–190, 205
Wood, Antony, 12, 13, 17
Woodstock music festival, 183
World War I, 59, 64, 66
World War II, 98–101; post-war effects, 98–122
Wounded Knee, 192

Wyclif, John, 22

Yale University, 36
Yeltsin, Boris, 236
Yemen, 237
Yippies. *See* Youth International Party
Young Americans for Freedom, 141
Young Intellectuals, 72–73
Young Lords, 268n.46
Younge, Sammy, 6
Youth International Party, 177–179
Yugoslavia, 162–63, 233–2235
Yüan Shih-k'ai, 65

Zagreb demonstrations, 63
Zaire, 240–241
Zambia, 197, 198, 240, 241
Zengakuren, 105–107, 123–126
Zimbabwe, 197–198, 240, 241